Acclaim for

Richard Bernstein and Ross H. Munro's

THE COMING CONFLICT WITH CHINA

"The fullest statement yet of the new, troubling assessment of China." —*Washington Post Book World*

"Important and challenging . . . convincing . . . appropriately alarmist. Bernstein and Munro have performed a vital service." —*New Republic*

"Brilliant. . . . Their argument is nuanced and farseeing . . . written in crisp, graceful prose. The first book to broach the delicate problem of the emergence of a 'New China Lobby'—academics and businessmen who have fallen in love with China in the Clinton era. . . . Timely and intelligent." —*Los Angeles Times Book Review*

"No recent book has blown a bigger hole in the proposition that the U.S. must follow a policy of 'positive engagement' with China than *The Coming Conflict With China*. . . . While unmistakably polemical, [it] is also persuasive." —*New York Review of Books*

Richard Bernstein and Ross H. Munro

THE COMING CONFLICT WITH CHINA

Richard Bernstein studied Chinese history under John K. Fair-banks at Harvard, reported from China for the *Washington Post,* served as *Time*'s first bureau chief, was a bureau chief for *The New York Times* in two different postings, and is now one of *The New York Times*'s daily book critics. He lives in New York City.

Ross H. Munro is a scholar, journalist, and longtime China watcher. He is the Director of Asian Studies at the Center for Security Studies in Washington, D.C. He was *Time* magazine's economic correspondent in Asia and its bureau chief in Hong Kong, Bangkok, and New Delhi. Earlier, he was Beijing bureau chief for the Toronto *Globe and Mail.* His e-mail address is ross@munrolink.com.

THE COMING CONFLICT WITH CHINA

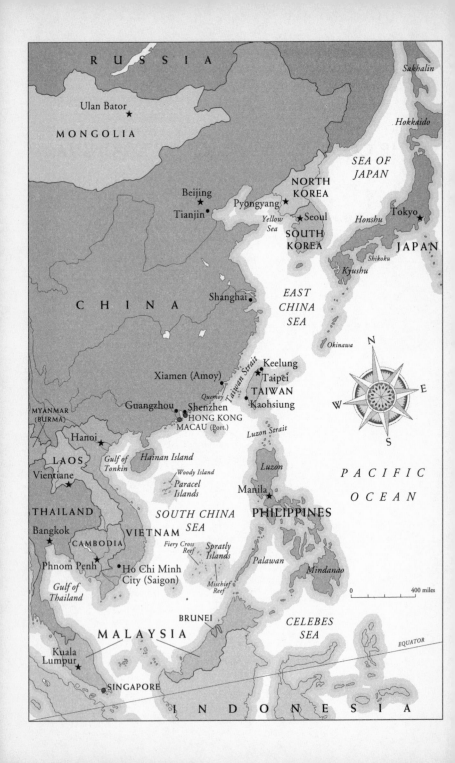

THE COMING CONFLICT WITH CHINA

RICHARD BERNSTEIN

AND ROSS H. MUNRO

VINTAGE BOOKS

A DIVISION OF RANDOM HOUSE, INC.   NEW YORK

FIRST VINTAGE EDITION, FEBRUARY 1998

Copyright © 1997, 1998 by Richard Bernstein and Ross H. Munro

The Library of Congress has catalogued the Knopf edition as
follows:

Bernstein, Richard, [date]
The coming conflict with China / by Richard Bernstein and Ross
H. Munro.—1st ed.
p.   cm.
Includes bibliographical references and index.
ISBN 0-679-45463-2
1. United States—Foreign relations—China.   2. China—Foreign relations—United States.   3. China—Politics and government—1976–   I. Munro, Ross H.   II. Title.
E183.8.C5B44   1997
327.73051—dc21   96-44434   CIP

Vintage ISBN 0-679-77662-1

Frontispiece map by David Lindroth, Inc.

Book design by Anthea Lingeman

Random House Web address: www.randomhouse.com

Printed in the United States of America

10   9   8   7   6

CONTENTS

PREFACE

TO THE VINTAGE

EDITION

SINCE THE PUBLICATION OF THIS BOOK at the end of February 1997, so many events involving China and the United States have occurred that the whole of the relationship takes on a kaleidoscopic quality. The book itself was vigorously and repeatedly denounced, its authors accused not only of fabricating their evidence but of being "white supremacists," as well, by a Chinese media that dragged into print all of the hyperbolic stock phrases usually used to deal with officially disapproved opinion. Even such top leaders as Jiang Zemin, apparently trying to improve the Sino-American atmosphere in advance of his official visit to Washington in the fall of 1997, denounced what came to be called the "China threat theory."

Among the major changes within China were, of course, the death of Deng Xiaoping, the paramount leader whose engineering of the country's free-market economic reforms had put China on the road to renewed wealth and power. And there was the return of Hong Kong to Chinese control after 158 years of British control, an event that occasioned a national patriotic celebration in China and that enormously enhanced Beijing's power and influence in Asia.

There were other developments as well, especially in the
United States, where a mood of hostility to China took hold
among a strange group of political bedfellows, ranging from
human rights advocates on the left, concerned with the continued repression of Tibet and the imprisonment of dissidents
like Wei Jingsheng, to Christian conservatives on the right,
upset about abortion in China and the intensified persecution of
Chinese Christians. In Congress, there was a renewed effort to
revoke China's most-favored-nation trading status, prompted in
large part by a widespread feeling that the Clinton administration and the business lobby (described in Chapter Four) had
made major concessions to China without getting any concessions in return. With the trade deficit exploding from roughly
$40 billion in 1996 to an expected $53 billion in 1997, House
Minority Leader Richard Gephardt led the anti-MFN battle in
Congress, misleadingly suggesting that China has generated its
huge trade surplus with the United States primarily by exporting goods made by two million prison laborers. Perhaps the
most sensational story involved charges, reportedly substanti-
ated by F.B.I. electronic surveillance, that China had sought to
buy political influence in the United States by funneling illegal
donations to American political campaigns.

In short, 1997 saw the final breakdown of a consensus that
had long prevailed in the United States in the shaping of this
country's attitudes and policies toward the People's Republic of
China. Ever since 1972, when Richard Nixon opened up relations with China, American leaders have assumed that friendly
and cooperative relations with China would stimulate the emergence of a new China with values and interests compatible with
those of the United States. The events of the past couple of years
have raised many doubts about that assumption, so that, for the
first time in a quarter of a century, the idea that China and the
United States were headed not toward cooperation and friendship but toward a multifaceted and potentially dangerous rivalry
took hold among many Americans. Needless to say, we are
among those advancing a skeptical and wary approach to China.

This does not mean that we agree with every alarm that has been sounded on the country in the past year. We do not believe, for example, that the trade surplus is due to prison labor; China's trade surplus, as we point out in Chapter Five, is due to the country's economic reform, its special export zones, and to its unfair barriers against American and other foreign imports. In the book, we argue against linking MFN with human rights, the policy attempted in the first couple of years of the first Clinton administration and then abandoned. Overall, we try in this book to focus on the strategic elements of the Sino-American relationship, rather than on what might be deemed the small annoyances or misunderstandings virtually inevitable with two large and proud civilizations like the Chinese and the American. We were prompted to do this work by the crisis in the Taiwan Strait of 1996, when it seemed that China's rise to great-power status was putting it on a course of intensified rivalry with the United States—a rivalry that could, if managed ineptly or with insufficient firmness, actually lead the two countries to war. One way that war could result, and the choices that a military conflict would present to the leadership in Washington, is outlined in Chapter Eight, "China Versus America: A War Game." Our assumption was, and remains, that China's ultimate goal, which is to establish its status as the dominant power of Asia, directly clashes with the American goal, which is to maintain a balance of power in Asia and to maintain influence in a vast region of the world where American soldiers have been sent three times to fight in the last half century, always to prevent an unfriendly power from becoming so strong that American interests were threatened.

Nothing has occurred within the kaleidoscope of events to alter that fundamental view. Indeed, while relations as of September 1997, just weeks short of Jiang Zemin's state visit to Washington, are less overtly strained, less tense than they were a year and a half earlier, the underlying Chinese effort to achieve dominance in Asia has continued unchanged. Moods will shift; the press will stress tension one day and rapprochement the next. Leaders of both countries will try from time to time, when their domestic political situations require it, to evoke an atmosphere of cooperation and harmony. But when one looks through the day-to-day ephemera, the quotidian clutter, China remains the emerging chief global competitor to the United States, and the events of the last year have furthered, not retarded, that underlying trend.

What are these developments? One, needless to say, was the reversion of Hong Kong to Chinese control. In the weeks following the reversion, the world looked, understandably, for signs of China's willingness to adhere to its "one country, two systems" vows regarding Hong Kong. Leading up to the reversion, China had already begun to put its unmistakable stamp on Hong Kong, abolishing, for example, its elected legislature in favor of one appointed by Beijing, and including several figures defeated in the earlier vote. The press was widely reported to be censoring itself, and Chinese interests had effectively forced the sale of key companies at bargain basement prices to Beijing's control. We predicted in the Introduction to this book that the transition of Hong Kong to Chinese rule was likely to go fairly smoothly in the initial stages, and it did, although there were some early ominous signs that, despite the "one-country two-systems" pledge, Beijing was already tampering both with the Hong Kong system and with the basic law that supposedly ensured its perpetuation. The police gained the authority to ban demonstrations. Laws extending labor rights were suspended by the "provisional legislature" appointed by Beijing, and China began putting into place an election law that would favor pro-Beijing groups in Hong Kong at the expense of the Democratic Party, who won the colony's pre-reversion election. "The design is not simply from the consideration of democratic ideals," said one Lau Siukai, one of the drafters of the new rules who, perhaps unwittingly, admitted the primacy of politics over law. "We have to consider . . . how to maintain good relations between the mainland and Hong Kong."[1]

Whatever happens to Hong Kong's way of life, there is no

question that for Sino-American relations the most important matter is the increase in China's power and influence that resulted from the reversion of one of the richest and most dynamic economies of the world to Chinese control. Hong Kong is situated geographically at the head of the South China Sea, midway between the Paracel Islands in the South China Sea (claimed by China and Vietnam) and Taiwan, the recovery of which the Beijing leadership has openly declared to be its next most urgent task.

While Beijing made its takeover of Hong Kong a spectacle for global television, the world paid much less attention to other parts of Asia where Chinese power and influence continued to grow. Only five days after the handover ceremonies in Hong Kong, the byzantine politics of Cambodia took a violent turn culminating in a significant additional increase in Chinese influence in Southeast Asia. Cambodia's Second Prime Minister, Hun Sen, launched a bloody coup that crushed his royalist "partners" in the coalition government and forced first Prime Minister Prince Norodom Ranariddh to flee the country. What was remarkable was the alacrity with which the Chinese—who had long sided with the royalists headed by Ranariddh's father, Prince Sihanouk, and who had denounced Hun Sen as a "Vietnamese puppet"—switched sides and went with the winner, Hun Sen. What counted was the opportunity to increase Chinese influence in Cambodia. As the first foreign government to embrace Hun Sen's seizure of total power in Phnom Penh, China doomed efforts by Western and ASEAN countries to pressure Hun Sen to back down. Indeed, Hun Sen subsequently shocked visiting foreign officials when, instead of placating them, he rudely demanded that their countries stop interfering in Cambodia's internal affairs, a stance he wouldn't have dared if he hadn't had China's backing.

The quick gains that China made in exploiting the opportunity offered by Hun Sen's Cambodia coup drew further attention to the strides the country was making elsewhere in Southeast Asia. Years ago, China effectively swept Burma into its sphere of influence by assisting Burma's widely loathed ruling junta at a time when all other foreign nations were keeping their distance. More recently, China showed a willingness to use its economic power in new ways. Indeed, China's very economic expansion, and its invasion of the export markets of other Asian countries, was one of the main reasons for economic difficulties in Southeast Asia, and for the full-scale economic crisis in Thailand in the summer of 1997. China's influence over the weakened Thai economy was signalled by two moves: exploratory efforts by PRC-controlled banks and corporations to buy up some key stakes in the Thai financial sector and the decision by Beijing to use some of its mountain of foreign exchange (gained largely via its enormous trade surplus with the United States) to participate in an International Monetary Fund bail-out of the Thai economy. Beijing contributed a billion dollars to the rescue effort and gave the green light to its new possession, Hong Kong, to do the same.

China's shadow also lengthened on its land borders to the northwest, as well. Less than four weeks before the Hong Kong takeover, China beat out the American oil companies Texaco and Amoco and bought sixty percent control of Kazakhstan's leading oil company. China committed itself to investing $4 billion in a major oil field over the next twenty years, as well as additional billions to build a pipeline to transport the oil to China. Although China's economic ties with Kazakhstan had been steadily growing, this deal established China as a central player in determining Kazakhstan's future.

The experiences of China's neighbors as varied as Kazakhstan and Cambodia have something significant in common. There was little if anything that other powers, including the United States, could have done to prevent China from increasing its power and influence over its neighbors on or near its land borders. A country of 1.2 billion, with an economy that has been growing at an average rate of about 10 percent for almost two decades now, China is going to loom large over neighbors with whom it shares a land border.

That is why we argue against what is commonly called "containment" policy toward China. Chinese power is going to grow, and any policy that is rigidly committed to halting that growth everywhere is bound to fail.

Instead, the central issue for the United States and its Asian allies and friends is whether an increasingly powerful China is going to dominate Asia, as its leaders intend, or whether the United States, working primarily with Japan, can counterbalance China's emergence to great-power and eventually superpower status. That issue will be resolved on Asia's eastern rim—in the band of territory that begins in the Russian Far East and continues through the Korean peninsula, Japan, and Taiwan, and probably the Philippines and Indonesia, as well.

None are more acutely aware that this is the central strategic issue than China's leaders and the military and strategic thinkers who advise them. Hence, for example, the fierce campaign that China waged in the summer of 1997 to protest modest improvements in American-Japanese security cooperation. In June, the two countries issued a joint draft of new "defense guidelines" that envisioned greater support by Japan for the United States in any future conflicts in the region "surrounding Japan." Tokyo committed itself to provide American forces with fuel and supplies, to repair American aircraft and ships, and, if necessary, to send minesweepers to assist the United States Navy. Japan would also allow American forces to use its civilian airports, seaports, and hospitals in the event of war.

These new guidelines, while actually a modest move for Japan toward taking more responsibility for security in the western Pacific, alarmed China, which correctly saw that Taiwan was to be included in the region "surrounding Japan." From an American and Japanese perspective that was commonsensical, since much of Japan's trade and almost all of its petroleum are routed through the waters around Taiwan. But China, with some justification, saw the proposed modest changes in the defense guidelines making it more difficult for China to take military action against Taiwan if it felt that was necessary in the future. Beijing invited prominent Japanese visitors to Beijing to declare that the guidelines should exclude the Taiwan area. After a top official in Prime Minister Ryutaro Hashimoto's government countered in August by reiterating, firmly but diplomatically, that the Taiwan area was included, the Chinese authorities furiously declared his stance "unacceptable."

The complex issue, largely ignored by the American press, has to do with the ability of the United States and Japan to work in concert to offset an increasingly assertive China precisely where conflict, or even a competitive show of military force, was most likely. The need for such cooperation became apparent early in 1996 during the Taiwan Strait crisis, when China carried out missile-firing exercises near Taiwan and the United States dispatched two aircraft carrier task forces to ensure that China did not transform the exercises into a full-scale Taiwan invasion. Since then, China has somewhat cooled its rhetoric threatening Taiwan, even as it has continued apace the world's most rapid ongoing military buildup. China increased its officially acknowledged military spending 12.7 percent in 1997 over 1996.[2] Increasingly, China is abandoning the long-held principle of self-reliance in developing military hardware and using its mountainous foreign exchange reserves to purchase state-of-the-art-weapons systems from foreign countries, first and foremost Russia, a practice detailed in Chapter Three. After the Taiwan Strait incident, China sealed a deal with Russia to purchase two destroyers equipped with missiles that were specifically designed by weapons scientists of the former Soviet Union to sink American aircraft carriers.

The obvious Chinese ambition reflected in its purchasing pattern is not to confront and threaten the United States directly, something it will not be able to do for a decade or more, but to reduce or eliminate the ability of the United States to constrain Chinese military actions in Asia, particularly against Taiwan. That ambition is also reflected in the renewal of calls by Chinese officials for an end to the American military presence in Asia. The Chinese formula for this ambition is summed up in an increasingly voiced slogan: "Asian security should be decided by Asians," reiterated by Foreign Ministry spokesman Shen Guofang in April 1997. China's position is a key change in attitude. Several years ago China saw an American military presence in Asia as stabilizing and in China's interest. This attitude persisted even after the end of the Cold War and the collapse of the Soviet Union. Now, by contrast, China is promoting a "new security concept" ultimately aimed at eliminating all bilateral security arrangements between the United States and its Asian allies.[3]

The Chinese leadership, in short, continues to work toward four interrelated goals that amount to a program for Chinese domination of Asia: first, is to gain sovereignty and control over Taiwan; second, is to expand its military presence and take control of the South China Sea; third, is to aim at inducing a withdrawal of the remaining American military forces in Asia—with the possible exception of a defensive force in Japan, whose purpose would be to prevent Japan's emergence as an independent military power; fourth, is to keep Japan, as we explain in Chapter 7, "China's Plan for Japan," in a state of permanent strategic subordination. The various initiatives undertaken by China in the last year, from Kazakhstan to Japan to Cambodia, all move it incrementally closer to achieving those goals. If it achieves them all, China, which will soon be the world's largest economy and one of the world's most powerful military powers, will have achieved a shift in the balance of power in Asia permanently in its favor. And that in turn would signal a basic shift involving American preeminence in Asia that has kept the peace in that region, while fostering both prosperity and greater democracy, for the last fifty years.

1 Rowan Callick, "World Silent as China's Powerful Shadow Grows, *Australian Financial Times*, August 5, 1997.
2 Steven Mufson, "China Raises Spending for Military," *Washington Post*, March 5, 1997.
3 Banning Garrett and Bonnie Glaser, "China Works on its Design for a New Asian Security Structure, *International Herald Tribune*, June 28, 1997.

THE COMING CONFLICT WITH CHINA

INTRODUCTION

*[As for the United States] for a relatively long
time it will be absolutely necessary that we
quietly nurse our sense of vengeance. . . . We
must conceal our abilities and bide our time.*
—LIEUTENANT GENERAL MI ZHENYU,
Vice Commandant, Academy of
Military Sciences, Beijing

THE PEOPLE'S REPUBLIC OF CHINA, the world's most popu-
lous country, and the United States, its most powerful, have become global rivals, countries whose relations are tense, whose
interests are in conflict, and who face tougher, more dangerous
times ahead. Only a decade or so ago, in the mid-1980s, the two
giants of the Pacific saw each other as actual and future strategic
partners, each of them interested in an alliance of necessity with
the other to prevent the domination of Asia by the Soviet Union.
But by the early 1990s, conflict came to dominate the relationship. And so, for example, a senior military official like General
Mi Zhenyu, writing in a widely published 1996 collection of es-
says by several Chinese officials, could speak of vengeance during a long-term battle for supremacy. "The authors are all tops
in their fields," the editor of the collection said. "Their views reflect the general debate in government and academic circles
about how China should greet the next century."[1]

If China remains aggressive and the United States naïve, the
looming conflict between the two countries could even lead to

military hostilities. The United States, after all, has been in major wars in Asia three times in the past half century, always to prevent a single power from gaining ascendancy there, and there seems little question that China over the next decade or two will be ascendant on its side of the Pacific. But even without actual war, the rivalry between China and the United States will be the major global rivalry in the first decades of the twenty-first century, the rivalry that will force other countries to take sides and that will involve all of the major items of competition: military strength, economic well-being, influence among other nations and over the values and practices that are accepted as international norms.

We base these conclusions on two propositions: One is that China, after floundering for more than a century, is now taking up the great power role that it believes, with good reason, to be its historic legacy. Within a few years, China will be the largest economy in the world, and it is on the way to becoming a formidable military power as well, one whose strength and influence are already far greater than those of any other country in the vast Pacific region, except for the United States. China is an unsatisfied and ambitious power whose goal is to dominate Asia, not by invading and occupying neighboring nations, but by being so much more powerful than they are that nothing will be allowed to happen in East Asia without China's at least tacit consent.

The growth of China's power and the aggressive pursuit of its interests conform not only to the country's sense of its historic role but to a deep-seated psychological need as well, one that the country's leadership is happy to exploit. China's ambitions are fired by a nationalism of historic aggrievement and thwarted grandeur, a nationalism that is strange and therefore little understood in the more satisfied and complacent West. China's rulers, striving to maintain dictatorial control in a world where dictatorial control is ever more obsolete, use xenophobia as a way of bolstering their power in a country that they portray as besieged and embattled. They believe that an appeal to patriotism, and the existence of a Great Enemy in the world that perpetuates the former imperialist insult to Chinese standing and pride, are a sure way of ensuring loyalty in a population that is otherwise subject to many domestic discontents. Anti-Americanism has become a matter of national dignity.

The second proposition is that the United States for at least one hundred years has pursued a consistent goal in Asia, which is to prevent any single country from dominating that region. Since this is precisely what China seeks to do, its goals and American interests are bound to collide, and they are colliding in an area that is rapidly eclipsing Europe in economic and strategic importance. The great game in East Asia involves, as it did in the nineteenth century, the balance of power, with China emerging to threaten a rough equilibrium, guaranteed and overseen by the United States, and that has endured since the end of World War II. When President Richard Nixon went to Beijing in February 1972, China was rhetorically threatening but militarily and economically weak. It was a paper tiger, as the Maoist propaganda used to say of the Soviet Union, China's enemy of those years—intimidating in its appearance but in reality incapable of projecting power outside of itself. That is rapidly changing, in large part, ironically, because China has abandoned the Marxist practices that made its image so fearsome a quarter century ago.

Whether the absorption of Hong Kong, the most freewheeling, laissez-faire entity in the world, by heavily bureaucratic, tightly controlled China goes smoothly or not—and our guess is that there will be a good deal of political repression but, at least initially, little economic chaos—it will provide China with the world's busiest deepwater port and container terminal, a major naval base, and an economic powerhouse that is the United States's thirteenth-largest trading partner, with $24 billion a year in two-way business.

In 1999, the Portuguese colony of Macau will revert to Chinese control, an event important only because it will complete Beijing's extension of its sovereignty to the entire historic Chinese Mainland. But Taiwan will remain as an unresolved irredentist claim, and that promises to keep generating tension between China and the United States. In March 1996, China conducted military exercises in the Taiwan Strait aimed at intimidating voters during a presidential election campaign on Taiwan, and the United States dispatched not one but two aircraft carrier groups to the region in a show of force specifically aimed at China. The incident was quickly forgotten by the American public. And yet it was a remarkable event, the largest military face-off in the Pacific since the end of World War II and unmistakable proof that a potential flashpoint exists for Sino-American conflict. Here is an area where the two countries not only have directly antagonistic goals, but each of them may one day find itself required to fight to attain its goals. The 1996 face-off in the Taiwan Strait could presage future face-offs as an ever more powerful, assertive, nationalistic China maneuvers to retake what it deems to be a part of its national territory.

In fact whatever the outcome, Taiwan will be a problem in Chinese-American relations. If China attacks Taiwan, the United States will have little choice but to come to Taiwan's aid or risk the collapse of its credibility with other friendly, economically important Asian countries, and that would mean real war with the People's Republic. In the unlikely event that the people of Taiwan agree to reunification with the Mainland, the takeover will be peaceful. But it will leave China in possession of yet another immense economic prize, the ninth-most-important American trading partner and the country with the globe's biggest foreign-exchange reserves. Moreover, Taiwan sits in the middle of the sea routes that supply all of the oil and raw materials to the United States's most important Asian ally, Japan. Complete Chinese reunification, in other words, would further upset the balance of power and vastly enhance China's economic and strategic strength.

The first years after the renewal of Sino-American relations in 1972 were marked by a happy tone of rediscovery, and relief on both sides that mutual hostility seemed to have given way to common interests. That mood is long gone. Nobody talks about strategic cooperation these days, but many are talking about the various ways in which the Sino-American relationship has become fraught with distrust and a pervasive sense of conflicting goals and interests. The details involve such things as Chinese missile tests near Taiwan and those two American aircraft carriers patrolling the seas not far from China's shores. There were dark warnings from Beijing to Washington about keeping out of the Taiwan Strait, an international waterway. There was even a sinister admonition from an unnamed Chinese official about nuclear missiles targeted on Los Angeles. The elements of antagonism also include ongoing Chinese human rights violations and the sales of missile technology to Iran and of special magnets that can be used in nuclear weapons building to Pakistan. China has built a secret, plutonium-capable nuclear reactor in Algeria; it has sold chemical weapons materials and nuclear technology to Libya; it has transferred large amounts of conventional weapons to both Iran and Iraq. The military equipment sold or transferred to countries that are American adversaries includes main battle tanks, antitank guided missiles, rocket launchers, fighter aircraft, and surface-to-surface missiles—this in addition to the help China has given to other countries in developing weapons of mass destruction.[2]

China at the same time has been nettled by American countermeasures and other gestures that the Chinese press, playing to an increasingly nationalistic population, has portrayed as interference in China's internal affairs reminiscent of the days of imperialist aggression. Washington obstructed Beijing's ardent bid to host the 2000 Olympic Games; it condemned China's policies on Tibet and gave reverential treatment to the exiled Dalai Lama; it allowed the president of Taiwan, Lee Teng-hui, to make a "private" visit to the United States; it warned of reprisals for Chinese arms sales abroad; it delayed China's entrance into the World Trade Organization. Arms sales to Taiwan continued, and Congress voted to support Taiwan in the event of a Chinese attack. The American press gave great play to reports by human rights organizations that China essentially murdered through intentional starvation large percentages of the children it keeps in orphanages. In May 1996, a lead story in *The New York Times* reported that federal officials were searching for and arresting officials from two of China's state-owned arms companies "on charges of smuggling 2,000 AK-47 fully automatic rifles into the United States."[3]

A couple of days before that, *The Wall Street Journal*'s lead story involved the McDonnell Douglas Corporation's massive effort to profit in the China market—an effort that not only failed economically for the company but produced charges in Congress that, in seeking to make profits, the company had given China secret military technology. Meanwhile, the trade deficit between the two countries was approaching $40 billion as China threatened to surpass Japan as the United States's largest trade-deficit country.[4] And China is just beginning its recovery from two generations of enforced economic stagnation. Equally important, China, unlike Japan, is neither a democracy nor an ally of the United States. As we will show, China's leaders after long debate have identified the United States as the country's chief adversary in the world. Whereas in the 1960s and 1970s China accused the Soviet Union of seeking "hegemony" in Asia, that accusation is leveled now at the United States, China's officially designated enemy, while rapprochement with the former Soviet enemy is well advanced.

There are moments when tensions seem to be relaxing, most important when Chinese and American negotiators agreed in June 1996 on mutual visits by the presidents of the two countries, Bill Clinton and Jiang Zemin, to take place in 1997. But China's peace offensive was a tactical move, one that might disguise but does not eliminate the basic disagreements between the two countries that had led to the tensions in the first place, disagreements that were well noted on the American side in Congress, the press, and among the public. China, a vast, potentially very powerful nation and the last of the great Communist powers on the planet, was seen to be conducting its business in a way that was inimical to the United States and to American values. Frank R. Wolf, a Republican congressman from Virginia, gave voice to the mood during House hearings on most-favored-nation status for China. He listed everything from the illegal sales of AK-47 assault rifles in the United States by Chinese companies ("Guns that could kill American boys and girls," he said), to Beijing's alleged purchase of SS-18 missiles from the former Soviet Union, to the persecution of Christians, the repression in Tibet, and the use in transplant operations of kidneys and corneas acquired from accused criminals executed after cursory, veritably pro forma trials. "In all three areas of concern," Wolf declared, "human rights, proliferation, and trade, the situation has worsened." The congressman's claim about SS-18 purchases remains unproven, even though Defense Secretary William Perry has publicly expressed the worry that China is attempting to buy these proven ICBMs from the Russians. There is no doubt that in the past couple of years China has bought something like $4.4 billion worth of advanced military equipment from Russia, including supersonic fighter jets, bombers, submarines and air defense systems.[5] Russia, whose arms sales grew 62 percent between 1994 and 1995, has outstripped the United States in arms sales to developing countries, and China is by far its biggest customer.[6] The irony is that China is acquiring some of the very arms that the former Soviet Union deployed as it pursued what China used to call its hegemonic ambitions.

Meanwhile in China, the propaganda machinery was cranking out more than its share of anti-American statements, along the lines that the United States was meddling in the internal affairs of China, portraying the PRC as a rogue nation, complaining about every aspect of China's behavior, fostering a "contain China" school of thought whose aim is to prevent the PRC from achieving its legitimate ambitions of reunification with Taiwan and economic development. "Whatever we do, you don't like it, and it seems an exercise to contain China" one foreign-affairs expert in Beijing said in an interview there in 1996. "In these circumstances it's not politically correct in China to say anything nice about the United States. In fact, it's very politically correct to describe the U.S. as a sinister superpower, a dangerous enemy, a superpower bully."

Even in the immediate aftermath of the announcement that Jiang Zemin would be invited to make a state visit to Washington, China's press and its leaders were using remarkably harsh language to denounce the United States as China's main adversary in the world. As though picking up that cue, five young Chinese intellectuals—paradoxically most of them veterans of past antigovernment democracy movements in China—wrote a book called *China Can Say No* that angrily attacked the United States and quickly became the talk of the Chinese nation. Among the book's numerous accusations: the Central Intelligence Agency is supporting "separatists" on Taiwan so as "to make any action by China condemned by the world as a threat to regional and world peace." One of the authors, Zhang Xiaobo, gave an interview to *The New York Times* in Beijing. "When we were students, we yearned for American novels and movies," he said. "But today, we find that country rather disgusting."[7]

Is this cooling in the China connection temporary, a brief downward jag in a rising line on the historical graph? Or have Chinese-American relations slipped permanently into conflict? Many experts, including many in the State Department and some of the leading China hands in the United States, contend that China and America have far more reason to cooperate than to collide, and therefore the relationship is fundamentally sound. There is a convergence of views between American officials and their Chinese counterparts on this subject. Moralistic congressional meddling, inconsistent policies emanating from the White House, and a sensationalist press are interfering in what ought to be a continued strategic partnership, goes this view. The United States is needling China, provoking it, annoying it, and getting nothing in return for this behavior. In fact, the argument continues, China is militarily weak and poses no threat of expansion, either to the United States or its neighbors. China is a defensive, easily offended nation that engages in a good deal of rhetorical bluster. But it needs the United States, both as a trading partner and as a source of stability in East Asia. Over the long run, China and the United States are fated to be global partners, even if, from time to time, as in the Taiwan Strait in March 1996, there are periods of tension.

Our hypothesis is different. We believe that China and the United States do indeed have common interests, especially in the area of economic exchange. China needs the United States for trade, technology, and the maintenance of a peaceful environment for economic growth. Moreover, despite the popularity of books like *China Can Say No,* there remains among the Chinese people an enormous reservoir of admiration and goodwill for America.

But these needs and good feelings, strong as they are, conflict with other needs and interests that we will describe here. We will show that growing Chinese economic and military strength, linked to the nation's ambitions and to its xenophobic impulses, are making it more rather than less aggressive. The important thing here is that Beijing's rulers will risk war with America not because it is in their country's interest but because it is in the interests of the governing clique. If economic growth slows down, if income gaps increase, if corruption continues to erode the reputation of the leadership, or if there is a new, internationally televised movement for greater freedom similar to the 1989 student demonstrations, the regime will wrap itself in the flag. And the major way of doing that is to blame the outside world, especially the United States, for China's problems.

Our argument is that China during the past decade or so has set goals for itself that are directly contrary to American interests, the most important of those goals being to replace the United States as the preeminent power in Asia, to reduce American influence, to prevent Japan and the United States from creating a kind of "contain China" front, and to extend its power into the South China and East China Seas so that it controls the region's essential sea-lanes. China aims at achieving a kind of hegemony. Its goal is to ensure that no country in its region—whether it is Japan exercising oil exploration rights in the East China Sea or Thailand deciding about visits of American naval vessels to its ports—will act without first taking China's interests into prime consideration.

That, in turn, fits into an even broader new global arrangement that will increasingly challenge Western and especially American global supremacy. China's close military cooperation with the former Soviet Union, its technological and political help to the Islamic countries of Central Asia and North Africa, and its looming dominance in East Asia put it at the center of an informal network of states many of whom have goals and philosophies inimical to those of the United States, and many of whom share China's sense of grievance at the long global domination by the West. Samuel P. Huntington, of Harvard University, has argued that this emerging world order will be dominated by what he has called the clash of civilizations. We see matters more in the old-fashioned terms of political alliance and the balance of power. Either way, China, soon to be the globe's second most powerful nation, will be a predominating force as the world takes shape in the new millennium, and, as such, it is bound to be no longer a strategic friend of the United States but a long-term adversary.

AN EERIE HISTORICAL COMPARISON asserts itself here. From 1941 until 1945 the United States maintained a strategic partnership with the Soviet Union, one of history's most repressive dictatorships, because such a partnership was necessary to defeat Nazi German aggression. With the war over, the alliance came to an end and was replaced by a more natural competition between the world's two superpowers.

In some ways, America's friendly relationship with China in the 1970s and 1980s parallels its wartime relationship with the Soviet Union. Both were alliances of opposites made necessary by a common urgent threat—in one instance Nazi Germany; Soviet expansionism in the other. Once the threat was gone, the strategic alliance fell victim to the underlying differences in values and interests between the erstwhile allies. The period of alliance, it should be noted, saw many professionals, academics, and journalists especially, but also government officials and State Department experts, viewing China through the same sort of illusory prism that was used during the American wartime alliance with the Soviet Union.

In the early 1940s, Joseph Stalin, one of the worst mass murderers in history, was transformed into a stubborn, stolid father figure. China's Deng Xiaoping, who benefited from a similarly generous evaluation, had several advantages. He had been purged from the ranks of China's leaders twice at the hands of Mao Zedong and his radical followers, and so when he returned to power, he seemed to embody the shift from a radical, anti-American China to a moderate, pro-Western China. Second, he was of such small stature, barely five feet tall, that he looked harmless. Third, and most important, Deng was in many ways a truly great and admirable figure, very unlike Stalin. He did not seek to expand China's control beyond its borders. He sponsored vastly more liberal policies than those that existed before. China changed tremendously during the nearly twenty years after Deng emerged from his second period of political disgrace. As all those cover stories in *Time* and *Newsweek* kept reminding us, China was taking the capitalist road. The world's busiest and most profitable Kentucky Fried Chicken opened only a stone's throw from the mausoleum that houses the earthly remains of Chairman Mao. Stock markets opened in Shanghai and other cities. Big Bird of *Sesame Street* visited China. One hundred thousand Mainland students came to the United States to attend universities. Inside China, metropolises sprouted in special economic zones that had only a few years before been production brigades on collective farms. Procter & Gamble sold more soap in China than it did in the United States. Motorola did a thriving business in cellular phones. Ten percent of Boeing Aircraft's entire production was sold in China, where the domains of private life and of cultural and intellectual freedom expanded dramatically.

The comforting notion that emerged from this vision of China was that the country, so unsettlingly different before, was coming more and more to resemble us, and insofar as it resembled us, we believed, our interests and its would be common, and conflict unlikely.

But that view ignored a great deal about China, especially as a country that, in fact, shares exceedingly little common ground with the United States. For one thing, Mao is still there in that mausoleum near the American fast-food outlet, still officially revered as the father of modern China. China probably has the largest number of political prisoners of any country in the world—it has officially admitted to three thousand. It is a country that broke up a student demonstration by ordering in tanks and armed infantry and shooting to death several hundred, possibly a couple of thousand, of its own people and then, even though the whole world had watched the military action on live television, launched a major propaganda campaign to deny that the killings had ever taken place. One of us was in Beijing during the 1989 Tiananmen student uprising and watched as Chinese soldiers put wreaths on street corners to honor the soldiers killed in the operation against what were suddenly being termed "counterrevolutionary hooligans." The dead students were never mentioned in the government-controlled media. When a Chinese man was shown on American television describing what he saw the day of the massacre, imitating the motion of the Chinese soldiers as they had fired their automatic rifles, he was promptly tracked down in a nationwide manhunt and sentenced to ten years in prison for spreading counterrevolutionary propaganda.

That imprisonment serves as a reminder of several surviving elements of the Chinese situation: one, the regime still resorts to the big lie when it feels threatened; two, it will stop at almost nothing when it feels that its monopoly on political power is at stake; three, there is no true due process of law; and four, however urbane, sophisticated, and reasonable may be the representatives of the Chinese Foreign Ministry who transact China's business with other countries, there is a hard line within the leadership that holds decisive power, and that, as we will see, views the United States, its values and its way of life, as threats to China.

China, of course, continues to occupy Tibet by force and to impose strict limits on the observance of the Tibetan religion and culture. In 1995, the authorities offered up to the rest of the world an incredible spectacle. The bureaucrats who run the Chinese Communist Party, and who constitute a kind of High Council of official "scientific" atheism, overruled the Tibetan religious authorities' choice of a six-year-old boy as the reincarnation of the Panchen Lama, the second-most-revered figure in Tibetan Buddhism after the Dalai Lama. China summoned some monks to Beijing and forced them to choose a different boy. The Tibetans' original choice, a herdsman's son, was kept in a secret location in Beijing. His parents were denounced by the press as conniving and deceitful. They disappeared and are assumed to be under arrest.

Chinese human rights violations are not the most important cause of tensions between China and America. But they illustrate three aspects of the overall picture: First, the extent of these violations in China today is a measure of the extent to which we deluded ourselves about China in the past, thinking that it was rapidly becoming a kind of free country, more and more like us. Second, the human rights issue illustrates the extent to which China, despite many important changes, remains unchanged in its essential political nature. Third, China's deliberate flouting of American entreaties, threats, and demands on human rights reflects both the country's increased power and its confidence in itself as the embodiment of an alternative to Western ways.

The hope of American policy makers has long been that over time China would become democratic. These optimists may be proved right eventually. The forces pushing toward global democracy are powerful, and China will probably not be unaffected by them forever. But there is no reason to believe that China will become democratic in the near future, for several reasons. The first is that it would be contrary to the Chinese political culture. China, in its entire three-thousand-year history, has developed no concept of limited government, or protections of individual rights, or independence for the judiciary and the media. It has never in its history operated on any notion of the consent of the governed or the will of the majority. China, whether under the emperors or under the party general-secretaries, has always been ruled by a self-selected and self-perpetuating clique that operates in secret and treats opposition as treason.

A second reason, related to the first, is that for there to be real democratic reform, the bureaucrats who hold power in China today would have to give up some of their power, and there is no sign whatsoever that they have ever been ready to do that. The Chinese tradition is that personal benefits stem from political power—whether the benefits involve a state-maintained harem (Chairman Mao had a twentieth-century version of one of those) or servants provided by the state or a Mercedes-Benz provided by a Japanese businessman in exchange for an import license—and the bureaucracy will not voluntarily relinquish those advantages for the sake of democratic principles imported from the West.

Moreover, China's leaders are probably sincere in their equation of democratic reform with social chaos. China has made great strides in creating a more prosperous life for tens of millions of its people, but it remains a potentially unstable nation where the gap between rich and poor is growing, where restlessness and unemployment are rampant, and the revolution of rising expectations has seized the minds of many people. The population seems at once to be happy over rising standards of living, but it is also discontented about corruption, crime, petty abuses of power by local officials, the precariousness of life now that many of the former guarantees provided under Communism have been stripped away. China's leaders, facing the prospect of social uprisings, can be counted on to stress patriotic solidarity and unquestioned leadership. They cannot be counted on to relinquish their monopolistic hold on power.

Finally, for China's government to subject itself to the concept of popular will would mean the loss of its control in areas where it feels its national interest allows no such loss. If, for example, Tibet were to be governed by democratic principles, rather than diktat from Beijing, the Tibetan people would create an independence movement that would challenge Chinese sovereignty

there. Democracy in China would force China's leaders to acknowledge the right of the people of Taiwan to be allowed to decide for themselves whether to keep their island's de facto
independence, to move toward de jure independence, or to become part of China with its government in Beijing. But the
granting of any such power to the Taiwanese themselves would
have two unacceptable consequences for Beijing: it would sabotage China's nonnegotiable insistence on reunification, and it
would provide an unwanted precedent for the people of the
Mainland who might ask, If the Taiwanese are consulted on the
issue of their political identity, why not the rest of the people of
China too? China's ruling clique is simply not prepared to suffer
the losses to its prestige and the undermining of its power that a
move toward real democracy would entail.

Even as they prepared to take over Hong Kong, for example,
the Chinese announced the abolition of Hong Kong's popularly
elected legislature. Some say that this decision was in itself democratic because it was taken by a Preparatory Committee of
Hong Kong residents appointed by Beijing. It was this group,
not the bureaucrats in Beijing, who voted to abolish the assembly. There was even a dissenting member of the Preparatory
Committee, one Frederick Fung, who voted against the abolition
of the legislative assembly. Fung, however, was informed the day
after his sole dissenting vote that he was being removed from the
Preparatory Committee and would not be able to participate in
its votes in the future. Given the importance to China of a har-
monious handling of the Hong Kong reversion, one might have
thought that China would actually have welcomed his sole contrary vote. It would have given the appearance that the results of
the vote involved a degree of free choice on the part of the voters.

But no. On matters relating to their hold on power, China's
Communist leaders have a great love of unanimity. Indeed, in
many detailed ways, China in the months preceding the Hong
Kong turnover was ensuring that its control would be unquestioned. When a retail clothing entrepreneur and newspaper pub-
lisher named Jimmy Lai ran articles that offended China in his

Hong Kong magazine, *Next*, the Beijing government promptly closed down his chain of clothing stores inside China to punish him and to send a warning signal to others. But in 1995, when Lai created a newspaper, *Apple Daily* (whose reporters were immediately banned from covering any officially sponsored China activity), the new publication rapidly became the second-most-popular newspaper in the colony, a sign that the people of Hong Kong themselves are more used to freedom than the Beijing regime realizes. Later, one of the arguments Beijing's authorities had with the British had to do with security on June 30, 1997, the day of the reversion itself, with the British expressing confidence in the Hong Kong police and the Chinese demanding to dispatch a force from their own Public Security Bureau. The reason is not Chinese concern about assassination attempts against the senior leaders who will be present, but over the possibility that pro-democracy forces will demonstrate against Chinese rule.

This is important in a general sense because if the history of the last two hundred years is any guide, the more democratic countries become, the less likely they are to fight wars against each other. The more dictatorial they are, the more war prone they become. Indeed, if the current Beijing regime continues to engage in military adventurism—as it did in the Taiwan Strait in 1996—there will be a real chance of at least limited naval or air clashes with the United States. Still, we believe the chances of actual military conflict to be small, and we can be thankful for that. There are other things to be thankful for. China does not seek to use military force to occupy the territory of neighboring countries or to attack the United States. There is no Eastern Europe in the picture here, no satellite countries, no puppet governments, no tanks stationed on the territory of neighboring countries. Moreover, because Communist ideology—as opposed to the power of something still called the Communist Party—is dead in China, the country has none of the messianic impulses that made the Soviet Union more threatening. China does not seek to spread its way of life to other countries.

Still, superpowers are more likely to conflict than they are to cooperate. China is not replacing the Soviet Union as a threat to the United States. It is emerging as a separate and different kind of challenge, more difficult to deal with in its way because, in striking contrast to the Soviets, the Chinese are not a powerful military power founded on a weak economy, but a powerful economy creating a credible military force. The key is the steady growth of Chinese power, not just in China itself, but throughout Asia and elsewhere in the world. The global role that China envisages for itself and the relations it is building with other rivals of the West are antagonistic to the United States. And there is a very specific potential flashpoint constituted by the complex and intractable problem of Taiwan. This is because the Taiwan situation comprises two irreconcilable elements: one, the people of Taiwan do not want to be ruled by the current Beijing regime, and two, Beijing has made reunification too high a priority for it ever to relinquish that goal. As China grows militarily, and as the regime runs out of patience, the possibility of an invasion—and of an American response—increases.

What happens if China, unable to achieve its goals regarding Taiwan by negotiation, tries to retake the island by force, possibly via a naval blockade, possibly by an all-out military assault? Can the United States stand by and consent to the use of military force after it has sternly warned China for years of its strong preference for a peaceful solution? If we do become involved in a conflict with China over Taiwan, what would be the scale of the involvement and its outcome? And if the United States does not come to Taiwan's aid and the island is overrun, what will be the implications for the survival of credible American power elsewhere in Asia and the Pacific? What will happen to the balance of forces in Asia that, with the United States assuring military security, has produced a remarkable period of peace and growth from Japan to Australia?

Those questions loom over the future. But already in the recent past, China's leaders have been increasingly prickly and aggressive

in their attitude toward the United States, engaging in a number
of provocative measures almost bound to increase tensions:

- It grabbed the disputed Mischief Reef from the Philippines
  early in 1995.
- It sold nuclear weapons technology to Pakistan and missiles to
  Iran, an American enemy.
- It has given moral, and sometimes material, support to just
  about any country that has trouble with the United
  States—Iran, the Sudan, Nigeria.
- It has issued diplomatic warnings to its neighbors that they
  must take China's interests ahead of the interests of "out-
  side" powers like the United States.
- It is a nuclear power that has hinted of weapons pointed at the
  United States, the only country in the world that has such
  targeted weapons.

As we will see below, China's self-conception and its vision of
the American role in Asia have changed markedly over the past
decade. Internal party documents have been circulating within
the Chinese leadership since 1992 portraying the United States as
China's real enemy. In 1995, China's foreign minister Qian
Qichen sent a chill through the annual meeting of the Association of Southeast Asian Nations by declaring it was time for the
United States to stop regarding itself "as the savior of the East."
Qian said: "We do not recognize the United States as a power
which claims to maintain the peace and stability of Asia."[8] The
statement signaled that China's strategic thinking had changed.
Before, it welcomed the American military presence in Asia as a
stabilizing force and a balance to the Soviet Union. Now its assumption is that an American withdrawal would leave China the
dominant power, and that is what it wants to be.

China's military buildup of naval, air, and amphibious forces
will enable it to seize and hold almost the entire South China
Sea, now divided among Vietnam, Malaysia, Brunei, and the
Philippines. Few Americans realize that China's stated goal is to
occupy islands and outcroppings so far to the south that Chinese

forces would be almost in sight of Singapore and Indonesia. That would not only alter the balance of power in Asia, but would also place China astride the only viable international sea-lane connecting the Pacific with the Indian Ocean. American warships and freighters traverse the South China Sea daily, as do tankers carrying nearly all of Japan's petroleum supplies.

Bitter conflict with China is not inevitable. But conflict seems to us to be the most likely condition of Chinese-American relations for the foreseeable future. The only clear-cut purpose in Asia that China and the United States share is preventing a second all-out war from breaking out in Korea. The two countries also have a substantial degree of mutual economic interest, though, as we will see, the economic relationship is also full of conflicts. In short, the United States and China have very little in the way of shared interests or shared values of the sort that provide commonality between the United States and Europe or the United States and other Asian countries—Japan, Thailand, the Philippines, Taiwan, and others. Moreover, China's political unpredictability, the always-present possibility that it will fall into a state of domestic disunion and factional fighting, especially in the absence of unifying leaders like Deng Xiaoping, make it prone to insecurity, to paranoia and arrogance, and to the use of bluster, threat, and xenophobic appeal as tools of foreign policy.

In 1995 and 1996 China behaved like a rogue country unbound by the usual rules of diplomatic moderation, unbound even by its own stated commitments. Within the next decade or two, China will become the second-most-powerful military power on earth, with economic power to match. Most unsettling of all, perhaps, China has given numerous signals that it views the West as its spiritual and practical adversary, and in this scheme of things, the United States and the West are one and the same.

CHAPTER I

AMERICA IS THE ENEMY

Once China becomes strong enough to stand alone, it might discard us. A little later it might even turn against us, if its perception of its interests requires it.[1]

—HENRY KISSINGER

IN THE EARLY MONTHS OF 1994, a large number of Communist Party officials from all of China's provinces were summoned to a meeting in Beijing. The secretaries and propaganda chiefs of party committees from every one of China's twenty-nine provinces and regions were there, and so were delegates from the major central government agencies and the provincial and big-city governments. The attendees, gathered in the Great Hall of the People, which squats massively on the west side of Beijing's immense Tiananmen Square, were soon told the reason for the meeting. It was to designate the United States as China's main global rival and to announce an eventual aim: setting up "a global antihegemonist united front at an opportune moment."

In the carefully crafted attack vocabulary of China, the word "hegemonist" has a special meaning. It refers to a country that is so powerful in Asia that China's independence and sovereignty is threatened by it. For many years, in fact, from the 1960s to the 1980s, the word had been reserved exclusively for the Soviet Union, China's chief enemy during those decades. But there was little question as to who the "hege-monist" in question was at this meeting in early 1994. The main address at the conference, given by Chief of the General Staff Zhang Wannian, was entitled "Reinforcing the Army, Accelerating the Army's Modernization, Firmly Opposing Interference and Subversion from Hegemonism, and Defending the Motherland." General Zhang's central statement: "Facing blatant interference by the American hegemonists in our internal affairs and their open support for the debilitating activities of hostile elements inside our country and hostile forces outside the mainland and overseas opposing and subverting our socialist system, we must reinforce the Armed Forces more intensively."[2]

Zhang's accusation, that the United States was giving "open support" to "hostile" forces inside China, involved the kind of language that, even given China's propensity for rhetorical posturing, has hardly been heard since the late 1960s, when America was still portrayed in endlessly repeated boilerplate phrases as the great imperialist enemy. Certainly it was the language of the sort of aggressive posture that China has assumed toward the United States, whether in testing American resolve on such matters as arms proliferation, violating international human rights standards, or engaging in an ambitious military buildup. As if to show that Zhang's language was no accidental burst of verbal excess, other speakers at that meeting made a point of echoing his anti-American phrases. Speaking for the Politburo, the highest expression of the CCP, the Chinese Communist Party, was Hu Jintao, a member of the Politburo Standing Committee. Hu told the assembled party bureaucrats: "According to the global hegemonist strategy of the United States, its main rival at present is the PRC. Interfering in China, subverting the Chinese government and strangling China's development are strategic principles pursued by the United States."[3] Ding Guangen, another Politburo member and the official guardian of party ideology, spoke on the "propaganda work" that now needed to be done. Some of his points:

- The anti-China strategy of the United States is aimed at strangling China's socialism and reducing China to a vassal state.
- The United States is interfering in China's internal affairs under the pretext of human rights and it makes judgments in terms of ideology. This is a subversive strategy.
- The United States supports and uses hostile forces and elements in China to carry out subversive and seditious activities.[4]

Blatant interference in China's internal affairs? More open support for hostile forces inside China? Strangling Chinese development? These were remarkably hostile remarks coming from a country that, on the public level at least, talks a great deal about developing friendly relations with the United States. What were the reasons for all of this hostility?

In fact, for years China has portrayed the United States as a kind of enemy, even when its official policy aimed, as it still officially does, at the cultivation of friendly relations. Indeed, no other supposedly friendly country has attacked the United States more strenuously or with more rhetorical excess than China has over the quarter century since relations between the two countries were restored. It is as if, with regard to the United States, there have all along been two Chinas: one the more outgoing, open, moderate, pragmatic, nonideological country that sees the United States not just as a strategic partner but an economic and technological helpmate; the other a calculatedly xenophobic, defensive, closed, angry, more ideological country that sees the United States both as a moral and cultural danger to China and as the ultimate obstacle to its national ambitions. Sometimes one, sometimes the other, attitude toward the United States prevailed. But that meeting in the Great Hall of the People in 1994 represented something different than this previous alternation. When the chief of the General Staff, a senior member of the Politburo, and the propaganda head of the Communist Party, the man responsible for the content of the newspapers and the broadcast media, stress to representatives of the party from all the corners of China that the United States is a hegemonist power bent on subversion and sedition, that is a departure, a step into a higher level of hostility than has been seen in recent decades. Moreover, it was a departure that was long in the making. It represented the culmination of a long battle over China's attitude toward the United States waged inside the leadership for nearly a decade. This battle involved several competing tendencies inside the ruling party and the politically powerful army. By tracing its stages, we can see how China, always ambivalent about the United States, always distrustful of the American influence, veered from an essentially friendly stance toward the superpower across the Pacific to an essentially unfriendly one in which the United States came to be designated China's main global enemy.

The story, which begins in the late 1980s, mixes several themes. There are the major changes in the world that took place since then, including the most momentous of all—the collapse of the Soviet Union, an event with enormous, veritably incalculable implications for China. But the story also involves a little-known struggle centering around the man most responsible for the shape and the look of China today, paramount leader Deng Xiaoping. As we will see, China's move to turn against America was powerfully but unsuccessfully resisted by Deng. Indeed, the anti-American rhetoric of that meeting in Beijing, the triumph of the idea that the United States is China's enemy, are signs that Deng, who died in February 1997, had lost the final battle of his long life.

NINETEEN NINETY-FOUR was the Year of the Dog in Chinese cosmology. It was also, from the American point of view, the Year of Bad China, the prickly, assertive China that ignored pleas and warnings from the rest of the world and went dangerously its own way. This view of the year's events was not due just to the sudden ferocity of the anti-American declarations of China's leaders, of the controlled press, and even of private groups and citizens in China who might be expected to feel favorably toward the United States. Some of these expressions of anger were fueled by the immediate situation. Nineteen ninety-four saw the debate inside the United States over whether to withdraw most-favored-nation (MFN) trading status from China because of the country's abysmal record on human rights. Americans were being especially outspoken at that time about China's policies of control and cultural extermination in Tibet, which China, as always, saw as gross interference in its internal affairs. But China was also defying arms proliferation agreements—which Beijing had not signed but was pledged to observe—by selling missiles and nuclear technology to countries like Iran and Pakistan and then repeatedly denying that the sales were taking place. Beijing provided Pakistan with nuclear weapons technology, flouting the widespread view that the nuclear arms race between India and Pakistan represents the world's gravest likelihood of nuclear war. When Secretary of State Warren Christopher visited Beijing in mid-March 1994, the Chinese subjected him to such humiliating treatment in private meetings that two and a half years later he had yet to set foot in Beijing again—an extraordinary fact for a man who has visited Damascus more than a dozen times.

There were numerous small incidents, none of historical significance in themselves but, taken together, showing a pattern of Chinese irritability, defensiveness, harshness, and defiance of American opinion. In February, China arrested a small group of foreign Christians for conducting unspecified "illegal religious activities" (apparently distributing some pamphlets), held them incommunicado for four days (in violation of China's consular agreements with other countries, requiring prompt notification of the arrest of foreigners), then stripped them of their possessions and five thousand dollars before expelling them.[5] In March, seventeen organizers of unofficial organizations, like the League for the Protection of the Rights of Working People, were arrested or simply disappeared. China began charging political dissidents with ordinary crimes from arson to disrupting traffic(!) and giving them what human rights monitors called "extremely harsh sentences."[6] On April 1, 1994, the Chinese authorities rearrested the pro-democracy dissident who was best known in the United States. Wei Jingsheng, having already served a fifteen-year sentence, imposed because he called for more democracy in China in 1978 and 1979, was jailed again shortly after going to a private meeting with an American human rights official, John Shattuck. During that year, China stopped talking to the Red Cross about opening its prisons for Red Cross inspection; it jammed broadcasts of the Voice of America, and it continued its lax policies toward the Chinese factories that were pirating tens of millions of dollars' worth of compact discs and computer software. In the months after President Clinton, in a major concession, waived the human rights requirements for MFN, *The New York Times* reported that "human-rights conditions have continued to deteriorate and relations with Washington remain mired in mistrust and contentiousness."[7]

In addition, 1994 saw a military cat-and-mouse game between the United States and China that, while not very serious on an absolute scale, was the first actual confrontation involving the armed forces of China and the United States since the Korean War of 1950–53. It took place between October 27 and 29 in the Yellow Sea, where an American naval task force, headed by the carrier *Kitty Hawk*, was making a show of force directed, not at China, but at North Korea's refusal to allow international inspection of some nuclear plants that the rest of the world worried were part of an arms-building program. China dispatched a 330-foot-long, 5,000-ton Han-class nuclear-powered submarine into the waters of the Yellow Sea, where, at one point, it got as close as twenty-one nautical miles from the *Kitty Hawk*. China even scrambled some F-6 fighter planes and flew them by the American task force before both it and the submarine returned to their bases. Later, while American officials played down the incident, China's controlled media lambasted the United States for "harassing" and "unreasonably entangling" the sub. Why, the newspapers asked, should the United States be operating at all in the Yellow Sea, which was "right in front of China's gate, a long way from the United States"?[8] Then even as the Americans con-

tinued to minimize the matter, a Chinese official dropped a conversation stopper at an otherwise friendly Beijing dinner party.
The next time this happened, he said, China would order its pi-
lots to "shoot to kill."[9]

The atmosphere, in short, was bad (it was to get worse in 1996
when China and the United States confronted each other over
Taiwan), and yet it does not seem to explain either the 1994 Beijing meeting or the many other signs that China was adopting a
stance toward the United States more hostile than at almost any
time since the two countries reestablished direct contacts in 1971.
The incident in the Yellow Sea took place after the Beijing meeting, so the two events seem to have been consequences of the
same underlying cause rather than causes of each other. The conflict over human rights had been much worse a few years before,
in the wake of China's brutal suppression of the student-led pro-
democracy demonstrations of 1989. Trade disputes had come
and gone between China and the United States, and while the
issue of MFN was particularly unsettling to China, it does not
seem by itself to justify the ferocious accusations of interference
and subversion being made in closed-door sessions by the country's top leaders.

China's harsh rhetoric and incidents like the one in the Yellow Sea are not so much temporary responses to a temporary situation but products of a fundamental change in the Chinese
attitude toward the United States. The use of the words "hegemonism," "subversion," and "interference" with regard to the
United States signals a change in China's strategic thinking. Before, Beijing saw American power as a strategic advantage for the
PRC; now it has decided that American power represents a
threat, not just to China's security but to China's plans to grow
stronger and to play a paramount role in the affairs of Asia.
China, in short, has determined that the United States, despite
the trade, the diplomatic contacts, the technology transfers, the
numerous McDonald's and Kentucky Fried Chickens open in
the People's Republic, despite even the limited amount of coop-

eration that still existed between the two countries, is its chief global rival.

That shift in thinking is central to this book. China, which thinks in very realpolitik fashion, assumes that relations among states involve spheres of influence, the balance of power, and struggles for domination. That is one reason why China's strategic thinkers have always been drawn to former secretary of state Henry Kissinger, who once said that there are only three possibilities in international relations: a balance of power, domination by one country, or chaos. Morality, good intentions, and friendly feelings play little or no role in this vision of the world, even if policies and protests are often put in exactly those terms for the sake of public opinion. And in China's view a clear struggle between it and the United States is what will give the world its shape in the decades ahead.

FROM THE AMERICAN point of view, this may seem difficult to believe, and, indeed, many people, including quite a few experts on China, do not believe it. One school of thought on China plays down the idea of strategic rivalry and tends to see the two countries' differences as temporary, aberrational, caused by American inconsistency and a misguided moralism, these differences bridgeable by shrewd, nonmoralistic, consistent diplomacy (which, in practice, has usually involved unreciprocated concessions to the Chinese). Many analysts would argue that the statements China was making in 1994 were a response to a temporary downturn in bilateral relations. Similarly, they contend, statements like those of Chief of Staff Zhang Wannian are merely attempts to exaggerate the threat from outside in order to garner a larger share of the national budget for the military— something that generals tend to do in other countries, including the United States.

The only problem with this analysis is that it ignores both what China's leaders say and what they are doing to prepare for a long-range conflict with the United States. Remarkably little noticed, for example, is the way the Chinese attitude comes through even when American officials are busily announcing great improvements in the two countries' relations. In July 1996, President Clinton's national security adviser, Anthony Lake, went to Beijing for high-level talks with Chinese leaders, after which he announced a dramatic lessening of tensions and a bright future. Chinese president Jiang Zemin (he is also general-secretary of the Communist Party and therefore in at least a titular sense the most powerful man in the country) would visit Washington; Bill Clinton, assuming he won the 1996 presidential election, would go to Beijing. Needless to say, given the atmosphere, the Americans were very enthusiastic about these developments, seeing them as a turning point, a breakthrough.

China did not reciprocate with warm statements of its own. Indeed, it has been common in China over the past few years for some diplomatic gesture to produce talk in the American press of improving relations while the Chinese papers run anti-American editorials of striking hostility. Even as the Americans were waxing optimistic after the Lake visit, China's *Liberation Army Daily* was sending a very different message to the Chinese people. The words, as they always are in China's controlled media, were chosen carefully:

> Driven by its hegemonic ambitions, the United States has been showing off its force more and more. The United States has time and again created disturbances against and interfered in China's internal affairs, and it connived with the forces calling for the independence of Taiwan.[10]

At the same time, there was this statement from the *People's Daily*, the official organ of the Communist Party:

> After the end of the Cold War . . . the strategic objective of the United States is to dominate the world. The United States will not allow the emergence of a great country on

the . . . Asian continent that threatens its power to dominate. Hence it views as its main opponent a country that in
its imagination is the most likely to pose a serious challenge
to it."

From the perspective of China's ruling elite, such charges had
the ring of truth. The United States for fifty years has enjoyed a
preponderance of military power in Asia practically unique in
world history. With Japan constitutionally limited to a defensive
force and China weak and poor, the United States has had no rivals capable of challenging its supremacy. The superpower role it
played guaranteeing the balance of power in East Asia was effectively undisputed. Now a more powerful and assertive China
does threaten the old order of things, an order that has allowed
most of the countries of Asia, recently including China itself, to
concentrate on economic development while the American tax-
payer largely bears the burden of military expenditures.

But that has long been the case, and China has not complained. The United States as of 1993 or 1994 or even 1996 had
not grown more powerful or more militarily aggressive in Asia.
It posed no new threat to China. The change in Beijing's rhetoric
therefore has to reflect a change, not in American actions, but in
China's vision of things. And the *People's Daily* editorial made
clear what that change is: "the emergence of a great country on
the . . . Asian continent that threatens [American] power to
dominate." There could not be a clearer statement from China's
official, party-controlled newspaper of the nature of the superpower conflict of the future. From the Chinese point of view, the
era of American domination in Asia, which was an undesirable
accident in the first place, should be coming to an end. China's
leaders are asking themselves: Why should distant, flawed, self-
interested America be the hegemon in a part of the world where
for the better part of two millennia China reigned supreme? As
far as we can tell, the entire leadership in Beijing has by now been
swept into the view represented by that question. The disagreement in Beijing is tactical, with moderates, including many in

the economic ministries and those responsible for foreign affairs, advocating a nonconfrontational policy for the next decade, so as to avoid a military clash and to preserve the Sino-American trade relationship. The more hawkish anti-Americans, especially in the military and the security apparatus, argue for a tougher anti-American line right away. But even the "doves" in Beijing acknowledge that China's goal of supplanting American power in Asia will put the two countries into likely conflict in the future. China recognizes it more clearly than America does; America, for reasons that we will explore, remains more wedded to the vision of cooperation with China than to the vision of antagonism.

In interviews that we conducted with Chinese strategic thinkers in 1996, there was little effort to disguise the consensus view that China and the United States have become rivals, and that the rivalry will intensify as China becomes stronger. Said one senior analyst at the Chinese Society for Strategy and Management Research in Beijing: "China is growing stronger in the world, and that is affecting the dominant role of the United States. . . . In the coming fifteen years there won't be fundamental conflicts between the United States and China, but after that fundamental conflict will be inevitable." Another scholar, this one a member of the Institute of American Studies, part of the Chinese Academy of Social Sciences, put it this way: "Nationalistic feelings are on the rise in China. More and more people don't have good feelings toward the Americans."

There is at least one influential school of thought in China that insists on moving fast, contending that China has only a short time to establish its domination over Asia—before it is blocked by the United States or by regional coalitions that will form to respond to the Chinese challenge. That is a theme of a remarkably revealing book called *Can the Chinese Army Win the Next War?* which was published as an internal, for-senior-officials-only document in 1993. The book was accidentally distributed to a Beijing bookstore and bought there by an American. It contains the kind of rhetoric that is filtered out of official statements, the goal of forcing the United States to accede to China's dominant power unmistakably expressed in its supposedly not-for-public-consumption pages.

"After the year 2000, the Asia-Pacific region is likely to gradually become an American strategic priority," the book warns, making the case for moving now, while Americans are preoccupied elsewhere. The immediate post–Cold War years inaugurated a "period of transition" that will last for a decade or a bit more, the authors of this book declare. "In other words, from the end of this century to the beginning of the next, the principal theme of world military confrontation will be local or regional wars throughout the globe. Thus whoever gains the initiative in this transition period will get the decisive seat in the future military order." The assumption, consistent with what is known about China's realpolitik philosophy, is that the international system is characterized by a constant struggle for domination and that China must engage in that struggle, its main adversary necessarily being the United States.

"While the conflict of strategic interests between China and the United States was overshadowed for a time by the 'tripartite great-power' relationship, it is now surfacing steadily since the breakup of the Soviet Union," the book says. "China and the United States, focused on their respective economic and political interests in the Asia-Pacific region, will remain in a sustained state of confrontation."[12]

RARELY HAVE CHINESE statements been so explicit about the United States being a strategic foe of China, but the idea of the United States as an enemy is far from new. To be sure, there have been times when the United States was portrayed favorably by the Chinese press—as, for example, when hundreds of Chinese journalists accompanied then–vice premier Deng Xiaoping on his historic visit to the United States in 1979. But America has always been a problem for China, a bigger problem than most Americans realize. We have always been displayed in one way or another as a source of subversive ideas and licentious practices, of pornography, drugs, social decay, as a threat to what China's press often calls "socialist morality." But when, in the mid-1990s, China began to refer to the United States not just as a moral threat but as a strategic threat as well, an enemy state, that represented a new turn of the rhetorical screw. It is remarkable the extent to which the United States has come to be officially identified in China's official media as a global adversary. And it would be a grave mistake not to look at what the Chinese say about us. Though sometimes ridiculously hyperbolic, veritably self-parodic, the Chinese commentary is a reflection of what China's leaders really think.

Indeed, the Chinese attitude toward the United States has at times been at the very center of China's political life, a defining element for the country's very identity, certainly a factor in the struggle for power that has erupted from time to time in Beijing. In the early 1970s, to take the most important example of this, party chairman Mao Zedong's decision to reestablish relations with the United States was tied to the life-and-death struggle he was waging with Lin Biao, the defense minister whom most of the world saw as Mao's closest comrade-in-arms, the figure who turned Mao's "Little Red Book" into a national icon and made the "Great Helmsman" the object of a cult of personality of a dimension not seen since Stalin's Russia. In fact, Lin's role in creating the cult around Mao and in first inciting, then quelling, the turmoil of the Cultural Revolution gave him power so great that it threatened to eclipse that of Mao himself.

But Lin was ideologically radical, so by definition he saw the United States as China's major enemy. For that reason, Mao's decision, made in 1971, to open up contact with the Nixon administration and to invite the American president to China was a direct, even crippling, blow against Lin. What happened next is still a mystery. Lin Biao seems to have attempted a coup d'état against Mao, and when that failed, he attempted to escape to the Soviet Union, dying when his plane crashed—or was shot down. In any case, Lin knew that the opening to the United States signaled an end to his power, and the end of a radical, anti-Western era in the Communist history of China.

Of course Mao, too, was a radical, a believer in Communism, but he also exercised the tightest control over his population of any major ruler in modern history, more even than Stalin. Mao was not a political leader so much as he was a kind of living God, the chief idol of a state religion whose worship was required for every person. He seems to have believed—though he was wrong and Lin Biao was right in this—that he could use the United States in the strategic balance against the Soviet Union, and as a club to destroy Lin Biao, without weakening Communist ideological credibility.

The truth is, however, that creating ties with the United States changed the very nature of life in China, and it produced an ongoing dilemma for the regime in Beijing that is mirrored in the propaganda. China has consistently wanted to gain benefits from the United States but in doing so faces the prospect that its own authority and power will be undermined. The very existence of the United States as a real entity for the Chinese people, rather than just a distant ideological abstraction, is a threat to Communist power in China. To some extent, this reflects the simple fact that the United States has tremendous appeal in China, not just for ordinary people, but for the Chinese elite as well. The Chinese word for America translates as "Beautiful Country" in Chinese. Millions of Chinese see the United States as a land of bounty and opportunity. Political dissidents draw inspiration from the American example. The bureaucrats who rule China themselves get rich in business deals with Americans or send their children here as students even during periods when the United States and its influence are being described as baleful.

But for the secretive, self-selecting clique that determines policy in China, an essential element of the Chinese-American relationship is this: the American values of freedom, of limited government, of unrestricted cultural creation, of the rule of law, of unhindered free expression in politics, sexual relations, music, dance, and the movies undermine the standing and legitimacy of

a Chinese government that by and large represents the opposite
of what America represents—discipline instead of freedom; control instead of rights; tradition instead of innovation. Especially
to a Chinese government turning to the appeal of nationalism as
a means of holding on to power, the United States is a handy natural enemy.

And so, even when formal relations between the two countries
have been good, China's propaganda machine has treated the
United States as a moral threat. In the fall of 1979, for example,
in the wake of Deng Xiaoping's celebratory visit to the United
States, the Chinese government conducted a large-scale campaign against American moral and material influence, which was
given the code name *jing-shen-wu-ran,* or "spiritual pollution." It
was probably not a coincidence that within months of the establishment of diplomatic relations, the first of China's several recent and vigorous movements of political protest sprang to life
in Beijing. This was the Democracy Wall Movement, centering
around a stretch of a main street in Beijing not far from the compound known as Zhongnanhai, where China's senior leaders live
and work. The chief official propaganda slogan at the time
called on China's people to achieve the Four Modernizations—
in agriculture, industry, science and technology, and the military.
But at the Democracy Wall, a young electrician named Wei
Jingsheng put up a poster calling for a Fifth Modernization,
democracy, without which, Wei argued, none of the other modernizations could be achieved. The problem posed by the
Democracy Wall, in the view of Chinese leaders, was traceable to
American influence. From their point of view, the United States,
without trying, has a nefarious impact on order, stability, and the
Chinese habit of obedience to authority.

China's effort to counter the American influence, to warn
against it, cannot usually be put directly into anti-American
form, not when the two countries enjoy friendly relations. There
can be no slogans along the lines of 'Resist the pernicious influence of American democracy and the example of American freedom.' Instead the anti-American message is coded in warnings

against "spiritual pollution" or "bourgeois liberalization" or, as it has been put more recently in China's press, "all-out Westernization." The alleged and, to some extent, the real targets of these campaigns are pornography, crime, drugs, prostitution, and corruption. The underlying target is the United States, the American example.

Indeed, if China complains that American news reporting on China stresses the negative, the same complaint could be made about Chinese coverage of the United States, which is full of stories about human rights violations (of Mexican immigrants, for example), of social disintegration, poverty among blacks and Hispanics, high divorce rates, the burning of black churches in the South, and drug use. "What makes people more dissatisfied is that with a poor human rights record itself, the United States criticizes many other countries in a high-handed manner," said one typical article in the English-language *China Daily.*[13] Another article in 1996, citing various press reports, accused the United States of being "one of the countries in the world today which has conducted inhuman large-scale experiments on humans," including many thousands of children, mostly black children.[14]

Pernicious cultural influences are another theme. "Certain foreign forces hostile to China and those who have ulterior motives have never stopped their infiltration and disintegration activities against China," said a typical 1996 article, referring to "the reappearance of dregs of colonial culture." "It is necessary to vigorously promote socialist culture," the article said, and to "hold high the banner of patriotism."[15] The United States, declared another article, this one in Shanghai's *Liberation Daily,* "is in relative decline, with ever more severe domestic problems and steadily declining capability to intervene in international affairs."[16] And here is the Chinese magazine *Pursuit of Truth* editorializing in March 1996 on the American ambition to keep China down:

The "Westernization" and "splintering" directed at China by Western countries led by the United States will not change and the powerful, united conspirators will not relinquish their plot to contain China's development. . . . They are plotting to destroy China as a fortress of socialism and subjugate China in an inferior position.[17]

THE SUBVERSIVE NATURE of the American influence in Chinese life has to be kept in mind in considering the changes that swept the official Chinese attitude toward the United States starting in the late 1980s. It is possible, by tracing the statements of major leaders and examining the documents of the time, to trace the battle fought inside China over the correct attitude to take toward America, and to link the stages in that battle with the colossal events taking place in China and elsewhere.

The first element in the picture is the most obvious: the fact that with the fall of the Soviet Union, both the United States and China found themselves freer to express their disagreements than before. When Richard Nixon went to Beijing in 1972, the Soviet Union was at the height of its power, a mortal threat to the United States but even more so to China, which was far weaker than the U.S.S.R., closer to it, and had engaged in armed conflicts with the Russians along the Amur River between Chinese Manchuria and Soviet Siberia. By the mid-1980s, however, with the Russians foundering in the Afghanistan war and the economy in deep difficulty, the Soviet Union no longer seemed so threatening. Moreover, Soviet leader Mikhail Gorbachev, as part of his ultimately unsuccessful plan to rescue the U.S.S.R. from collapse, made a historic public declaration during a visit to Vladivostok in 1986: The Soviet Union, he said, was offering an olive branch to China. After nearly a quarter century of animosity, the Sino-Soviet split, which was the basis for Sino-American rapprochement, showed signs of being healed.

The issue was an important one for China, which was then divided between those who saw China's future in close collaboration with the United States and those who saw the Americans as a future obstacle to Chinese ambitions. The country's two leading liberal modernizers, Prime Minister Zhao Ziyang and Communist Party secretary Hu Yaobang, were wary of drawing too close to a Soviet Union whose political and economic system epitomized what they were seeking to change in China. Instead, they argued that China should continue leaning toward the United States, which, in stark contrast to the Soviet Union, had the money, the markets, and the technology to assist in China's economic modernization.

But Gorbachev's overture resonated with China's paramount leader, Deng Xiaoping, who favored mending fences with the Soviet Union, primarily so that China could reduce the enormous military expenditures required on its northern borders to defend against a potential Soviet invasion. In any event, by 1987, Hu Yaobang had been purged, and Zhao Ziyang was under attack for his attempts to dilute the power of the Communist Party. The way was open for Deng to pursue his strategy of equidistance, his calculation being that China could maintain good ties with both the United States and the Soviet Union while playing them off against each other.

But major events interfered with Deng's plan and led eventually to the emergence of the United States as China's chief adversary. One was the massive student uprising against the regime that took place in Beijing in 1989 and was ended by an infantry and tank assault carried out by the People's Liberation Army (PLA). Another was the actual fall and disintegration of the Soviet Union. A third was the awesome display of American technological might during the defeat of Iraq in the Gulf War in 1991. Taken one by one:

- TIANANMEN: The strength and duration of the student occupation of Tiananmen Square in 1989 were profoundly disturbing to the Chinese leadership and had several consequences. One was the cashiering of the moderate leadership of Prime Minister Zhao Ziyang, probably the most pro-American senior Chinese leader in recent history. A second was the sense among hard-liners that the demonstrators, whose goal, they believed, was to bring down the

Communist Party, had been inspired in part by the United States, and in this they were not wrong. Remember that the symbol of the movement was the "Goddess of Democracy" (essentially a replica of the Statue of Liberty), which students constructed on the square only a few days before the military crackdown. When China's brutal suppression of the movement produced a tremendous negative global response, Beijing saw America—where the Bush administration declared that it was suspending all high-level contacts with China* and granted blanket asylum to any student leaders who succeeded in escaping the Chinese police dragnet—as the leader of an international chorus of denunciation. The blame for all of this, hard-liners made clear, lay with Deng's policy of opening China to foreigners, particularly Americans, who brought with them their poisonous ideas about democracy.

- THE WEAKENING AND THEN THE FALL OF THE SOVIET UNION: The weakening of Russia freed Beijing from the trammels of a strategic relationship with the United States, but the fall of the Communist empire to the north brought with it a lesson. The political reforms, especially the tolerance of free debate allowed by Mikhail Gorbachev and his willingness to dilute the Communist Party's monopoly on power, had led to the ousting of the Soviet party altogether, a result that the Chinese Communists hardly wanted to emulate. They felt that to be soft, as Gorbachev had been, was to lose power. That was the reasoning behind the purge of the pro-American Zhao Ziyang and the military's decision to use tanks and automatic rifles to quell the Tiananmen demonstration. Zhao was seen as a kind of Gorbachev, a figure who would make too many concessions and then be cast aside, dragging the entire party down with him. The intellectuals had been trouble-

---

*In fact it was later revealed that Bush the very next day dispatched two senior advisers, Brent Scowcroft and Lawrence Eagleburger, to Beijing to explain the American actions to Chinese leaders.

some for an entire decade, ever since the 1979 Democracy Wall Movement. Moreover, the Tiananmen Movement had brought out many sympathizers from within the heart of the government and party bureaucracy—reporters from the *People's Daily*, for example. So the regime wanted to deal with this unfortunate tendency once and for all, lest groups of students join with others behind some figure like Zhao and bring him to power in the way demonstrators in Moscow assured the triumph of Boris Yeltsin after he moved to seize power from Gorbachev.

■ THE GULF WAR: Military and strategic experts around the world stress the importance that China attached to the awesome technical-military power shown by the United States in the Gulf War. The Chinese understood, for example, just how far behind they were, that such weaponry as the Americans used in Iraq could be used against China if it came into conflict with the United States, and that China would have to master the techniques demonstrated by the Americans if it was to pose a credible threat of its own—in the disputed islands of the South China Sea or, more important, if it ever came to a military expedition to "liberate" Taiwan. The Gulf War gave new focus to China's military modernization, involving such things as the development of accurate medium-range missiles of the sort that were fired near Taiwan in March 1996.

These events, occurring within two years of one another, stunned and shook China's elite. China's Communist system, to which they owed their power and privilege, seemed besieged both within and without. Most important, these epochal changes strengthened the elements in the leadership that stressed a highly nationalist, even chauvinistic, stance toward the rest of the world. There has always been a xenophobic strain inside the Chinese leadership, a strain that is especially powerful among what the Chinese call the old revolutionaries, the original cadres who were soldiers in the Communists' march to power and have long been dismayed at China's abandonment of Mao-style socialism and the embrace of so many foreign ways.

The old revolutionaries are joined by forces inside the military, by China's vast and powerful security network, and by others who glow with pride when the banner of patriotism is held high to form a political force that is powerfully suspicious of almost anything foreign and capitalist. These are the groups hidden from the delegations that come from foreign countries and companies that descend on Beijing every week. These are the groups that, when they held power in the past, punished their fellow citizens for having any contact with foreigners at all, that believe in the depths of their beings that foreigners have only brought destruction and moral decay and are intent on profiting from China while keeping it weak and subservient.

This force always exists inside China even if it is largely unseen by foreigners. But it is there, and its influence is especially strong on any issues that involve, or appear to involve, the question of Chinese sovereignty, reunification with Taiwan, or national pride. China's particular brand of patriotism, what we have already called a nationalism of aggrievement and thwarted grandeur, is rooted in the long, humiliating century during which foreign imperialists carved out spheres of influence, sold opium to the Chinese masses, enjoyed the protections of their own police and courts in their enclaves on Chinese soil, and frequently embarked on armed invasions of China to punish the Chinese for some act of disobedience. China is quick to take offense and to view disagreements that other countries might take more easily in stride as assaults on the national dignity, requiring an uncompromising response. One situation tailor-made to intensify the Chinese nationalist impulse was triggered by a decision made by the Bush administration in 1992 to sell 150 F-16 fighter planes to Taiwan, which must maintain a modern air defense system if it is to have a credible deterrent against the vastly larger PRC air force. The sale, driven both by election-year politics (for Texas, it meant jobs) and by the American interest in maintaining stability in Asia, was felt by China to be an assault on the very idea of Chinese nationhood.

In this sense, China's strategic understanding of its conflict

with the United States dovetailed with a more emotional nationalist antagonism spurred by the series of actions and statements in the United States that affected the national pride—and
were exploited by the conservative, old revolutionary, military-
security factions. Here in the United States, newspaper readers
and television viewers witnessed a series of disturbing Chinese
actions that changed the standard American attitude toward
China. In the early days of Sino-American relations, when the
two countries cooperated in the great task of confronting Soviet
power, China benefited from a favorable image in America, an
image perhaps best exemplified by the panda bear. Like the bear,
China seemed charming and inoffensive, eager for friendship,
militarily unthreatening, and open for peaceful contacts. There
were television and movie specials that fostered that image—
From Mao to Mozart, with Isaac Stern; a public-television special
involving Big Bird in China, and the visit of Luciano Pavarotti
to China, which brought with it scenes of Chinese standing and
applauding Italian opera.

In the months and years after the crackdown on Tiananmen
Square, however, that image was replaced by a different one: the
lone and brave young man who stood on Changan Boulevard on
June 4, 1989, before a row of Chinese tanks. Congress and private groups criticized the Chinese for numerous misdeeds and
dangerous policies, from the smuggling of AK-47 assault rifles
into the United States, where they might have found their way
into the hands of gang members and drug dealers, to China's
nonobservance of the nonproliferation treaty.

In other words, there was a response, especially from the
United States, to China's more muscular and ambitious role in
the world, a response that took several different forms and that
as a whole rubbed raw the national pride of China. Secretly the
Chinese leadership must have worried that certain statements
frequently made in the United States might turn out to be true.
Most of those who advocated "engagement" with Beijing rather
than "containment" predicted an outcome that represented the
Chinese leadership's greatest fear: namely, that the growing con-

tact between the two countries would inevitably lead to democ-
ratization and an end to the Communist Party. In fact, that is
precisely the outcome that would most alarm the governing elite
in China, the outcome that they are willing to slaughter their
own students in order to avoid.

TO SUM UP: Chinese actions resulted from changes in the
world, from the need to stifle dissent and maintain power for the
Communist Party, from the growth of China's regional ambitions, and the very energy and unscrupulousness with which
China pursued wealth and power. These actions produced an
unfavorable response in the United States. The steady stream of
criticism in turn produced a surge of anti-American sentiments
inside China, a widespread belief that the United States had an
ulterior motive—to keep China powerless, poor, and subservient.

For a time after the Tiananmen episode, anti-Americanism
reigned in party and government circles in Beijing. The official
media were full of articles warning against "peaceful evolution"
—code words for an alleged American plot to use the pluralism
and freedom of the growing market sector of China's economy
to subvert Communist Party rule. Fierce anti-American diatribes
were being circulated internally among government and party
officials. Typical was a secret ten-point document attacking the
United States that was jointly drafted in late 1991 by the Communist Party's propaganda department and the Foreign Ministry. It warned Chinese officials to be wary of all forms of
contact with the United States and accused the United States of
seeking to achieve global hegemony by weakening China and
other foreign countries.[18]

Despite this angry reaction, Deng Xiaoping and his supporters tried to moderate the anti-American feelings of many others
in the leadership, and at that time, they did have enough power
to prevent the anti-American feeling from dominating China's
leadership circles. For several weeks in 1992, in an event that
many believe saved China's policy of economic reforms and rel-

ative openness to the outside world, Deng traveled on a well-publicized tour of southern China, declaring that economic reform should not only be resumed, it should be accelerated. By late 1992, he had used his enormous prestige to see his vision prevail inside the party. He convinced the leaders in both Beijing and in the provinces that the only way they could be sure of retaining power and avoiding the fate of their Soviet counterparts was to achieve rapid economic growth. And the only way that could be achieved, he argued, was by moving quickly toward a market economy. If that meant shrinking from confrontation with the United States, which was China's biggest export market and a major source of investment capital and technology, so be it. Early that year, Deng had declared that while "China and the United States are different in ideology, there is no conflict between their fundamental interests."[19]

Deng won half the battle. China's political and military leaders accepted his prescription for rapid economic growth, but most of them continued to press for a policy of confrontation with the United States. Deng had disappointed the military leadership in particular by resisting calls for a full-blown confrontation with the United States in August 1992 when news of the F-16 sale to Taiwan made its way to Beijing. Leftists were also frustrated by Deng's unwillingness to declare ideological war on the United States after the newly elected Bill Clinton announced that he would use trade as a weapon to force China to improve human rights and move toward democracy. Now that the leftists and the military leadership agreed that the enemy was America, it was only a matter of time before that became official, albeit unannounced, Chinese policy.

The tide was visibly turning against Deng by April 1993, when 116 high-ranking People's Liberation Army officers wrote to him and party secretary Jiang Zemin demanding an end to China's policy of "tolerance, forbearance, and compromise toward the United States."[20] The letter deplored China's failure to retaliate against the United States over the F-16 sale to Taiwan and Clinton's trade threat. On the eve of May Day, dozens of PLA generals signed another letter to Deng, entitled "Take Action and Oppose the Hegemonists' Political and Economic Blackmail and Challenge against China."[21] A document explaining the reasons for the military's disaffection argued: "Because China and the United States have longstanding conflicts over their different ideologies, social systems and foreign policies, it will prove impossible to fundamentally improve Sino-American relations."[22] Then in October 1993, the security apparatus joined the anti-American chorus by convening a nationwide antispy meeting at which officials accused the United States and its alleged accomplices, Japan and Taiwan, of operating extensive espionage networks within China. "The United States," State Security Minister Jia Chunwang said at the conference, "carries out espionage activities by making use of hostile elements, diplomats, and journalists, and exchanges of academic personnel."[23]

The trend to identify the United States as China's official enemy gained momentum at an extraordinary closed meeting in Beijing that began on November 25, 1993. For eleven days, China's top foreign- and military-policy specialists, representing the Communist Party, the People's Liberation Army, and civilian think tanks, together with leading members of the Communist Party's Central Committee, were closeted at Beijing's Jingxi Hotel to discuss Chinese grand strategy. A detailed report on the meeting that is considered accurate by Western analysts was published by a Hong Kong journal, *Cheng Ming*, which has frequently served political factions in China as an unofficial organ of leaked information. The report began: "Whom does the Communist Party of China regard as its international archenemy? It is the United States."

The final report of the special meeting contained a blueprint for China's long-term strategic policy toward the United States and the rest of the world. The report said:

From the present stage to the beginning of the next century, the major target of American hegemonism and power politics is China. . . . Its strategy toward China is, through eco-

nomic activities and trade, to control and sanction China
and force China to change the course of its ideology and
make it incline toward the West; to take advantage of exchanges and propaganda to infiltrate ideology into China's
upper strata; to give financial assistance to hostile forces
both inside and outside Chinese territory and wait for the
opportune moment to stir up turbulence; to support and
encourage western groups to impose economic sanctions
against China with a view to reaching their political goal; to
fabricate the theory of a China threat toward neighboring
Asian countries so as to sow dissension between China and
countries like India, Indonesia, and Malaysia; and to ma-
nipulate Japan and South Korea to follow American strategy
toward China.[24]

The consensus of the closed meeting, also reflected in the report, was that China should seek to counter its American foe by
seeking alliances with Third World countries and, above all, with
Russia. *Cheng Ming* reported that older military leaders, many of
whom had trained in the Soviet Union early in their careers,
were particularly enthusiastic about an alliance with Russia. In
any case, China has moved steadily in that direction as its hostility toward the United States has become increasingly evident.
In April 1996, Boris Yeltsin journeyed to Beijing, where he and
Jiang Zemin signed a declaration announcing "a long-term
strategic partnership" aimed at counterbalancing U.S. world
power. By then, Russia had become the chief foreign supplier to
China of advanced military equipment and technology, including intercontinental ballistic missiles, advanced SU-27 fighter
planes, and Kilo-class submarines. In addition, thousands of
Russian scientists and technicians are now working directly or
indirectly for China's own military industries.

The statements made in closed-door sessions by Chinese officials were echoed in the press and even by what passes for public
opinion in China. In a kind of tit-for-tat struggle, America was
blamed for numerous crimes of its own. There were articles in

1996 charging that the United States was using China as a dumping ground for its more lethal garbage. (This was a distortion, intentional or not, of American wastepaper shipments to Chinese recycling plants.) Another media battle involved American cigarette exports to China, in which the Chinese people's sense of historical grievance was joined to present-day xenophobia. "We are actually facing a second Opium War," a Chinese researcher was quoted as saying, apparently forgetting that state-owned factories in China manufacture dozens of cigarette brands. "The dumping of cigarettes today by Western manufacturers into the Chinese market in all feasible ways, legal or illegal, could be likened to the pouring in of opium in the mid-eighteeenth [sic] century. The difference only lies in that today under China's open-door policy, Western powers no longer need gunships to knock open our doors."[25]

By the mid-1990s, China's propaganda machinery and the speeches of China's leaders showed that nationalist anti-Americanism was gaining strength. The word that emerged most frequently to describe the harmful American strategy toward China was "containment," meaning a policy aimed at preventing China from becoming a powerful country, to keep it weak, without influence, and poor. Actually, as one American scholar pointed out, the two Chinese characters commonly translated as "containment" could more accurately be translated as "throttling." In any case, China came to use that word as a kind of all-purpose accusation attached to almost any American action that China officially dislikes. When, for example, in 1996 the United States moved to strengthen its security ties with both Japan and Australia, China's press criticized the moves as "containment." Even American moves to strengthen relations with Vietnam and India, and its complaints against China on the pirating of computer software, have been labeled "containment" by the Chinese media.

In late May or early June 1996, shortly after the face-off between China and America in the Taiwan Strait, *China Can Say No* quickly became one of the hottest sellers in recent Chinese history. The highly nationalist, anti-American manifesto, according to some of those we interviewed in Beijing shortly after its appearance, reflects the views of many young Chinese. The fact that the book, written by a group of unknown young intellectuals, was published means in Beijing's controlled environment that officialdom wanted it on the market; indeed, China's first-ever ambassador to Washington, Chai Zemin, wrote the introduction. The book presents the United States as an arrogant and inveterate enemy, and it urges that China take these steps, among others:

- Fight back against American cultural and economic imperialism.
- Join with Russia in an anti-American alliance.
- Boycott American wheat and other products.
- Demand compensation from the United States for its use of gunpowder, paper, and other Chinese-invented products.
- Declare that China is ready to do without most-favored-nation status and impose high import duties on American products.

In the face of the anti-American consensus hammered out by party and military leaders, an already feeble and fading Deng retreated in the early months of 1994. He continued to plead for a moderate attitude toward the United States, whose markets were vital for the economic development that was still Deng's major goal. He wanted China at the very least to soft-pedal its anti-American feelings, while it built up its military might so it could achieve its international objectives.

That is not very different from what the anti-American faction wanted as well, though it has been less cautious about expressing its annoyance with the United States than Deng has thought wise, a fact that has been noted by a few American commentators. James Woolsey, for example, the former director of the Central Intelligence Agency, told a Japanese journalist that the Chinese government seemed to have fallen under the influence of "people in the decision-making process who want conflict with the United States. . . . In my judgment, there is no other rational explanation."[26] A year earlier, sinologist Orville

Schell wrote that "as a surrogate source of legitimacy, many leaders have shamelessly tried to fan aggressive forms of patriotism and nationalism,"[27] while Willy Wo-lap Lam, a Hong Kong journalist who specializes in Chinese politics, observed: "At the dawn of the post-Deng era, a leadership thin on legitimacy and power base is playing the 'nationalism card' to the hilt." Only that, Lam continued, could explain why the Chinese media were likening China's defense of its position in its trade dispute with the United States to a struggle "to safeguard national sovereignty and the self-respect of the Chinese race."[28]

Even after the Clinton administration assured China that it would no longer tie its MFN status to human rights, the angry anti-American tone of the Chinese media continued. The hardline nationalists, ignoring Deng Xiaoping's advice, believed that China could have it two ways—both preparing to confront the United States militarily and politically and at the same time benefiting from trade and investment ties with the Americans. Their tactic, as we will see, is a complicated and many-faceted one, involving intensive lobbying in the United States, the use of economic warfare, and a self-description that stresses China's Third World status, its relative weakness and puniness in comparison with the American giant. The next step was represented by national party conferences like the one that took place in Beijing early in 1994. China is gambling that it can prepare for the coming conflict with the United States even while publicly denying its ultimate objectives. So far the strategy has been remarkably successful.

CHAPTER 2

"WE WILL NEVER
SEEK HEGEMONY"

*To fight and conquer is not supreme excel-
lence; supreme excellence consists in breaking
the enemy's resistance without fighting.*
—SUN TZU,
The Art of War

A SLOGAN THAT HAS BEEN A CONSTANT since the heyday of
Chairman Mao is "We will never seek hegemony." Indeed, that
slogan, a statement of China's peaceable intent in its foreign relations, is one of the few that has remained in use in China as the
country has passed through its various political stages, from radical Maoism to the era of Deng Xiaoping. All along, China's official position has been that it seeks to develop a world-class
economy, to maintain military force only for defense, and to refrain from interfering in the internal affairs of other countries.
For three decades, China has promised never to attack another
country first—only to counterattack if another country attacks
it. It has vowed never to be the first to use nuclear weapons. It
proclaims itself to be a struggling Third World country with no
superpower capabilities or ambitions.

The ancient military strategist Sun Tzu, the author of the bril-
liantly aphoristic *Art of War,* which is still read by Chinese military officers and strategic thinkers, put denial and deception at
the center of any successful nation's protection of its interests.

"When capable, feign incapacity; when active, feign inactivity" is how Sun Tzu, the Chinese Machiavelli, put it. Is that concept still useful in figuring out China's goals and ambitions and whether they conflict fundamentally with those of the United States?

China heaps scorn on those who believe that China has long-range hegemonic ambitions. The propaganda machinery accuses those who do not share the official vision of China as weak and struggling as members of a nefarious anti-China lobby that seeks illegitimately and aggressively to "contain China." And so, for example, there has been a steady stream of articles in the controlled press denouncing what is called the "China threat theory," calling it a "colossal absurdity." "China's only target in its foreign affairs in political and military fields is to promote world peace and development," the New China News Agency intoned on June 27, 1996. A typical statement along these same lines was made earlier that year by Xing Shizhong, the commandant of the National Defense University of the People's Liberation Army. "China's socialist character ensures that it positively will not strive for hegemony [and] that China will unswervingly pursue a defensive national defense policy and military strategy.[1] "In November 1995, Jiang Zemin, China's president and party general-secretary, reassuringly told the parliament of South Korea: "To allege that a stronger China will pose a threat to other countries is groundless. China will never take part in an arms race, never engage in expansion, and never seek hegemony."[2] And then there was this statement by a senior official at the China Institute of Contemporary International Relations: "Economic construction shall remain the government's priority. Consequently, its security strategy is to maintain a favorable environment for the economy and make utmost efforts to prevent military confrontation, whether within or outside its borders."[3]

Many American specialists accept statements like those, reasoning that even if China's leaders do harbor the ambition to dominate all of Asia, economic growth will remain the government's priority for so long that the "China threat" will recede into the background, in practice if not in theory. But there are at least three good reasons for skepticism about this optimistic and naïve vision. One is that China is now beginning the passage into a new phase of its history, what might be called an era of restored national greatness. Two, China is so big and so naturally powerful that it will tend to dominate its region even if it does not intend to do so as a matter of national policy. Three, and most important, China has pursued initiatives and framed strategic goals that belie its claims of modest Third World status. In sum, China's historic sense of itself, its basic material and human conditions, and its own assessment of its national interest combine to make a Chinese move toward Asian hegemony virtually inevitable.

WE LIVE IN A WATERSHED moment in global history: the moment when China passed from a period of national decline lasting two centuries to a renewed period of international strength and power. Indeed, China was a kind of sick man of Asia for such a long time that it had ceased to seem an aberration for it to be poor and weak. But for the greater part of its long history, China has been among the world's wealthiest and most powerful nations. Historically, moreover, China has sought that wealth and power as a way of gaining supremacy in what was to China the entire known world. China's vision kept it at the center of the world (the translation of the Chinese term for "China" literally means "Middle Kingdom"), with all of the states on its periphery paying tribute to China's rulers in much the same way that vassals paid tribute to European or Japanese feudal lords.

But starting during the late eighteenth century, with the central government corrupt, venal, and weak, and outlying states (the European imperialist powers in this instance) relatively strong and vigorous, China went into one of its regular periods of decline, a decline that lasted nearly two hundred years and persisted through several tumultuous stages.

The difference between the last dynastic cycle and previous ones was that this time China faced a new world dominated by

expansionist, colonialist, technologically superior Europe. Trying to meet that challenge, influential figures of the mid–
nineteenth century attempted to reform the imperial system from
within. Under the terms of a formula invented for the purpose—
"Western learning for practical things, Chinese learning for the
essence"—China borrowed selectively from the technologically
superior Western powers even as it kept the Confucian system of
government and social organization in place. The attempt failed.
China remained defenseless in the face of European, and then
Japanese, aggression, and in 1911, the decayed and obsolete imperial system fell to a political movement created and led by Sun
Yat-sen. The dynasty was replaced by a republic, or, at least, what
was called a republic, but one that soon fell victim to internal
disunion and external, namely Japanese, aggression.

During the first quarter of this century, China's leading
thinkers came to the painful conclusion that China ("a sheet of
loose sand," in Sun Yat-sen's memorable phrase) would have to
change profoundly in order to reachieve wealth and power. The
idea of "Chinese learning for the essence" gave way to a probing
and critical examination of China's very values, which, in the
minds of these intellectuals, encouraged passivity, slavish obedience to authority, and unscientific and undemocratic attitudes.
One product of the tremendous ferment of that period was the
Chinese Communist Party, founded with Soviet help in 1921.
Another product was the Nationalist Party, or Kuomintang, that
still rules on Taiwan. The Kuomintang, too, was nurtured by the
Soviet Union in the 1920s, until it came into the open conflict
with the Communists that has still not ended.

After World War II, with China finally free of the Japanese
aggressors and European imperialists alike, the Nationalist government, led by Chiang Kai-shek, tried to reestablish a kind of
free-market authoritarianism as a means to national restoration,
but that effort was crippled by civil war. Then when the Communist Party marched to victory in 1949, putting all of China
under strong, unified rule for the first time in roughly half a
century, a system of central planning and rigid ideological con-

trol was put into place that brought China to Soviet-style economic failure. The Communists' policies were made worse by the style of rule of party chairman Mao Zedong, the peasant from Hunan Province who started as a revolutionary and ended as a kind of emperor, fomenting constant strife inside the walls of the old Imperial City, where he lived surrounded by sycophants and concubines.

Mao's perpetual and increasingly radical campaigns both for ideological purity and the elimination of political rivals created national chaos. The newspapers, the magazines, the movies, the loudspeakers blaring in every rural hamlet, proclaimed constant progress, rapid growth, bountiful harvests, diplomatic triumphs, spreading national happiness—or, as the ubiquitous slogan put it, "Ever greater victories!"But the truth was that for the better part of thirty years, China stagnated—economically, technologically, militarily, and culturally. During the half century of turmoil, several "new" Chinas were proclaimed, several born-again nations, but each in turn failed to live up to the promise made for it by its leaders. The most important progressive magazine of the 1920s was called *New Youth.* The main effort by the Kuomintang to regenerate the country was the New Life Movement. When the Communists took over, they created the New China News Agency. Maoist campaigns attacked the Four Olds and praised again the birth of a new China, but, in fact, Mao by the end of his life was a veritable reincarnation of the old, becoming the dictatorial head of a corrupt, venal, and stifling system.

The historic moment that we live in today began soon after Mao's death in 1976 and the elimination of leftist radicals by Deng Xiaoping, who returned to power after two periods of political banishment. Deng was one of the most significant figures in the twentieth century, perhaps the last of the giants, like Lenin, Roosevelt, Stalin, Churchill, and Mao, who gave our era its shape. Deng managed an astounding feat: to maintain national unity and internal order while abandoning central planning in favor of truly visionary economic reforms. By allowing the creation of a mixed economy, Deng instigated one of the most explosive bursts of economic growth in human history—indeed the decade and a half since China's first free-market experiments began may represent the most massive period of economic growth in all of history. After the 1970s, the overused and by-now-empty word "new" was no longer so commonly spoken, but the fact was that a new China did finally emerge. This new China was something that the world had never seen before, a Marxist state dominated by a Communist Party, but a state that was nonetheless becoming an economic powerhouse. Deng presided over the definitive arrest of China's long decline and the restoration of its historic greatness.

There is a remarkable paradox here. Under Mao, China conveyed the image of a country imbued with a messianic, world-conquering mission that frightened the rest of the world, when, in fact, it was a weak giant—intimidating by virtue of its size and ideology but possessing no world-class military or economic power and therefore unable to influence events outside of its borders. Only by abandoning its ideology, accepting a modified sort of capitalism, loosening controls on its own people, and giving up the messianic rhetoric of Communism did China gain strategic and economic power. The irony is that when the West was most fearful of China, China was actually stagnating and ineffectual. The West welcomed China's reforms, thinking that it would become more moderate, reasonable, more like other countries, and therefore less dangerous, but in fact China's growing strength enabled it to threaten Western, especially American, interests more seriously even than during the Korean and Vietnam Wars.

THE LAST HALF CENTURY in short saw China acquiring the conditions for renewed historic greatness. First came the elimination of foreign exploitation and invasion. The great contribution of the Communist revolution to Chinese history was that it completed the tasks of national consolidation and domestic stability. Communism also restored a great deal of Chinese national pride, since, under it, China was able for the first time in more than a century to defend itself against foreign interference. But it was only when Deng Xiaoping jettisoned orthodox Marxist economics that China was able to begin realizing its potential. And that potential is vast, given the country's basic elements. Indeed, they are the same elements of size, population, and economic resources that ensured it superpower status in the past and will ensure it superpower status in the future.

First there is the land. China is a continent-size country that looms over the entire Asian landmass. Not counting the Asian parts of Russia, China occupies 70 percent of the land of East Asia. It borders on Korea, Russia, several of the newly created states of Central Asia (specifically Kazakhstan, Kirghistan, and Tadzhikistan), as well as Mongolia, Pakistan, Afghanistan, India, Nepal, Burma, Laos, and Vietnam. China stretches from the Siberian tundra of the northeast to the lush tropics of Southeast Asia. It encompasses within its borders three of the great river systems of the world—the Yellow, the Yangtze, and the Pearl Rivers—as well as one of the world's vastest deserts, the Takla Makan, and its highest mountains (Mount Everest forms part of the border between China and Nepal). China looms close even to the Asian countries with which it does not share a border. Singapore and Indonesia may be several hundred miles away, but that distance is created by the South China Sea. And it will disappear if China succeeds, as most objective analysts suspect it will, in establishing its claims to islets in the South China Sea that border on Indonesian territorial waters.

And there is the sea. China's maritime history is spotted with tales of heroic explorers, grand armadas bent on conquest, and boldly led pirate fleets, but the explorers failed to pave the way for empire, the pirates came to no good end, and the most famous of the armadas, destined for the conquest of Japan, was torn apart by what the Japanese called *kamikaze*, or "heavenly wind"—a word famously used again in World War II. The fact is that China, despite its immense coastline, stretching from the tropical waters of the South China Sea to the colder Yellow Sea in the north, was not much of a maritime power. It failed to grasp what the British understood centuries ago: that sea power is the key to world power.

This is changing as China realizes that to be a major power in the world is to use its geographic endowment. Much of China's recent military and diplomatic policy has been aimed at exploiting a maritime geography that would enable it to flank Asia's major sea-lanes and trading routes. In other words, China's geography and the nature of the modern world are propelling the country to become a maritime power in a way that it never was before. China claims sovereignty over a far-flung group of islands in the South China Sea, many of which are quite far off its coastline and are occupied by others, who have no intention of giving them up. The stakes here have to do with oil exploration and fishing grounds, and with the projection of naval power into one of the most heavily trafficked sea routes in the world—one from which, for example, Japan and the other economic "dragons" of East Asia, South Korea, Taiwan, and Singapore, receive most of their oil and raw materials. The land and sea combination, as Colin S. Gray put it in a 1996 study, gives China the basic conditions for superpower status:

> The emerging Chinese superstate is located in Eurasia, as the eastern "rimland" of the historic "heartland," while its long seacoast flanks the principal sea lines of communication of the great maritime, manufacturing, and trading empire of Japan. China has weight and position. Unlike the unlamented, erstwhile USSR, China is not a landlocked power, and she cannot be landlocked by a prudent U.S. containment policy. . . . Because of size, character of territory, population, social habits, and location, it would be difficult to exaggerate the potential positive or negative contribution of China to international order.[4]

And there are the people. China's population, as it is often stated, is at roughly 1.3 billion, by far the largest in the world— 400 million more than the second-most-populous country,

India; more than four times the American population, five times that of Russia, about ten times that of Japan. Roughly 20 percent of the people of the world live in China, and there are tens of millions of Chinese scattered throughout the countries of Southeast Asia and the United States. The people, endowed with enormous talent and the values of hard work and achievement, are what give the huge piece of real estate known as China its tremendous weight, especially now that they have happily, and for the first time in four decades, been freed from the crippling restrictions on their activities imposed during the era of Mao. This has great implications not only for China's domestic strength but also for the influence it can wield abroad, in part because there are large Chinese populations living abroad that are culturally and economically oriented toward the mother country. The overseas Chinese communities, especially the economically powerful ones in Indonesia, Singapore, Malaysia, Thailand, and the Philippines, are part and parcel of what Samuel P. Huntington and others have called "Greater China," a kind of undeclared coprosperity sphere in which the wealthy overseas communities have been at the center of a dramatic expansion of economic ties to China.[5]*

That leads to wealth, or to the simple fact that sometime early in the next century, China will almost certainly become the largest economy in the world, vastly bigger than any of its neighbors, bigger in absolute terms, though not in per capita terms, than the United States and Japan. This does not mean that China is a rich country on a per capita basis—indeed, in that sense, it is still quite poor,[6] and, moreover, China is beset with enormous problems of unemployment, inefficient industries, a low level of average education, overpopulation, and continuing

---

*In Indonesia, according to Huntington, ethnic Chinese are less than 3 percent of the population but hold about 70 percent of the private domestic capital; the Chinese in Thailand are 10 percent of the population but control nine of the ten largest business groups and are responsible for half of the GNP.

poverty, especially in its naturally poor rural areas. But China is so big that its absolute figures make it a great economic power even when its per capita figures remain low. Still, since 1979, China's economy has been growing at an average rate of 10 percent a year, a figure unmatched by any other large country in the world. And Hong Kong possesses the biggest and richest container port in the world and one of the most important axes for air transport in Asia. If China retakes control of Taiwan, it will add the world's nineteenth-biggest economy to its already-massive totals, a state that enjoys a trade surplus of $7 billion with the United States and that possesses many high-tech industries as well as an extremely well educated, highly entrepreneurial population of 21 million people.

But even without Taiwan, the China of the future will have more trade than any other country, the greatest output of cheap consumer products, and numerous rapidly growing industries. China's vast territory is rich in important raw materials, including oil, iron, and coal, and the territory it claims in the South China Sea may contain large reserves of oil. China will pollute more than any other country as well. Indeed, pollution in China, which will be a direct product of its economic size, is a major international issue lurking in the wings. Until now, China has been unwilling to pay the cost of pollution controls, with disastrous results already. In the future, China will burn more hydrocarbons, emit more carbon dioxide, spew more chemical residue and industrial waste, than any other country in the world, with consequences for the atmosphere, the ozone layer, and acid rain that are easy to predict. In the more general sense, the Chinese economy, like the land and the people and the nearness of the sea, will make China paramount in Asia whether the government makes domination a goal or not.

CHINA'S GROWING and potentially rich economy could lead the country down any one of a number of paths in the future. One, hopefully predicted by many (though not by China's leaders), is that as China becomes more prosperous, it will also be more democratic and more moderate in its behavior, more dependent than ever on international order and stability, less likely to engage in aggressive or reckless behavior. And certainly there are forces working against the indefinite perpetuation of a Chinese authoritarian state: the growth of independent economic power in the provinces and the consequent loss of influence by the central government; the vast amount of uncontrolled information that pours into China from the outside world; the pressures for democracy from within, including the election of local officials and the modest growth of a national parliament, some of whose members actually have on occasion voted against the central authorities.

Another, and we think far stronger, possibility is that China's economic power and leverage will push it to greater aggressiveness, further defiance of international opinion. As we will show clearly, China even now effectively uses its newly built economic power, threatening to withhold contracts or to turn to other markets as a tool of great power diplomacy, especially to fend off criticism of its human rights record. Exactly what form China will take in the future is, of course, impossible to predict—just as almost nobody predicted in the mid-1970s that it would, by the mid-1990s, have become a great trading nation with a rapidly growing economy, the kind of place where the middle class plays the stock market and provinces send commercial delegations to do business in New York and Nigeria. But a very likely form for China to take—we would say the most likely—is a kind of corporatist, militarized, nationalist state, a state with some similarity to the fascism of Mussolini or Francisco Franco, stripped of the elements of racial superiority and the armed messianism that Hitler made a part of fascism. Indeed, because of Hitler, fascism is perhaps too loaded a word to apply here.

And yet China seems moving toward some of the characteristics that were important in early-twentieth-century fascism. There is a cult of the state as the highest form of human organization, the entity for whose benefit the individual is expected to sacrifice his own interests and welfare. There is the emergence of the army as the most powerful single institution in the country, the one with ultimate political authority that, as we will see below, has created a large number of business enterprises and become influential in Chinese economic life as well. There is also the continued rule by a highly disciplined party that controls information and demands political obedience. There is as well the alliance between financial interests and the interests of the state, a vast interlocking directorate by which the sons and daughters of the senior political leaders control the state corporations, the arms manufacturers, and the banking operations. Important in the Chinese picture is the powerful sense of wounded nationalism that we have already mentioned, a belief that there are historical grievances that have yet to be redressed, an intense, brittle, defensive kind of national pride, and a powerful suspicion of foreigners. Most of all there is a convergence of interest between the party leaders and the army in their desire to maintain undisputed power, to insist on order, that order maintained by a vast and highly effective security and police system operating in close cooperation with a compliant, entirely non-independent judiciary.

China has other characteristics that complicate this picture, but they do not lessen its nature as an authoritarian, nationalistic, and increasingly powerful and assertive state. Among them is a growing gap between rich and poor, and that could lead to unrest and violence. Even a temporary, cyclical economic slowdown could further threaten the stability and legitimacy of a government whose prestige has already been seriously damaged by corruption and high-handedness. China, once incorruptible and poverty-stricken, is wealthier now by far, but it is also a country where a kind of squeeze, an incessant gift giving, is an element of daily life. There are tens of millions of roaming unemployed in China, often men and women who used to be supported at subsistence levels on agricultural communes, but who no longer have work in the countryside now that private farming has replaced collective agriculture. The entire country remains short of amenities. The big cities have fancy shops that did not exist before. But they are also places where people wait in long, melancholy, endless lines on icy winter nights for the overcrowded bus that will eventually take them to the decrepit, dark, and dingy cement cubicle that is home.

One reason often given for the ability of the Communist Party to stay in power is that the economic reforms have until now been successful. But if there is a collapse, or even just a slowdown, the consequence could be political turmoil or even chaos. In the event of economic stagnation or political decay, the Chinese people will not respond passively. They will continue to pursue, in whatever way they can, the high expectations recently kindled in them for a better life. They will emigrate in large numbers, often illegally, paying bribes to the owners of "snake boats" to take them to New York or Brazil. An upsurge of illegal activities such as international drug trading, already entrenched in parts of South China, will follow. So too will old-fashioned, officially protected piracy, already a problem in the seas near China, as well as the information-age piracy epitomized by the Chinese factories still illegally reproducing computer software and music CDs. Ordinary crime will also increase, as it has been doing as an unwanted accompaniment to economic reform, with all of the attendant problems of insecurity that crime brings with it.

A China in turmoil would present even more daunting problems for Sino-American relations than a China that is prosperous and stable. Such a China would be even more likely to be presided over by an authoritarian government dominated by the armed forces and the police. And such a regime would almost certainly be increasingly nationalistic and assertive, if not outright adventurist in its foreign policies, following its need to stir up patriotic sentiment by blaming China's problems on "spiritual pollution," or "containment," or other forms of harm that come from abroad.

WHATEVER CHINA'S precise future situation, its basic conditions ensure that it will reach regional superpower status whether or not it seeks to achieve that goal as a matter of deliberate national policy. But in fact to achieve superpower status is deliberate national policy even if China's propaganda machinery constantly denies that to be the case. China's goal is to become the paramount power in Asia and to supplant the United States in that role.

One key sign of that is the country's military spending and its military ambitions, even though many American analysts dismiss the Chinese military as so large and backward that it will never be a threat to the United States and possibly not even to its neighbors. An important American school of thought contends that for many years China will not have the wherewithal to mount a successful military operation aimed at gaining control over Taiwan, much less threatening its neighbors, Japan, or the United States.

"China is doing little to acquire force projection capability" is the way one American military analyst put this to us, using military jargon for the ability of a country to fight for an extended time far from its own territory. "It lacks the legs, lacks the logistics, and lacks the firepower." China's force of jet aircraft is very large but outmoded, and its acquisition of SU-27 fighter jets from Russia, while important, does not give it a first-class air force. It has gotten a few Kilo-class submarines from the Russians, but its naval force of fifteen destroyers and thirty-five frigates is small and has limited long-distance supply capability. These ships lack air defenses, so that any naval operations China does undertake would have to be conducted within the range of land-based airplanes, which also clearly limits force projection capability. "They do not appear to be spending the money to show a major military modernization push," the American analyst said. "They have adopted a gradual, slow-paced, more cautious approach."

Some of this argument is correct, but most of it misses the point. China will not become a military power to rival the United States in the next decade. But the essential measure of any country's military strength is not its absolute power but its power relative to others, and in this sense China is already by far the most powerful country in Asia, and it is rapidly becoming even more powerful. It faces no credible military threat from any of its neighbors, almost all of whom are relatively weak, and its defense spending is growing faster than that of any other major country.

Indeed, the fall of the Soviet Union put both China and the United States into similar military positions, though the one's position is measured globally, the other regionally. With the Russians out of the picture, unable, for example, to put down the local Chechen insurrection, American military power became unrivaled, American technology, satellites, aircraft carriers, and missile systems giving it a reach and a power unprecedented in world history. World War II had long before led to the effective long-term offensive disarmament of Germany and Japan, the only two other world powers that would otherwise have been able to challenge American military might. And so with the Soviet collapse at the end of the Cold War, the United States suddenly found itself in an unchallenged international position.

Those same developments, especially the limits on Japanese military power and the enfeeblement and impoverishment of Russia, gave China analogous advantages in Asia, where Beijing also suddenly found itself comparatively stronger than it had ever been before. This could change. Russia could rise again. Japan could rearm. But for the time being at least—and almost certainly for at least the next decade or more—China will be militarily dominant in Asia. It is the only Asian country that deploys nuclear weapons; indeed, it is the world's third-largest nuclear power in the number of delivery vehicles in service, having surpassed Britain and France in this category by the late 1970s.[7] It has the largest army, navy, and air force in Asia and is spending more both absolutely and relatively than any other nearby country. In other words, it is a country whose relative strength gives it the ability to intimidate regional foes and to win wars against them. In the future, as China continues its rapid military modernization, only it will have the ability to challenge American power in East Asia, and only the United States will have the influence to counterbalance China's regional ascendancy.

WHILE CHINA has always believed in the struggle for domination, its way of waging the struggle has drastically changed in recent years. Until Mao Zedong died, Chinese strategy was dominated by his doctrine of People's War derived from the strategy and tactics the Communists used to achieve victory in China. By the 1960s, the doctrine boiled down to three related beliefs: (1) that the only serious military threat faced by China came from the Soviet Union, (2) that the main thrust of a Soviet attack on China would be a land invasion, and (3) that China, whose military hardware couldn't match the Soviets', should allow the invader to drive deep into China before China launched its main counterattack, using relatively small units to grind up the Soviets gradually. China devoted a large portion of its military budget to preparing against the perceived Soviet threat. Many of its best fighting units were stationed along the Soviet border or in southwest China and in Tibet facing India and Vietnam, countries that were allied to and armed by the Soviets. China, in short, was partly circled by unfriendly countries that, taken together, had far larger offensive power than it had.

By the mid-1980s, Chinese strategic thinkers concluded that the chance of a Soviet invasion had become very small, as had the possibility that China would become involved in a major or nuclear war. The two most militarily powerful Asian states on its borders, India and Vietnam—both of which fought short wars with China, in 1962 and 1979 respectively—had effectively lost their most important ally. By the late 1980s, the Chinese accordingly determined that future conflicts were not likely to take place inside Chinese territory itself but, more likely, near China's borders or China's shores. This set the stage for the Chinese People's Liberation Army to revise its overall defense doctrine and the very organization of its fighting forces.[8]

This proceeded slowly at first in light of the constraints of the military budget, particularly until 1989. Then came the Gulf War of 1991, which had a deep impact on China's planners, as described by David Shambaugh, an American expert on China who held what he has called "numerous discussions with personnel at the Academy of Military Sciences and National Defense University during the spring of 1991 and subsequently." According to Shambaugh, the Gulf War

> had a jarring effect on the PLA. The military nature of Desert Storm and the swiftness of the allied victory stunned the Chinese high command. Before the war they had been predicting that U.S. forces would become bogged down in a ground war similar to the Soviets' experience in Afghanistan. Every element of the allied strategy and capabilities left the PLA aghast and hammered home as never before the backwardness of the PLA. The PLA was forced to confront the elements of modern warfare: precision-guided munitions; stealth technology; electronic countermeasures; precision bombing of military targets with minimized collateral damage; airborne command and control systems; inflight refueling; the minimum loss of attack aircraft and life; the use of satellites in anti-ballistic missile defense; strategic targeting and intelligence gathering; early warning and surveillance; the use of command centers half a world away; the use of anti-ballistic missile defense; massive airlift and rapid deployment capability; the ability of troops to exist in desert conditions; the use of special operation commando squads; and so on. This was the PLA's first exposure to a high-tech war, and they were stunned.[9]

The new maxim quickly became "Fighting modern local wars under high-tech conditions in the future." All three branches of the PLA began the process of procuring new weapons. The emphasis on investing in high-tech weapons permeated not only the senior officer corps. The top political leaders had little choice but to support the drive for military modernization. The weapons builders themselves were feted as heroes of China. On June 21, 1996, Jiang Zemin, in his role as chairman of the Central Military Commission (a position arguably more important than the presidency), appeared with other commission members to congratulate military scientists and technicians at "the first grand Army specialized technology awards ceremony in Beijing." None of the awardees were named, none of the technological breakthroughs were identified, but it was clear this was a major event.[10]

Not all the weapons builders were Chinese. According to a senior American military officer whose job responsibilities included monitoring the Chinese armed forces, the American intelligence community around 1993 was hard at work tracking the increasing number of top weapons scientists and technicians of the former Soviet Union who were working for China. It was a difficult puzzle. The best guess then was that about eight hundred were living and working in China full-time. But there were many others who visited China often, working as paid consultants. Finally, there were scientists and technicians, both individually and in groups, who remained in Russia but worked for the Chinese.

Some of them interacted with their Chinese employers on the Internet, sending the products of their research to China and responding to requests from China. Those falling into the two latter categories—those not living permanently in China—were the hardest to count, the American officer said. But together, he estimated, they probably totaled in the neighborhood of ten thousand. Whatever the exact number, it is clear that American contingency planners must assume that China can obtain any military-related high technology or advanced weapons system that Russia has in its labs or in its armed forces' inventory. The Russian military-industrial complex, staffed by some of the world's best, suddenly underemployed and underpaid, minds in military technology, is so corrupt and so desperate for cash that everything seems to be for sale.

In 1995, for example, there were reports that Chinese agents, paying bribes to staff members of a Russian base near Vladivos-

tok, obtained "truckloads" of plans and technical documents for
Russia's two most advanced attack helicopters, the Kamov KA-
50 single-seat ground-support helicopter and the Kamov KA-52
two-seat trainer combat aircraft.[11]

That kind of acquisition would help China in a local war. A
more terrifying possibility is that the Russian government is unable to control the transfer to China of its most fearsome and advanced strategic weapons. In May 1996, American defense
secretary William Perry announced that China had asked Russia
and possibly also the Ukraine for "components of SS-18 technology."[12] The sole purpose of this highly advanced, 6,800-mile-
range, multiple-warhead missile would be to hit the United
States. "We vigorously oppose and have vigorously opposed such
transfers," Perry said.[13] Any sale of SS-18 technology by Russia
would violate the START II agreement between the United
States and the former Soviet Union, under which the SS-18s are
slated to be dismantled by the year 2002. It would also violate the
Missile Technology Control Regime of 1987, under which
twenty-seven countries are supposed to obey restrictions on the
missiles or missile technology they can sell or transfer. Much
more important for practical purposes, it would give China a
proven and tested strategic weapon, the kind of weapon that was
a central element of the nuclear balance of terror that prevailed
during the Cold War.

Could the Russians actually sell such a weapon to China? An official Russian spokesman who went before the press supposedly to
deny the information cited by Perry actually added to the American fears. "To my knowledge," declared Deputy Foreign Minister
Aleksandr Panov, "Russia is not selling any such thing to China."
Nevertheless, he added, since the technology could have been
leaked from "nonstate" sources, "this needs to be reviewed."[14]

"Nonstate sources"! By the admission of the official Soviet
spokesman, one of the most lethal weapons of mass destruction
ever built might have fallen under the control of freelancers inside the Russian military-industrial complex or operating outside of government control.

China's successful efforts at scooping up all the high-tech military gear the former Soviet Union has to offer reflects the ambition underlying China's military buildup. In July 1996, *Ming Bao*, one of the Hong Kong newspapers with a reputation for access to accurate insider information in China, reported that the objective of the Chinese high command is "to reduce the military technology gap with Western countries from more than twenty years to around ten years" by the end of the century.[15] That would be a remarkably fast pace. But as we shall see, whether or not China "catches up" to the West is not the important question. China is already essentially unchallenged militarily in East Asia, and yet its military expenditures continue to grow at more than 10 percent per year.

JUST HOW MUCH those military expenditures are is another disputed matter. China's official defense spending annually is $8.7 billion, which, compared to the $265 billion spent annually by the United States, would seem to be a very small figure. The United States General Accounting Office, in a 1995 study, found that the Chinese defense budget increased by 159 percent between 1986 and 1994, but when adjusted for inflation, the real-terms increase was only 4 percent. However, the study concluded that "China's official defense budget does not include its total defense profits from defense sales or PLA commercial activities, nor does it include costs of major weapons acquisitions funded from other budget accounts." The GAO, citing other estimates, concluded that China's actual defense spending is two or three times the announced result.

We believe that the multiple is much higher—indeed, that it is between ten and twenty times the official figure. The figures for defense expenditures released by Beijing conventionally exclude many items that are normally contained in the defense budgets of Western countries, such as weapons research, equipment, and pensions.[16] The official budget, for example, does not include the cost of the People's Armed Police, presumably because this force of 600,000 is used largely for domestic order. But the PAP consists mostly of former army soldiers demobilized to reduce the size of the army itself and serves as a kind of reserve available for use in an international conflict. The official budget also excludes nuclear weapons development and soldiers' pensions. In 1995, when the Chinese purchased seventy-two SU-27 fighter jets from Russia, at a value of about $2.8 billion, the entire amount was covered by the State Council and was not deemed a defense expenditure.[17] The numbers provided by China also fail to include the cost of research and development, with, for example, part of the cost for development of nuclear weapons belonging to the budget of the Ministry of Energy, and part of the money in aircraft development coming from the Ministry of Aeronautics and Astronautics Industry. Nor does Beijing count into its calculations its proceeds from arms sales, even though China by 1988 had become the world's sixth-largest arms vendor, selling more than $5 billion worth of arms from 1991 to 1995.[18]

The Chinese figures also leave out the proceeds earned by businesses and industries owned and operated by the army, which, indeed, has quietly become a major player in the global economy with unknown and largely unaccounted-for resources. According to *Institutional Investor,* the army controls "a loose network of some 20,000 companies—a virtual PLA Inc." It "operates as an integral part of the nation's military, and the People's Liberation Army has become the ultimate brand name in China. PLA Inc. exists essentially above the law, and military units engaged in business enjoy privileges that often give them a decisive commercial advantage."[19]

In addition, realistic analyses of defense budgets of China, or any other country, for that matter, have to take into account what is called purchasing power parity. If, for example, China's labor costs for one soldier amount to one hundred dollars, and the Pentagon's cost for a soldier of equivalent ability is three thousand dollars, then the comparable Chinese cost is actually thirty times the actual cost. This holds true for everything from food supplies to steel as well as for weapons systems that are "purchased" by the PLA at state-set prices that do not cover the cost of production. Indeed, a white paper on defense issued by the State Council in late 1995 claimed that 68 percent of China's defense budget is devoted to salaries, food, uniforms, training, construction, and maintenance of facilities, as well as water, electricity, and heating,[20] all of which would be vastly more expensive in any Western country.

How much does China spend in its military modernization program? The most conservative estimates require a multiple of three. The International Institute of Strategic Studies in London in 1995 concluded that China's actual defense spending is at least four times greater than the official figure.[21] If the People's Armed Police is added in, the IISS estimate would go up to a multiple of five. With a conservative calculation for purchasing power parity, we would double that again, arriving at a multiple of ten. The official Chinese military budget for 1996 was 69.8 billion yuan, or about $8.7 billion.[22] The most conservative Western analysts would multiply that figure by three, to reach a $26.1 billion amount. That is already close to half the Japanese defense budget, which is roughly $50 billion. Our multiple of ten would put China's actual defense spending at around $87 billion per year, which would make it nearly one-third the amount of American spending. Moreover, the 1996 figure was 11.3 percent higher than 1995, which was 14.6 percent higher than that of 1994. Even taking inflation into account, it is a high figure. In any case, no other part of the Chinese government budget has increased at anything close to the rate of increase in defense spending, whether inflation is taken into account or not.

THE RISE OF CHINESE defense spending is recent. Until the Tiananmen uprising of 1989, and because of the undisputed power of Deng Xiaoping, the army in China remained under the control of the party, and its budget was kept secondary to the budgets of other departments, including those for economic development. Indeed, one of the reasons for Deng's restoration to good grace in the mid-1970s was Mao's need to restore control over the army after the Cultural Revolution and the attempted coup d'état by Defense Minister Lin Biao. Mao died in 1976, and Deng, after a successful struggle for power with Mao's immediate successors, made the army subordinate to the larger goal of economic growth. Defense expenditures actually dropped in real terms between 1984 and 1988.[23]

The officer corps had reversed that trend by the end of 1989, cashing in the chip it earned from the party leaders when they used the army to crush the Tiananmen demonstrations. Ever since then, the military budget has continued to grow in both nominal and real (after inflation) terms. When Deng, by 1994, became too feeble to influence decision making, the armed forces' political power increased further, and its share of the overall budget has continued to grow in real terms, even when other parts of the budget were reduced.[24]

One key element of China's military buildup has actually been a cutback in manpower from the 4 million underequipped troops in service in the mid-1980s to a more effective, modern force of 2.5 million envisaged by 1998.[25] Some railway, engineering, and capital construction corps continued performing their functions after simply being "civilianized," and many soldiers "retired" to the People's Armed Police. Nevertheless, many of the cutbacks were real and, as one article put it, will "remarkably increase the outlay for research on new weaponry particularly high-tech electronic weapons."[26]

Overall, the focus is on what Western analysts of China's armed forces have called "pockets of excellence," specifically nuclear and missile forces as well as air, naval, and marine forces that can project Chinese military power increasingly farther from China's shores. Among them, for example, is the development of what China calls M-9 and M-11 missiles, which are deployed in Fujian Province facing Taiwan. These are medium-range mobile missiles fired from rail- or truck-mounted launchpads and then moved quickly to another location. The chief military lesson of the Chinese missile firings near Taiwan in March 1996 was that these missiles have attained a high degree of accuracy. The PLA leadership is also creating elite units of combat-ready rapid-deployment troops. Among them are so-called Quan-tou, or Fist Troops (the name suggesting their punching power), rapid-deployment units capable of amphibious and airborne operations—in other words, units that at short notice can land on foreign (or Taiwanese) shores or be parachuted onto disputed islands in the East and South China Seas. Altogether, these Rapid Reaction Forces, which numbered 15,000 in 1988, had expanded to more than 200,000 by the mid-1990s.[27]

Another reflection of China's new, outward-looking military posture has been the construction of new airfields (as well as improved port facilities) along the Chinese coast and on offshore islands. These new airfields greatly extend the combat range of Chinese warplanes. The most striking example has been the 2,600-meter-long runway completed by China in July 1990 on Woody (Yongxing) Island in the Paracel Islands in the South China Sea. This new air base regularly accommodates thirty or forty Chinese fighters and bombers and boasts storage depots for aircraft, fuel, and air-to-air missiles. This base puts several Chinese warplanes within combat range of the disputed Spratly Islands.[28] In March 1994, China constructed an early-warning-radar installation on Fiery Cross Reef in the Spratlys for the purpose of supporting future PLA operations in that disputed area.[29]

Among the warplanes that would see action over the South China Sea is the SU-27, China's first major purchase from a desperate Russia's cut-rate arms bazaar. The SU-27 jet fighter was the former Soviet Union's answer to the American F-16. The People's Liberation Army Air Force initially obtained twelve SU-27 fighters, which arrived in China in June 1992. China dickered skillfully with the Russians, offering to buy more if the Russians would transfer modern aircraft technology to China, as well as components and parts, so that the planes could be assembled in China. The Russians complied in 1993, and the first SU-27s assembled in China were reportedly delivered to the air force in

August 1995.[30] As of March 1996, China's air force had deployed at least twenty-seven SU-27s. Another sixty had been purchased or assembled, but how many of them had been deployed was unknown. One hundred fifty additional SU-27s were scheduled to be manufactured in China in the next ten years, with Russia's providing sophisticated avionics, engines, and other equipment.[31]

The SU-27 deployments reflect China's goal of controlling the entire South China Sea. The plane can fly from China's Woody Island base in the Paracels to the contested Spratly Islands far to the south and patrol the area for at least an hour.[32] The SU-27 is capable of long-range missions and, if it was supported by an aircraft carrier or in-flight refueling, could put all of Asia within striking distance of the Chinese air force. There have been signs that China may be seeking to acquire or build an aircraft carrier, and it has been developing in-flight-refueling ability. Chinese tanker aircraft, along with at least fifteen warplanes capable of receiving fuel aloft, are expected to be operational in 1997, which alters the military balance of power for all of China's Asian neighbors.[33] The air force's projection capabilities will also increase thanks to the purchase of ten Russian Ilyushin IL-76s—cavernous transport aircraft that could serve as tankers, as "airlift" for rapid-deployment troops, or as AWACS (airborne warning and control system) support for SU-27 warplanes to improve their combat capability.

To repeat, China already has not only the largest Asian military force, but also the only one that has deployed nuclear weapons. Its medium-range missiles already worry India, with whom China went to war in 1962. For now, concern in Japan is muted by the "nuclear umbrella" created by the U.S.–Japan security pact that commits the United States to come to Japan's aid if it is attacked. Nor do China's missiles currently pose a dire threat to the United States. Most of the long-range missiles currently deployed by China are liquid fueled, meaning they're most useful for retaliatory strikes, since preparing liquid-fueled rockets for launch takes a good deal of time and is observable by spy satellites. It is also doubtful that China can launch missiles capable of hitting cities on the American East Coast. But this is changing rapidly. China was pressured by international opinion finally to agree to a new nuclear test–ban treaty in 1996, but during the negotiations, it implemented an ambitious program of nuclear tests. The objective was to develop smaller and more reliable nuclear warheads that could be placed on its new generation of missiles capable of reaching the United States.

Indeed, various investigations of China's nuclear program have concluded that Beijing has focused on developing and testing missiles with ranges of five thousand to eight thousand miles.[34] China has built several generations of Dongfeng (East Is Red) missiles, the DF-31 particularly concerning China's neighbors because it is not only mobile but propelled by solid fuel. In practice, what that means is that China will have a nuclear missile that it can move around China, probably undetected, so that it is within range of virtually the entire territory of any neighboring country—including Russia, India, and Japan—and capable of being fired at short notice.[35] China's reported goal for the year 2000 is to have thirty missiles in hardened silos that are propelled by solid fuel (that is, capable of being launched at short notice) and MIRVed (carrying multiple independently targetable reentry vehicles). On the principle that it is slightly better to overestimate your rival than to underestimate him, American planners must assume that the one hundred–plus warheads will be targeted, or are capable of being targeted, on the United States.[36]

Is this description of China's nuclear program alarmist? In 1995, a Chinese official whispered to a visiting American, Chas W. Freeman Jr., that the United States would not risk defending Taiwan if the price for that defense was a nuclear attack on Los Angeles by China. Numerous American officials were quick to dismiss that comment as unofficial, and Freeman himself later downplayed its importance. But the Chinese official was in fact telegraphing part of China's plan for neutralizing the American military presence in Asia. With an arsenal of nuclear-tipped missiles that could reach the United States, China could threaten to "go nuclear" if the American military intervened to prevent a Chinese offensive against Taiwan. This may seem irrational, given the huge American advantage in nuclear weapons. But some American analysts argue that, for decades, Chinese leaders have deliberately fostered the idea that China's decisions to use nuclear weapons cannot be predicted by a conventional and Western calculation of risks and benefits.

Most disturbing of all is the possibility that China has acquired SS-18 missiles, or at least the ability to build them, from Russia. This is a proven missile. By acquiring it, China would shave several years off the research-and-development time that would otherwise be needed to develop an equivalent missile from the ground up. Indeed, some of the reports of the Chinese's developing indigenous missiles may well prove to be bogus cover stories deliberately concocted by China's military establishment to obscure its acquisition of the SS-18, which will probably be renamed as part of the Dongfeng series, in order to compound uncertainty over its origins.

The navy has never enjoyed higher priority in China than it does today. Its acquisitions of new weapons epitomize a recent and key trend in the Chinese military buildup: the increasing pace at which new weapons systems are being deployed. One scholar has pointed out that, until the late 1980s, "the PLA's efforts to upgrade its antiquated conventional warfare hardware were limited mostly to 'window-shopping' and research and development."[37] But this changed in the 1990s. Since 1991, for example, the PLA Navy has launched at least four new destroyers, five frigates, and nine fast-attack missile boats. In 1994, thirty-five additional modern warships were under construction, and forty-six additional acquisitions were planned.[38]

GIVEN CHINESE ACTIVITIES, some experts on China's military began to revise the views they held up to the early 1990s, taking up instead the position that Beijing's policy was no longer modest and defensive but far more threatening to the Asian military balance in general. Others continued to believe that China's endeavor consisted of a sensible and overdue modernization of an antiquated system. Again, this focus on absolute rather than relative power seems to miss the point. China, for example, has 9,200 tanks; Vietnam has 2,000; the Philippines 126. China has fifty-one submarines: Vietnam and the Philippines none. China has fifty destroyers and frigates—Vietnam seven, the Philippines one. China's 5,845 combat aircraft are mostly outmoded compared to the American force, but in any air war, numbers alone count for a good deal, and neighbors like Vietnam and the Philippines have 190 and 43 airplanes in their forces respectively.

For many years, military experts noted that China's leaders like Mao spoke bombastically but were actually very cautious in their use of military power. They went to war in Korea in 1950 because they genuinely feared that the United States was planning an invasion. They used troops in 1962 in disputed territories on their border with India, but only after warnings that China would retaliate if India continued military probes in the region. China also engaged in some minor skirmishes with Soviet troops along the Amur River in the mid-1970s. But all these armed engagements involved what China perceived as active threats to China's own territory and did not represent any real projection of power to other countries. They seemed to prove the rule of China's essentially defensive posture and its caution.

But China has become more assertive in recent years. In 1974, it seized several of the Paracel Islands in the South China Sea from South Vietnam. In 1979, it broke its still-frequently-reiterated promise never to be the first to resort to arms when it attacked over the North Vietnamese border. In 1988, the Chinese sank three Vietnamese ships in the Spratlys area. More than seventy-five Vietnamese sailors were killed or missing. Since then, China has gradually occupied additional islands in the Spratlys. In 1994, there was the episode in the Yellow Sea involving a Chinese submarine and American ships, described earlier. In 1995, China sent an armed naval force that seized Mischief Reef from the Philippines. In 1996, it fired missiles off the coast of Taiwan in an attempt to intimidate the residents of the island during the presidential elections there—a bit of saber rattling taken seriously enough in Washington for the Clinton administration to respond. During the Taiwan episode, China warned the United States to stay out of the Taiwan Strait, which is an international waterway.

China, in short, is willing to use military force outside its borders in what seem to be at least probing efforts, attempts to gauge what the response of other countries will be, how strong their political will is, and who, if anyone, will come to their aid. It chose Vietnam as a target in part to see whether the Soviet Union would retaliate. In the Mischief Reef incident, it seemed to be testing whether the Philippines's closest friends—its treaty ally, the United States, as well as its neighbors among the Association of Southeast Asian Nations—would respond. So far, the attacks have been minor, but they have also demonstrated China's determination to extend its power deep into the strategically crucial South China Sea.

A look at a map will quickly show the enormous forward thrust China would gain by controlling the islands that it claims in what is effectively an inland waterway that connects most of the countries of Southeast Asia and governs the most important sea routes from Japan to the Middle East and Europe. Mischief Reef is in the southeast part of the South China Sea, about 800 nautical miles from the nearest point in undisputed Chinese territory, Hainan Island, but about 135 nautical miles from the nearest point in the Philippines, the coast of Palawan Island. Fiery Cross Reef, in the Spratly Islands, where China has now built radar installations, is even farther south.

Hong Kong offers naval vessels free access to the best deepwater port in all of Asia, one poised at the northern entrance of the South China Sea. As part of the arrangements for the handover, the British paid for construction of a new naval base at Hong Kong's Stonecutters Island, with four hundred meters of deepwater frontage capable of taking even aircraft carriers. Some British analysts believe that China plans to turn Stonecutters into a major southern naval base, from which it could extend its control over the entire South China Sea.

Increasingly China is looking abroad, not only to Russia, but now also to Western European countries, to purchase advanced military hardware that will rapidly increase its power projection capabilities. The latter half of 1996 witnessed an upsurge in such deal making, very likely prompted by the PLA's failure to intimidate Taiwan with its military exercises and missile tests early that year. The fall of 1996 saw widespread reports that China was close to acquiring the aircraft carrier *Clemenceau* from France, reportedly with completely upgraded electronics and radar systems. Although years will pass before the Chinese navy assembles all the other ships needed to constitute a modern aircraft carrier task force, the acquisition of the *Clemenceau*, particularly one with up-to-date electronics, would be a milestone.

China also moved late in the year to catch up in airborne early-warning-radar systems, a key element of modern warfare. In August, it purchased six to eight Searchwater surveillance radars from Racal, the British defense and electronics company. The systems are used primarily by maritime patrol aircraft to hunt submarines. In October 1996, China was also negotiating with both Britain and Israel to buy the airborne early-warning systems needed to convert its IL-76 aircraft into AWACS, which use radar and high-powered computers to detect enemy aircraft and coordinate attacks among air, sea, and ground forces. In short, the planes would constitute a "force-multiplier" for Chinese warplanes over the Taiwan Strait or the South China Sea.[39] These were all cash deals, as were the earlier multibillion-dollar purchases from Russia. As we shall see, the necessary cash came from the United States.

In addition, in a little-noted move, China has been building a rail link from southwestern Yunnan Province through Burma to the Bay of Bengal. This would allow the Chinese to supply naval vessels in the Indian Ocean. Such a move would dramatically alter the balance of power in China's favor in both Southeast Asia and South Asia. China's military would have a presence on all of Southeast Asia's land and sea frontiers. As for South Asia, Indian military planners have told us of their alarm over the prospect that China will be able to position a fleet sitting off their east coast. Already, the Chinese have personnel stationed on Burmese islands in the Indian Ocean monitoring Indian air and naval operations.

CHAPTER 3

SPEAK LOUDLY
BUT CARRY A
SMALL STICK

*If you always stand straight, then your
shadow can never be crooked.*

—LIU QING, former political prisoner

AMERICANS TEND TO LOOK at defending human rights in
other countries the way they might see optional surgery—
worthwhile to undertake as long as the risks are not too great.
American idealism pushes us to push others to create a world in
which governments respect the rights of their citizens and refrain
from committing atrocities against them—as long as other interests, like trade and security, are not jeopardized. As China
contemplates its relations with the United States, however,
human rights are vitally important. This is because criticism of
China's human rights record goes to the heart of the several subjects that are not negotiable for China's current leadership,
namely sovereignty, territorial integrity, noninterference, national pride, and, above all, the undisputed power of an authoritarian government that still operates within the framework, if
not the original ideology, of the Communist Party that seized
power in 1949.

For China, therefore, resisting pressure on human rights is a
matter of political survival for the sake of which Beijing has

waged an unremitting, sometimes-oblique, always-multifront war against the United States. It is a war that has involved fierce diplomatic pressure on other countries, appeals to Pan-Asian cultural solidarity, energetic lobbying inside the United States, and, most effective of all, the adoption of a cunning system of economic rewards and punishments aimed at bringing American corporations onto China's side.

There is a paradox here. The method used in the past by the United States was to threaten Beijing with high import duties on its products sold in America—resulting from a withdrawal of China's most-favored-nation status—unless the regime stopped jailing its political dissenters. That initiative, little more than a clumsy and ultimately transparent bluff, failed abysmally. China in its way inverted the American approach. Beijing threatened to impose the equivalent of economic sanctions against the United States—an effective boycott on the purchase of high-technology products and curbs on American investments in China—unless it dropped its policy of pressure and threats. The difference is that China's bluff was taken seriously, and its strategy has been remarkably successful.

As of the end of 1996, China had made no significant concessions to the United States on human rights. Indeed, it had found several ways to publicly defy and even to humiliate the United States. "Humiliate" is the correct word. In 1994, while the Clinton administration was deciding whether or not to extend most-favored-nation treatment to China and whether to link that decision to human rights, China released some political prisoners in what was certainly an effort to influence the American decision. As soon as the administration announced "delinkage," agreeing that China would have MFN no matter what its treatment of political dissent, the Beijing security apparatus swung into high gear, making new arrests, holding political trials that had earlier been postponed, cracking down on people who, supposedly, gave away "state secrets" to foreigners. "During the year the Government continued to commit widespread and well-documented human rights abuses," the annual State Department report on China found for the year 1995. "Overall, in 1995, the authorities stepped up repression of dissent. By year's end, almost all public dissent against the central authorities was silenced by intimidation, exile, or imposition of prison terms or administrative detention."[1]

What is not appreciated in the United States is the extent to which Beijing's crackdown has been part of a struggle against Western, and specifically American, influence, a struggle that China's growing economic strength and diplomatic clout have enabled it to win. Chinese arrests and imprisonments have been timed in such a way as to highlight American impotence in affecting China's domestic policies. In the most recent instance of this, the Chinese in the fall of 1996 sentenced Wang Dan—the leading student activist of the Tiananmen demonstration still in China—to eleven years in prison. The "Intermediate People's Court" of Beijing handed down the sentence literally hours after the departure of a White House and State Department delegation that had been in Beijing to make plans for the visit of Secretary of State Warren Christopher scheduled for several weeks later. The American delegation had brought up human rights in general and the case of Wang in particular during the discussions. Wang had been held incommunicado for seventeen months and presumably could have been tried and convicted at any time. By trying and convicting him when they did, China forced the United States into a familiar predicament: it had to either make a show of canceling the Christopher visit to protest Wang's imprisonment or make a show of not canceling it. In the former instance, it would hold matters of vital importance hostage to the treatment of a twenty-seven-year-old former student; in the latter instance, it would publicly renounce its former demands that China improve its record in order to have normal relations.

In the case of Wang Dan, the United States chose the second course. The very day that reports reached the United States of Wang's sentence, Washington declared that the Christopher visit would go ahead. In so doing, the United States brought to completion a long-term process of backing down on human rights in the face of China's power to defy it. Beginning with the Tiananmen massacre in 1989, American policy under President Bush had been to maintain correct state-to-state relations with China, including the occasional top-level meeting, but to keep a certain distance from the leaders, specifically Prime Minister Li Peng and President Jiang Zemin, responsible for the massacre, the round-ups, the televised confessions, and the jailings that followed it. During the 1992 election campaign, candidate Bill Clinton had criticized that policy as weak and inadequate. "Instead of leading an international effort to pressure the Chinese government to reform, the Bush administration has coddled the dictators and pleaded for progress, but refused to impose penalties for intransigence." In his State of the Union address in January 1994, Clinton announced to applause: "As we build a more constructive relationship with China, we must continue to insist on clear signs of improvement of that country's human rights record."

In the light of subsequent actions, which have involved a fair amount of "coddling the dictators," those ringing declarations now seem part of a determination to speak loudly but carry a small stick. First came the 1994 decision permanently to "delink" MFN from China's human rights record, a gesture that was followed by a renewed crackdown on dissenters in China which included the rearrest and eventual imprisonment of Wei Jingsheng as well as numerous other dissidents, including a group of fifteen promoters of free labor unions. Then came National Security Adviser Anthony Lake's trip of reconciliation to Beijing in the summer of 1996, after which the Clinton administration cheerfully announced its invitation to Jiang Zemin to exchange state visits in 1997, a gesture that put an end even to the appearance that the United States was keeping its distance from those leaders directly responsible for the worst of China's human rights abuses. "I think it would be fair to say that my policies with regard to China have been somewhat different from what I talked about in the campaign," Clinton admitted to *The New York Times* a few months later, just as the new presidential campaign was getting under way—that expression "somewhat different" being one of the major understatements of the president's career. Then with the Wang Dan case, and the decision for the Christopher visit to go ahead as planned, the United States took a step toward even greater "delinkage." From now on, there would not even be the most pro forma diplomatic protest against China, no matter how cruel its human rights crackdown became. Beijing's victory was complete, the American surrender unconditional.

It is worth noting several other aspects of the Wang case. Wang, for one, had already spent four years in prison immediately after Tiananmen. His new eleven-year sentence meant that he would most likely be in prison for all but about a year of the eighteen years between his twentieth and thirty-eighth birthdays, all for urging democratic reform on his own government. The specific charge against him in 1996 was sedition, or, as the court put it in its announcement of his sentence, of "plotting to subvert the government," which he did in part by writing and publishing articles "in overseas newspapers and magazines and distributing them in China to mold public opinion." One of those articles had been published in 1993 on the op-ed page of *The New York Times.* It was written at a time when most Chinese human rights activists abroad were fighting against a bid by China to host the Olympic Games in the year 2000. But Wang wrote that he favored Beijing's Olympics application. China, he argued, would be "more likely to adjust its conduct in line with international norms" if it ended up hosting the games. By contrast, if China was ostracized, Wang warned, "conservative forces in the Communist Party [would] further stir nationalistic, xenophobic sentiment and attack factions that have been closer to America and Europe."[2] Wang's prescient warning about "conservative forces in the Communist Party" suggests the underlying reason for the cruel treatment he received. It is an expression of the political struggle in Beijing in which anti-Western hardliners have gained the upper hand.

Our argument here is not that the United States should place human rights above every interest in its relations with China. The threats of economic sanctions—specifically to link China's performance on human rights with America's granting of most-favored-nation status—was a bad idea in the first place. It was a policy with no teeth, and it was contrary to the other American goals of building an economic relationship with China and gaining its strategic cooperation.

But the amateurish, fumbling, and inconsistent policy toward China adopted by the Clinton administration highlights several characteristics of the Sino-American relationship. For one, it sent a clear message that in any test of wills, the United States will back down in the face of the inflexible determination not to yield. It showed too that whatever policies the administration in Washington may adopt, human rights will remain a source of serious conflict between the two countries, unless Beijing makes genuine democratic reforms. There will always be powerful groups within the United States and a certain element of public opinion that will want to punish China for its rights violations, and those groups, which include the Congress, human rights organizations, and much of the press, cannot be ignored in the White House or the State Department. Friction on human rights will continue indefinitely into the future.

Most important, the Clinton administration's weakness and waffling on human rights and its invitation to Jiang to come to Washington are more likely to ensure than to deter future conflicts. The ultimate American objective on China is to induce China to behave responsibly and to become more democratic. The rapprochement with China inaugurated by the Lake visit to Beijing was a gift to the current Chinese leadership, whose hardline approach both to the United States and on human rights will have been vindicated. Jiang and the leadership group around him were strengthened, their hard line against the United States vindicated. In the summer of 1996 Jiang was pressing inside the leadership to be given the same title, Party Chairman, that Mao Zedong had held, even while he remained the head of state. He was reaching for a level of formal power in China that surpassed even that held by Deng Xiaoping during the 1980s, indeed, that nobody has held since Mao himself—a level of power that does not augur well for the chances of democracy in China. Jiang might fail. But if he succeeds, he will owe his success at least in part to the stunning victory over the United States granted him by the Clinton administration, a victory that enhanced his prestige at a time when defying American wishes appeals to nationalist Chinese sentiment.

THERE ARE THOSE who argue, not without reason, that what is called engagement, that is, maintaining a full and growing array of normal contacts and exchanges with China, opens up a far-wider avenue toward change for the better in China than any policy of criticism, sanctions, and isolation. That position gains in strength because China has changed enormously in the nearly two decades since the United States has had full diplomatic relations with it. China was once a place, to take just one example of this change, where homosexuals were jailed and, in some of the more radical periods of Maoist rule, executed. Now there are gay bars in Beijing, just one indication of the way in which the grip of party control over personal life has been almost entirely loosened. Even formerly imprisoned dissidents of the Democracy Wall period, while under near-constant surveillance, are allowed to run businesses and to grow rich in China's new world of free enterprise. In the past they would have been subject to constant study and indoctrination meetings, to readings and discussions of the latest editorial in the *People's Daily*, and to public attack in their work unit whenever the party authorities called for a campaign to ferret out the class enemy.

These are very meaningful differences with the recent past, the most meaningful being that the Chinese people, rather than having to endure state-mandated poverty, materially stark and uncomfortable lives, have gained the right to improve their economic conditions. This includes studying in China and abroad, seeking a job, moving to another city, having a telephone, renting an office, going into business. China in essence has changed from a totalitarian society, where every aspect of life was regulated, to a dictatorship, where regulation and prohibition apply only to political life. The truth, and it is a bitter truth for those who care about China's imprisoned dissenters, is that the average person in China is rather apathetic about human rights the way they are defined in the West. The indications are that the people, gratefully released from the terrible intrusions of the past, are happy with their government, and this happiness depends more, as it does in other countries, on its economic performance and its ability to maintain law and order than on its respect for civil liberties.

This is true even though the penalties for infractions of the political rules are swift and harsh. China has no independent judiciary. The courts may have all of the trappings of the solemnity and due process of Western courts, but they merely rubber-stamp the actions of the security police. There are almost no acquittals in Chinese courts, certainly none in political cases. Nobody wins on appeal. There are no newspapers or magazines not closely controlled by the government. No organization, club, or association, not even a religious or recreational one, can exist without official authorization. No crusading newspaper editor will take up the cause of a wrongfully convicted defendant, unless he is prepared to go to prison himself. Once you have run afoul of the authorities in China, you are isolated, without recourse or succor or comfort; you are alone in the face of the undisputed power of the leviathan state. China remains a country where, under certain circumstances, its own laws, procedures, and guarantees of protection—indeed its own Constitution—are violated. Human rights organizations whose compilation of data about China has always been accurate in the past estimate that there are about three thousand political prisoners in the country, though the truth is nobody can know this for sure. That number would be a vast reduction from Maoist days when hundreds of thousands were sent to work camps in remote regions because some party functionary, needing to fulfill his quota of "rightists" in his organization, willy-nilly designated 5 or 10 percent of his workforce as political criminals. But China remains a country of arbitrary

police authority, cruel punishments, Kafkaesque legal procedures, and Orwellian justifications, all of it presided over by the
man who, unless the current course is changed, will be honored
at the White House sometime in 1997.

In about 1995, the phrase "strike hard" came into frequent use
in China's press. It designated a stepped-up campaign against
crime, which was on the increase. The words were meant to
apply especially to the "relentless pursuit" of ordinary criminals—murderers, thieves, rapists, embezzlers—and unprece-
dentedly large numbers of people accused of those crimes were
arrested, convicted after trials that normally lasted twenty minutes or so, and then, in thousands of instances, publicly executed
with a bullet in the back of the head.

But "strike hard" also suggests the way in which the regime
has tightened its political controls, especially since the Tiananmen Movement of 1989. The regime evidently felt, in the wake
of the student uprising, that it needed to adopt more unmistakably tough policies on dissent if it was to be able to take the risks
involved in the unabated liberalization of the economy. In the
mid-1990s, especially, with Deng Xiaoping passing from the
scene and the possibility of a power struggle looming in the near
future, a series of harsh policies were adopted that affected
China's human rights record across the board.

ON MAY 6, 1996, shortly before Anthony Lake was in China
engineering Sino-American rapprochement, a Chinese "work
team" showed up at Ganden, which is one of three major Buddhist monasteries in Lhasa, the capital of Tibet. The work team
was present to enforce compliance with a directive issued the
month before, ordering the removal of pictures of the Dalai
Lama from all monasteries. The Chinese refused to negotiate
with a group of monks at the monastery. The monks began to
sing and dance in the monastery courtyard and eventually to
throw stones at the Chinese. A scuffle ensued during which there
were a few nonfatal injuries on both sides.[3]

That night, ten truckloads of Chinese troops surrounded the monastery. Other troops in the surrounding hills began firing into it. In the morning, the soldiers invaded the compound and over the next couple of days arrested at least eighty-six monks, three of whom suffered gunshot wounds. Then the Chinese authorities offered substantial monetary rewards for information about other monks who remained in hiding. They closed the monastery, which houses about five hundred to seven hundred monks, for what was called "consolidation and rectification," and an announcement was made to the effect that the arrested monks were being "educated." Similar episodes of invasion and arrests took place in other monasteries around Tibet. An editorial set the tone for the crackdown: "Everyone in the region must understand clearly that the struggle against the Dalai Lama group is a long-term, bitter, complex, 'you-die-I-live' political battle with no possibility of compromise."

The 1996 operation by the Chinese army was of course only the latest and far from the harshest incident of repression in Tibet by China, which has waged a war of attrition against Tibet since 1959, when its army was sent to crush an independence movement centering around the Dalai Lama. The Chinese have moved to eliminate any remaining influence by the Dalai Lama, who went into exile in India after the invasion. The most ridiculous recent incident involved China's virtual imprisonment of the six-year-old boy Gendum Choekyi Nyima, who had been chosen by Tibetan monks, in consultation with the Dalai Lama, as the new incarnation of the Panchen Lama, Tibet's second-most-revered religious figure. Months after his disappearance, China's ambassador to the United Nations in Geneva acknowledged that the boy had "been put under the protection of the government at the request of his parents." This was done, the New China News Agency reported, because the boy "was at risk of being kidnapped by Tibetan separatists and his security has been threatened." Needless to say, Chinese solicitude for the welfare and safety of the young boy did not include any information about his or his parents' whereabouts, much less any statement from them confirming that they had requested protection for their son.

Tibet to be sure has for centuries been a kind of feudal theocracy about which much Western sentimental nonsense has been written. The portrait of a happy people ruled over benignly by a gentle Buddha-king is no more accurate than rhapsodic portrayals of American Indians as peoples of superior spiritual qualities. But even if the Tibetans, like the Indians, are not saints, they have a two-thousand-year-old culture and way of life that is being destroyed in a way analogous to, though with less outright warfare and far less actual killing than, the way the Indians were destroyed in North America in the last century. China's policy on Tibet since the territory was essentially annexed in 1959 has involved large-scale colonization of Tibetan land, the eradication of many aspects of the Tibetan culture, and ruthless suppression of any expressed sentiment in favor of the Buddhist leader recognized by all Tibetans as a kind of supreme spiritual authority, the exiled Dalai Lama. In the past, during the cruelest period of Tibetan cultural eradication, from the late 1950s through the 1960s, celibate monks were forced to copulate and to use pages from the Buddhist sutras as toilet paper. All but 13 of the 6,254 monasteries that used to exist in the country have been closed, according to one student of Tibetan affairs. The Potala Palace, which for centuries served both as a seat of government and a religious center, is open these days only to tourists, who are taken by Chinese guides on rapid, partial tours while, as a visitor there noted, "Tibetans stood plaintively outside."[4]

China's policy on Tibet is no secret to American leaders. In the 1992 campaign, Bill Clinton spoke of the "harsh persecution" that Tibetans continue to suffer "under their Beijing oppressors." During his confirmation hearings, Secretary of State Warren Christopher, urging that the United States "be more effective with China in respect to Tibet," said "the violations of human rights there are very striking." The Chinese, typically, have accused the United States of seeking malicious ends because of such critical remarks, the official New China News Agency in

1996, for example, claiming that "the U.S. government and the Congress have been backing the separatist activity of the Dalai Lama for a long time."⁵ Since 1994, the Chinese have applied that familiar term "strike hard" to what the newspapers call "splittism" or "secessionism" in Tibet, and they have become more and more strident in their association of the Dalai Lama with both of those crimes and with what the propaganda organs call "terrorism." Bai Zhao, the president of the Tibet Higher People's Court, said in June 1996: "We must develop the 'Strike Hard' campaign to end secessionism in all its forms and halt the terrorist activities of our enemies."⁶ (Bai, though no doubt a distinguished jurist, did not spell out what these terrorist activities were.) The Tibet *Daily*, reporting around that same time on the ninth Five-Year Plan for Tibet, declared: "We must expand and deepen and publicly expose and criticize the Dalai Lama, stripping away his cloak of being a 'religious leader.'" The newspaper continued: "We must ensure that the broad masses of the people clearly understand that what he is advocating with his so-called 'Tibetan independence,' 'high-level autonomy' and 'greater Tibetan region' is really opposition to the Communist Party."⁷

In fact, in repeated statements, the Dalai Lama has stated that he is willing to acknowledge Chinese sovereignty over Tibet and to give up any calls for independence on the condition that Tibet is given a meaningful degree of autonomy. But while China's policy is theoretically one of autonomy (indeed, the official name of Tibet within China is Tibetan Autonomous Region), the actions taken over the past several years indicate a policy of Chinese settlement and cultural extermination.* That explains the raids against monasteries, the banning of the Dalai Lama's

---

*China's heavy-handedness in Tibet so discredited the notion of an "autonomous region" that Beijing, while promising Hong Kong a high degree of "autonomy" after its reversion to China in 1997, came up with a new term, "special administrative region," if only to avoid cynical allusions to China's other "autonomous regions."

photograph, the "reeducation" of monks, and the importation into Tibet of all the institutions of the party and the government, the rubber-stamp court system, the phony People's Congress, and the propaganda organs that exist in China.

It is as if some foreign power had occupied Italy, stripped it economically, forced the pope to escape into exile, closed down the main churches, banned the pope's pictures, writings, and opinions, and rounded up priests and bishops to be "educated," all the while declaring that Italy was an autonomous region whose culture, religious beliefs, and traditional ways of life were being fastidiously respected by the occupying authorities.

CHINA'S SUCCESSFUL RESISTANCE of American human rights pressure begins with the adoption of hard-line battle tactics in Beijing around late 1993 or early 1994, soon after China's anti-American hard-liners had gained prominence in the central government and the Communist Party. They argued that the human rights question represented an opportunity to confront the United States, demonstrate its lack of resolve, and get away with it. They wanted to fight the Clinton administration's major demand, namely that China show progress on human rights or be penalized with high tariffs on Chinese exports to the United States.

Clinton himself had prepared the ground for the conflict even before he became president by making an issue of the Bush administration's China policy and by making public references to China's leaders as "oppressors" and "tyrants." Candidate Clinton's key adviser on China was Winston Lord, a former aide to Henry Kissinger and also a former American ambassador in Beijing, as well as a lifelong Republican who had broken with the Bush administration over its China policy. Lord had played a key role in the 1980s in promoting what was then the conventional wisdom on China among both governmental and academic specialists that post-Mao China was evolving quite naturally and, by virtue of the logic of late-twentieth-century political development, away from Communism and toward both a market economy and a more liberal political system.

It is difficult to exaggerate the extent of Western optimism about China in those days. The country, which had been so rigidly controlled throughout the 1960s and most of the 1970s that it was virtually impossible for a foreigner to have a private relationship of any sort with any Chinese person, was rapidly changing, and American experts were understandably elated. The expansion of contacts with the United States, which included trade, tourism, student and scholarly exchanges, and binational marriages, was doing exactly what it was supposed to do in theory—make China itself more open and more democratic. And since so many welcome changes in China came with the rapid growth of ties with the United States, it was easy to see a causal relationship. The belief was that a peaceful revolution was under way, one spurred by the American example as well as by the natural talents and aspirations of the Chinese people.

Things changed abruptly with the Tiananmen massacre of June 4, 1989. Journalists in China at that time whose experience in the country dated from the mid-1980s were shocked by the sudden emergence of a doctrinaire regime that gunned down its own people in a full-scale military operation, engaged in mass arrests, and waged a vast media campaign consisting entirely of lies and distortions. To those who had been in China during the late 1970s and early 1980s, however, especially during the crackdown on the Democracy Wall Movement of 1978–79, the China that emerged after the Tiananmen massacre was eerily familiar. Nobody wanted to talk; Chinese friends disappeared from foreigners' view; literally overnight a festive atmosphere was replaced by a regime of fear and intimidation.

Lord, who left Beijing as ambassador a few months before the massacre, was disillusioned. He began to appear on television and in the press as an outspoken critic of the Chinese government, but also as a prophet of its quick demise. He declared that the regime's days were numbered, at one point suggesting it was "a matter of weeks or months" before China's leaders were swept from power. Many other sinologists also misread the implications of Tiananmen and were uncertain about the regime's future. But two years later, Lord was still suggesting that once Deng Xiaoping died "we're going to see a major move towards a more pragmatic and reformist government, a move towards a more pluralistic, if not democratic, system."[8]

Around that time, Lord rejected the Bush administration's kid-glove China policy and later became a Clinton supporter. Specifically, he spoke out in favor of the main campaign statement that Clinton was making on China (not a major theme of the campaign but nonetheless widely noted in the press) to the effect that Bush's policies had been shamefully weak and that his would be tougher. Lord's belief that those leaders some Democrats were calling the "butchers of Beijing" would soon be replaced echoed a deep, persistent Western faith that eventually our example will lead the Chinese to become more like us, to turn from bureaucratic dictatorship and become free-market liberals. The Chinese had gone so quickly and so far in that direction in the 1980s that it seemed impossible even after Tiananmen that westward-leaning momentum would not resume, just as soon as the abhorrent group in power disappeared, which seemed imminent given the great age of the paramount leader Deng Xiaoping.

This expectation rested on the assumption that a policy of condemnation and warnings against China could be carried out with no risk. If the regime was going to fall in a year or two, then confronting that regime, however abrasively, would entail no worsening of America-China ties. Indeed, it would encourage the reform forces in China waiting to take power, who would then be grateful to the United States for its unfriendliness toward the old regime. It was a logical assumption, and it might even have proved to be true had China not played the game more skillfully and with far greater clarity of purpose than Clinton did. In fact, the approach of the new administration brought about something close to the opposite of the intended result—a hardening of China's position on human rights at considerable cost to the United States.

Clinton elaborated his China policy in a formal executive order of May 1993. It served notice on China's leaders that they had exactly one year to improve human rights in several specific areas, from allowing emigration of family members of dissidents to reducing the mistreatment of the Tibetans to better accounting of political prisoners. If there wasn't "overall significant progress" in those areas, Clinton threatened, China would be removed from the list of most favored nations.

In fact, "most favored nation" is a misnomer given that all the world's major trading nations are on the American "most favored" list, meaning that standard tariffs are imposed on their exports to the United States. Countries that are not on the list, such as Libya and Iraq and a few other hostile states, have to pay such burdensome tariffs on their exports to the United States that most trade is effectively cut off. Roughly one-third of China's exports go to the United States, which is by far its largest single national market. To have put China into the off-list category would have meant a virtual end to the large and growing trade surplus that China had built up with the United States, but Chinese retaliation would also have cut down on American exports to China.

In other words, if Clinton had actually taken away China's MFN status, two major consequences would have followed: one, the United States would have cut itself off from the biggest and fastest economic expansion in world history; two, China's export-driven economic takeoff, based on private business and the explosive growth of an independent Chinese bourgeois class, would have been gravely harmed by the closing to it of the American market. In other words, Clinton could not have carried out his threat without imposing an excessive penalty on China and without incurring American losses out of proportion to the gains that would have accrued. And so the American president was putting himself into a position where he would have to choose between two almost equally unattractive alternatives: carry out the ultimatum or find a pretext to retreat from it.

The Chinese seem to have understood this fact. Their words and their deeds and what we know about the secret meetings that took place in Beijing at that time (described earlier) leave little doubt that by late in 1993 the Chinese leadership decided to call what amounted to an amateur's bluff. Clinton, however, unaware of the view that was coming to prevail in China and having taken little action during the first few months after he issued his ultimatum, dispatched State Department officials to Beijing in an attempt to gain Chinese compliance with it. First, in late February 1994, went John Shattuck, the Clinton administration's top human rights official. Shattuck met with Chinese officials and, in an attempt to publicize the American concern for human rights, also extended his now-famous invitation to Wei Jingsheng to meet with him.

Wei had emerged during the Democracy Wall Movement of 1978 and 1979 as the major theoretician of democracy for China. He was for about a year and a half the editor of the best known of the unofficial magazines published during that period and probably the most effective leader of the fledgling movement. In late 1979, he was given a fifteen-year jail term for his "counterrevolutionary" activities and he had only been released, almost all of his term served, a few months before Shattuck's arrival in Beijing. The American invitation in hand, Wei evaded heavy surveillance and met secretly with Shattuck. When Chinese officials later learned about that event, they were infuriated at what struck them as a sneaky American attempt to embarrass China.

In the meantime, in mid-March, a still more senior American official arrived in Beijing to press the Clinton administration's hard line on human rights. This was Secretary of State Warren Christopher, whose purpose in China was to reiterate the American ultimatum, the deadline for which was now only ten weeks away. In an attempt to underline his seriousness, the no-nonsense Christopher adopted an even sterner style than usual. He spurned the offer of a Chinese limousine, a normal courtesy extended by the hosts, and opted for an embassy vehicle instead. He informed the Chinese he didn't want to attend any of the usual banquets. And he refused to stay at a guest house reserved for senior VIPs like himself, opting instead for a suite at the China World Hotel. Most important, perhaps, was Christopher's hard-line rhetoric, consisting of words that the American secretary of state would soon have to swallow. "I will reiterate that overall significant progress on human rights remains necessary if I am to recommend the renewal of Most Favored Nation trade status for China," he told a business group in Tokyo just before his flight to Beijing. "What we seek in China should not be regarded as extraordinary. What we seek is no more than the recognition of the most basic universally recognized human rights."[9]

In China, Christopher wasted no time in getting down to business. Reporting on the first meeting between the secretary of state and his hosts, one journalist said that the opening conversations consisted of "harsh and acrimonious exchanges."[10] Christopher bluntly told the Chinese that the administration was ready to impose harsh trade penalties unless they made substantial progress on human rights, and the Chinese just as bluntly told him they considered such threats outrageous. Beijing's response led Christopher to feel that he'd had enough. It took the American ambassador Stapleton Roy to talk Christopher out of leaving China after only one day in the country. Christopher at one point did shutter himself in his hotel room all day.

Chinese authorities followed up the Christopher meeting by defiantly taking exactly the steps that the administration was warning against, and not only in human rights. It made a shipment of chemical weapons to Iran and of missile parts to Pakistan, defying American warnings about arms proliferation.[11] As for human rights, China's Public Security Bureau arrested Wei Jingsheng and sent him to prison. A few weeks after that, the authorities amended China's public order law, broadening what were already sweeping police powers to detain, or restrict the activities of, democratic and labor union activists as well as leaders of religious and ethnic minorities.

The fact that China's leaders had reached a consensus just a few months earlier that the United States was the country's principal global rival does not satisfactorily explain why China chose to be so defiant not only of American diplomatic pressure but of global public opinion on its human rights policies. The truth is that China, ever cognizant of foreign depredations during the period of imperialism, is extremely prickly when it comes to what the Chinese see as interference in their own affairs. Moreover, many in China, and not only in the leadership, genuinely believe that granting Western-style human rights would create disorder in China. From their perspective, their market-driven economic policies allow enough freedom and create enough disorder. Adding an element of democracy to this volatile mix would make it combustible, as it did in 1989 at Tiananmen Square.

But the Chinese leaders defied American pressure and threats because they believed they could get away with it. And that in turn was because they had come up with a way of turning their burgeoning economic power into a political and diplomatic weapon. Briefly put, the Chinese dangled billions of dollars' worth of trade and investment deals in front of American corporations, and they threatened to, and in some instances did, go elsewhere to punish the United States for its human rights meddling. Many deals were concluded well before the MFN deadline in early June; others were still being negotiated but close to agreement; yet others were only at the early stages of discussion. But in every case, the Chinese made it clear that these deals would collapse if the Clinton administration carried out its threat to suspend MFN for China. The American business community, naturally eager for a larger share of the China market, was unhappy about the threat of economic retaliation for Chinese human rights abuses. In just a few months, China transformed several Fortune 500 companies into a formidable New China Lobby.

We will turn to that in the next chapter, with this dramatic foreshadowing. The lobbying involved some of the wealthiest tycoons in America, men who live lives of material abundance unimaginable to most other inhabitants of the planet, standing shoulder to shoulder with dictators and warning of the extreme unwisdom involved in their government's speaking out on behalf of a few people kept in dungeons because of the peaceful expression of their political views. Bill Gates of Microsoft, then the second-richest man in the world, met with Jiang Zemin in April 1994 and declared, first, that his goal was to increase sales in China by 50 percent a year and, second, that "it's a little strange to try to tie free trade" to human rights issues. "It is basically getting down to interference in internal affairs," he said.[12]

Perhaps Gates is correct. The argument could be made, and is made, that over the long run, Microsoft software will do more to change China than all global preachments on human rights combined. We do believe that China one day might accept the principles of Western-style liberal democracy that have become the global norm, and when it does, the economic change fostered by trade with the West will have been instrumental in bringing about that result. A tightly controlled authoritarianism cannot indefinitely sustain itself within an essentially free-market capitalist system.

But that happy outcome cannot be expected for a long time, if, indeed, it ever comes about. What recent experience has shown is that the Chinese leadership can use the wealth and power stemming from economic reform to quell demands for political change and to battle against foreign pressure. Trade with the West, including with Microsoft Corporation, has a double edge. It brings in practices and ideas that ought to lead to political reform. But it also enhances the power of the regime to resist and suppress political reform and to force other countries to drop their demands for it. In 1996, China succeeded in prevent-

ing the United Nations Commission on Human Rights in
Geneva from even considering the question of China's human
rights record as part of its annual meeting. China accomplished
that goal via a gigantic, global lobbying effort that included enlisting the support of corporations in the effort to remove human
rights from the agenda. In this sense, a figure like Gates, standing side by side with China's president and the head of the
Communist Party so that the two of them together can accuse
the West of interfering in China's internal affairs, reflects, not an
inclination toward long-term change in China, but a power to
resist that change.

Human rights in this sense take on a practical dimension. Stable democracies are more likely to behave responsibly and peace-
fully in international affairs than are dictatorships. But there is
the moral dimension as well, the notion that when somebody's
spirit is crushed by tyranny, it is everybody's business at least to
speak out and possibly to refuse to do business as usual with the
crushers of that spirit. That is the idea that animated American
policy in the former Yugoslavia as well as in the former Soviet
Union. It should have animated the policy of the West when
Germany was annihilating the Jews, but sadly it didn't. At the
very least, rich and privileged American corporate executives
who dismiss the human rights issue as a kind of unwarranted domestic interference in somebody else's affairs ought to reflect on
the people who are in prison for their beliefs as well as on the
consequences of resisting efforts to have them released. There are
the oppressed Tibetans, who are the worst Chinese human rights
offense. There are, in addition, as we have noted, as many as
three thousand other people in prison in China today because
they expressed the wrong opinion or belonged to the wrong organization. Nobody knows them better than a slight, short, be-
spectacled, and very brave man named Liu Qing.

Liu works in a small office in New York to publicize China's
violations of human rights, violations that he has experienced
firsthand. He spent eleven years in the Chinese Gulag, three of
them undergoing what the Chinese euphemistically call "strict

supervision." It meant that he was required to sit all day every day without exception on a narrow chair made out of rope cables that dug into his flesh, not moving, watched over every minute by his prison guards. When he slept, he was required to do so in a regulation position, on his back, hands to his sides, and if he shifted, he was rudely awakened. But Liu endured his punishment to the end, reciting to himself a Chinese proverb to give himself courage. "If you always stand straight, then your shadow can never be crooked."

Liu's crime dates to 1979, when he was the deputy editor of the *April 5 Forum,* one of the leading short-lived free magazines that came out during the Democracy Wall period. He was a close associate of Wei Jingsheng, and when he published the statement that Wei made on his own behalf at his trial in October 1979, Liu was arrested and imprisoned for three years without trial, the Chinese Public Security Bureau taking advantage of a provision in Chinese law that allows for up to thirty-six months of "administrative detention" of any person deemed by the authorities to require it, with no trial, no defense lawyer, no possibility of appeal. Later Liu managed to write a two-hundred-page account of his arrest and imprisonment, and, with the help of an inmate being released from his labor camp in Shaanxi Province, he smuggled it out to the West. Eventually it was translated and published at least in part in twenty-eight countries. Not surprisingly, the official spokesman of the Foreign Ministry declared that the Liu manuscript was a "crude forgery." Back in Shaanxi, Liu was put on trial as the author of this "forgery" and sentenced to eight additional years in prison for "disseminating counter-revolutionary propaganda."

Liu served three years of administrative detention and his eight-year sentence, and when he was finally released in 1990, he and his wife were able to go to the United States. Eventually Liu got a job as the head of a small organization called Human Rights in China, which collects information on political prisoners, publishes newsletters in both English and Chinese, and tries to distribute that information in China itself and around the world.

Liu, as a member of a nongovernmental organization, attends various meetings on human rights, such as the annual session of the United Nations Commission on Human Rights in Geneva, where effective global lobbying has succeeded in preventing China's human rights record from being officially considered by that august body.

Liu fights on, his phone in his windowless cubbyhole in Manhattan ringing all the time with new stories of arrests, disappearances, torture, and mistreatment of dissidents in China. He represents one side of the human rights debate, the side that wishes to keep up a certain pressure on the Chinese government, that does not have faith that the simple act of engagement with China will lead to democracy there. On the other side of a very unequal match is the Chinese government itself, which has devised numerous highly effective ways of overcoming American objections to its policies on human rights and other matters as well, a campaign so effective that it forced even the president of the United States within a matter of months to reverse himself on the question of China.

CHAPTER 4

THE NEW
CHINA LOBBY

FOR AMERICAN CORPORATE executives who wanted to reap the fabled profits of business with China, it had never been easy. Eager Chinese officials would tell them, "Let's deal." But often the deals ran into postponements that went on for years, as the company provided answers to innumerable questions, turned over technical specifications, and saw promised tax abatements and import-duty waivers granted and then suddenly withdrawn. Some lucrative deals were nonetheless made, but in the first months of 1994, American business was inking agreements with China at a faster pace than had been seen before, or has been seen since. These early months of 1994, as we have pointed out, were the time when the Clinton administration was threatening to cancel China's most-favored-nation trading status, and the Chinese had figured out a way to stop him with an economic offensive aimed at enlisting American corporate support on behalf of China. And so:

In January 1994, China floated a total of $1 billion in bonds in American financial markets, or, as Reuters reported, China was "finishing the last leg of its roadshow in the United States," organized by "its lead underwriter Merrill Lynch Capital Markets."[1]

In February, the Ford Motor Company was deep in talks with China regarding joint ventures in that country for component-part manufacturing and possible entire-vehicle assembly. "China is of major importance to us," a Ford executive said, "and the establishment of this organization [Ford China Operations, whose formation was announced at that time] demonstrates our serious intention to be a key player in the development of the Chinese automotive industry."[2]

In April, the Chinese held up the prospect of billions of dollars' worth of deals that drew seven hundred businesspeople from three hundred American corporations to Chinese "trade and investment fairs" in New York and Los Angeles. The Chinese later claimed that they had signed contracts and agreements worth $11.1 billion with American companies.

Also in April, Chinese officials in Shanghai hosted senior executives from Time Warner, Inc., and discussed a joint endeavor to open an amusement park in China. On April 28, Vice Premier Zou Jiahua journeyed to AT&T's offices in New Jersey to sign contracts that were expected to generate more than $500 million for the company.

A few days later, IBM revealed that it had reached several agreements with China, including joint-venture agreements. IBM chairman Louis V. Gerstner Jr. had visited China in March to negotiate with senior Chinese officials.[3]

In May, The Wall Street Journal reported that Boeing was "within weeks" of completing a $5 billion sale of commercial jetliners to China. For weeks, Boeing executives had been openly pushing for continuation of China's most-favored-nation status.[4]

Not so coincidentally, shortly before that, in early May, the then Speaker of the House, Tom Foley, broke publicly with his fellow Democrat in the White House, saying Clinton shouldn't link trade with human rights. "It's very public and challenging and confrontational," he said. Foley represented the Spokane area of Washington State, the home of Boeing. Indeed, there are no China critics in the congressional delegation from Washington State.

The day after Clinton's announcement, Kentucky Fried Chicken president John Cranor announced in Shanghai that the fast-food chain would invest $200 million in China over the following four years, and he explicitly linked the investment decision to Clinton's announcement: "By permanently delinking human rights and economic investment, President Clinton has removed uncertainty from our China business."[5]

While many congressmen reflected the pro-China stance of companies in their home states, other key political leaders received delegations from China who impressed them with the potential economic benefits of a cordial relationship between the two countries. New York governor Mario Cuomo signed a framework agreement in April 1994 to facilitate high-technology exports to China by corporations in his state. A senior state official responsible for promoting exports said at the time: "They are the ones who approached us. They made several overtures." Cuomo's announcement made clear that he wanted Clinton not just to delink MFN from human rights but to extend it unconditionally to China.[6]

The Chinese even sent lobbying delegations to the federal government itself after accurately discerning a split in the Clinton administration between the human rights promoters at the State Department and the business-first elements elsewhere in the government. In mid-April, Commerce Secretary Ron Brown signed an agreement with visiting Foreign Trade Minister Wu Yi to establish permanent working groups for bilateral trade and investment. Acting as Madame Wu's host and promoter in all but name was the U.S.–China Business Council, composed of companies with business interests in China who were at the same time pressing strenuously for a continuation of China's MFN status. At a luncheon at the council, attended by fifty Chinese officials, Madame Wu spoke tantalizingly before the two hundred businessmen present with prospects of huge profits for American investors in capital- and technology-intensive projects.[7]

Only one voice in the business community sounded a different note. Levi Strauss & Co. had announced in the spring of 1993 that it would no longer do business in China because of China's "pervasive violation of human rights." It stopped purchasing about $50 million annually in trousers and shirts from Chinese contractors. However, it neatly avoided sacrificing its main source of potential profit: it conceded that it would continue allowing its distributor Jardine Marketing Services to sell its prized jeans in China.[8]

As the campaign for delinkage, skillfully, subtly orchestrated by China, turned into a juggernaut by late April 1994, Winston Lord jettisoned the approach to China that he had championed until then. In a letter he wrote to Secretary of State Christopher that was promptly leaked to the press, Lord declared, in effect, that the policy he had fostered—of making trade benefits for China contingent on its human rights record—was a failure. Indeed it was: on May 26, a chastened Bill Clinton declared that he would extend China's most-favored-nation trading status without regard to China's human rights record, thereby marking one of the most complete turnabouts in recent American diplomatic history. After months of intensive effort, China had won a complete victory over the United States on human rights, a victory that was crowned two years later by the 1996 invitation to Beijing's previously spurned top leader to make an exchange of state visits with Clinton in 1997.

ALL COUNTRIES of course strive to influence public opinion and policy making in the United States. Still, there are four special characteristics to Chinese lobbying and public relations campaigning in the United States that, taken together, make it different from these efforts by other countries.

One of them, the most important, is that China is in so many ways an adversary, a dictatorship, an emerging superpower whose interests are at odds with those of the United States. Second is the ferocity of China's efforts to influence American actions, the tone of virulent aggrievement with which it greets disagreement, and the breadth of its activities in the United States, which include not just propaganda, threats, and bluster, along with intense private lobbying, but also efforts to buy or steal technology and transfer it to China. (More on this subject later.) Third, an extremely influential group of American former high officials have come to dominate the public debate about China even as they profit from the policies that they advocate. And finally, China has used to great effect the threat of economic warfare to enlist behind it one of the broadest business efforts to influence national policy in all of American history.

In the background of most of these efforts is the lure of profit and the concomitant threat to deny profit if China does not have its way. When Prime Minister Li Peng punished Boeing and bought $1.5 billion worth of Airbus Industrie Airplanes in 1996, he couldn't have been more explicit as to the reason. He praised European leaders because "they do not attach political strings to cooperation with China, unlike the Americans who arbitrarily resort to the threat of sanctions or the use of sanctions."[9] The irony is that China itself has effectively used sanctions, or overt promises of economic benefits or threats of economic punishment, as means of exerting pressure on the American government, even as it issues dire warnings against the United States's doing the same thing, warnings that are repeated in vociferous tones by the businessmen who stand to suffer from Chinese sanctions. The members of what has come to be a powerful new China lobby never acknowledge that it is precisely the linking of economics and politics, the granting and the withholding of profits, that has made China's policy toward the United States so remarkably effective.

With the important exception of strong congressional support for defending Taiwan against Chinese military intimidation— arms sales have continued despite strong Chinese protests— China's multifarious lobbying activities have been very successful.

China in particular has managed to force Washington to back down on practically every threat to take action against China for some violation of international norms. Some might cite another exception, having to do with American willingness to impose sanctions on China for the pirating of music CDs, movie videos, and computer software. But, in fact, despite renewed Chinese promises to crack down in this matter, the signs by mid-1996 were that the billion-dollar pirating industry, well protected by powerful figures in the provinces and in the army, was continuing to thrive.

In any case, on all of the various questions regarding human rights (the Clinton administration in 1994 said that there were seven specific categories, including treatment of Tibet), on poison gas shipments to Iran, on missile sales to Syria and Pakistan, on nuclear help to Iran and Pakistan, and on trade practices that, as we will see in the next chapter, are aimed at maximizing technology transfers to China and the trade deficit in its favor, the United States has threatened and blustered but in the end taken very little real action. There are many reasons for this, but one of the most important is the effectiveness of what could be called the New China Lobby, a multifaceted, loosely correlated network actively encouraged and manipulated by China mainly by promising or withholding money.

"One of our biggest problems in China is that our friends in Europe and Japan hold our coats while we take on the Chinese, and they gobble up the contracts," a frustrated Winston Lord said, acknowledging the failure of American efforts to force China to halt arms sales to American enemies and to respect its trade commitments.[10] Another senior official told staffers of *Risk Report,* a newsletter on arms proliferation, "We haven't really been tough on the Chinese. They pay lip service to the rules, but they still violate them—sometimes blatantly. The reason we are looking the other way is market potential."[11]

The New China Lobby, though based largely on money, is not based only on money. It also has to do with access, which in certain circles leads to the deals that translate into money.

The Chinese for decades have had a word for this: *guan-xi* (pronounced GWAN-she), which means "relationship" or "connection." If somebody has *guan-xi,* it means that he has an advantage. Among the Chinese themselves, this might be because he has a friend or a relative in the right place—the party secretary of the best local school or the head of the neighborhood committee who assigns available apartments or the assistant to the provincial government who controls licenses to create joint foreign-Chinese companies with the right to send hard currency abroad. If you are a foreigner, your *guan-xi* might involve your friendship with Rong Yiren, who is the chairman of the China International Trust and Investment Corporation (CITIC), China's state-run merchant bank, or with Jiang Zemin himself.

A related expression, commonly used in China since the country was taken over by a Communist bureaucracy (but with its roots in imperial China), is *zou-hou-men,* literally "go the back door." The phrase expresses the realistically cynical view that qualifications, skill, and the lower price mean less in China than the ability to skirt the official rules and to slip into the Palace of Power via the rear entrance.

Foreigners able to carry out special activities in China have long benefited when they have had *guan-xi.* In the 1950s and 1960s, for example, foreign access to China was reserved almost exclusively for a small group of foreign writers and journalists who were designated "friends of China"—translation: propagandists for the Communist revolution. The Eurasian novelist Han Suyin, a Swiss citizen, was one of these "friends." Another was Edgar Snow, for years one of the very few American citizens who could go to China and, while he was there, enter the holy of holies, the meeting room where Chairman Mao met with foreign guests. There were others: the American journalists Agnes Smedley and Anna Louise Strong, the New Zealand writer Rewi Alley, the Australian Communist Wilfred Burchett, the French novelist and, later, minister of culture André Malraux. With a couple of exceptions (like Malraux), almost all of these people had access to China because of their status as "friends," a status that could easily be revoked if they engaged in "unfriendly" behavior, like telling the truth about the ongoing power struggle, or about the cult of personality around Mao, or the misery brought about by the Maoist version of voodoo economics. People like Han Suyin glowed with admiration for one man in power only to have to condemn that person a few months later and glow with admiration for somebody else who had until then been officially designated a class enemy, a capitalist roader, a black hand of the running dogs of American imperialism, a freak and a monster.

The "friends of China" wrote and spoke about China the way Chinese officials wanted to be written and spoken about. They did this because they actually believed what they said or, if a more cynical interpretation of this behavior is correct, because they needed to protect their *guan-xi*, their access to Beijing's bureaucratic pinnacle. Whatever the case, China itself skillfully created an exclusive club of supporters, rewarding them with visas, with travel permits, with meetings inside Zhongnanhai, the walled annex to the old Forbidden City, where Mao and the other revolutionary progenitors lived and worked. When some specially invited guest betrayed the leadership's hospitality, that person would be denounced as a villain and a scoundrel and held up as an example for others.

Such was the case of the Italian filmmaker Michelangelo Antonioni, a member of the Italian Communist Party who was allowed to film a documentary in China in 1972. When the resulting film, *China Is Near*, showed the Chinese the way they actually were, rather than as heroic figures in a revolutionary tableau, a campaign of vituperation was waged against him that lasted for months. Edgar Snow by contrast made a film about the building of a bridge across the Yangtze River that would not endanger his next visa. More recently, when Mao's former doctor, Li Zhisui, wrote memoirs that vividly described Mao as a cruel tyrant and a lecher, the doctor, who was living in the United States, was denounced as a liar, as was Columbia University professor Andrew Nathan, who wrote a foreword to Dr. Li's volume.

American scholars and writers who have publicly criticized the Chinese leadership for human rights violations have been denied visas to visit the country or made to enlist the support of famous Americans in a virtual publicity campaign before the visa is granted. Orville Schell, the Chinese-speaking author of several books on China, has had troubles along those lines since the early 1990s—no doubt because of his association with Human Rights Watch. In August 1996, Perry Link, a leading scholar of Chinese literature who teaches at Princeton University, was detained overnight in a hotel room and then flown out of the country the next morning. Four Public Security Bureau officers took turns sleeping in the bed next to Link's, he reported. "They cut the telephone line in the room so I couldn't call my friends in Beijing who were waiting for me," he said.[12] Similarly, another well-known China expert, Ross Terrill, who over the years has written more and more critically of China's human rights policies and has befriended dissidents, has found his visa applications turned down. The Australian-born Terrill, who, like Schell and Link, speaks very good Chinese, is an interesting case, because in the early 1970s when China was just starting its opening-up to the West, he wrote favorably of Mao's China and benefited from special access of the sort normally reserved for "friends of China." But he was refused a visa in 1995 when he was assigned by *National Geographic* to do an article on the Yangtze River gorges. He was turned down again in 1996 when, once again, *National Geographic* commissioned him to write an article, this time about Hong Kong and its connections with Guangzhou. Still later, he was invited by the Chinese Academy of Social Sciences to attend a conference in Beijing on Mao's poetry. He sent the letter of invitation and a visa application to the Chinese consulate in New York. After a delay, he received a handwritten note on plain, nonletterhead stationery informing him that he needed another letter from his host in China, but by that time the conference had already begun.

"They clearly are not above refusing visas as a punishment for people who do not toe the ideological line on certain key issues,"

Schell wrote. "By and large, I think they are quite successful at this. There is indeed an intimidation factor that makes many watch what they say out of fear that they will become persona non grata. But this is something we are already acquainted with in the Party's treatment of its own intellectuals. The threat of ostracism is powerful, not less so for foreign journalists and writers who depend on access to China to make their livings."[13]

There is a contingent of a half dozen or so senior scholars of China whose careers have flourished, in part because of their skills as analysts but also in part because they have been granted access at a high level in China. They consult informally at the White House, escort American corporate or political bigwigs on trips to China, and write scholarly analyses of Chinese politics. These academic specialists bear only a glancing similarity to the likes of Han Suyin or Edgar Snow, who were straightforward apologists for the Chinese regime at a time when it was most dictatorial and brutal. But given the nature of the Chinese government, today's academic experts face the prospect that they will be cut off if they offend the Chinese on certain subjects. It would be unfair to say that Beijing requires flattery from American scholars in exchange for access. China's leaders are more sophisticated than that. The political scientists who maintain excellent contacts with Chinese officialdom also learn how China's leaders think about issues, and that is valuable knowledge. They write useful articles on Chinese politics. But on certain subjects, like the reputation of Chairman Mao or the questions of human rights, China's military intimidation of Taiwan, and Chinese control over Tibet, it is best either to flatter or to remain silent. Beijing pays close attention. Those who play by China's rules continue to meet with vice premiers in Beijing's Great Hall of the People. Those who don't, don't.

THAT GENERAL RULE applies more strictly to the world of business than to any other, and here the Chinese have been masterful in using access to influence American policy. Among the remarkable aspects of this Chinese success is the way in which a politics of accommodation has been urged on the public and the government by the very people most likely to profit from accommodation.

It works like this: Former government officials—the most conspicuous of whom in this regard are former secretaries of state Henry Kissinger and Alexander M. Haig Jr. but include others like former deputy secretary of state Laurence Eagleburger and former national security adviser Brent Scowcroft—become counselors to companies doing business in China. The job of a counselor is to give advice. But in China, where business enterprise and the licenses needed to do business are controlled by a self-interested and self-perpetuating political elite, a crucial role of outside advisers is to make contacts with that elite.

"If a consultant wants to get a competitive contract for his client—say, the chairman of a major American corporation—part of the deal is that the consultant will speak out for China or that he will deliver Congressional or media delegations to China," said James Lilley, a former American ambassador to Beijing. The consultant knows the Chinese leaders; the American company gets a meeting with the relevant ones; the consultant gets paid by the corporation, and in order to solidify his all-important access to Chinese power brokers, he makes public statements supporting the policies that Beijing favors. "It's never explicitly stated in the contract," Lilley said, "but everyone understands the deal."[14]

Within a couple of days of the Tiananmen massacre in 1989, Kissinger issued a series of statements and wrote op-ed articles that put him squarely into the "friend of China" tradition. "I wouldn't do any sanctions," Kissinger told Peter Jennings of ABC, speaking at a time when Congress was calling for sanctions, and the Bush administration was, to a limited extent, going along with that demand.[15] The very day after the massacre Kissinger's syndicated column referred to Deng Xiaoping as "one of the great reformers in Chinese history" and a man "who chose a more humane and less chaotic course"[16] for China. In fact,

Kissinger's statement was not wrong, though it did seem a bit sycophantish when the blood was not yet dry on the paving stones of Tiananmen Square. More to the point, Kissinger's advice to President Bush was to avoid taking any measures against China that would jeopardize "vital American security interests." In another syndicated column, Kissinger criticized Congress for approving anti-Chinese sanctions that went beyond those recommended by President Bush. In that column also, he made this extraordinary statement: "No government in the world would have tolerated having the main square of its capital occupied for eight weeks by tens of thousands of demonstrators," a condition of disorder and chaos that made a crackdown "inevitable." China, Kissinger concluded, remains "too important for America's national security to risk the relationship on the emotions of the moment."[17]

Kissinger did express shock at the "brutality" of the crackdown, but his very brief statement along those lines was perfunctory. His analysis did not include the basic idea which everybody in China understood: that the regime's way of dealing with unarmed student demonstrators was intentionally brutal and murderous, a planned means of eradicating once and for all any inclination the intellectuals might have had to threaten the party's power or to cause public disorder. The general trend of his statements was to find excuses for the Chinese authorities. In late July, Kissinger wrote his column recommending against anti-Chinese sanctions. In November, he was in China, meeting with Chinese foreign minister Qian Qichen, who praised the former secretary of state for having "the courage of a statesman and the foresight of a strategist." One of the people Kissinger and his group (he was accompanying a business delegation) met with on that trip was Deng Xiaoping, with whom he exchanged cordial jokes about being private citizens no longer in power.[18] And after returning to the United States, Kissinger had dinner at the White House, where he reported back on his conversations at the highest level.

In a single year, Kissinger may go to China several times, and the door is always open. In September 1990, he met with Li Peng, the man deemed most directly responsible for ordering the Tiananmen assault on students, who gave him and Nancy Kissinger a banquet complete with warm mutual toasts.[19] The next day, Kissinger went to see Jiang Zemin, who noted that Kissinger was making his eighteenth visit to the People's Republic of China. And so it has continued. In April 1996, weeks after China bracketed Taiwan with missiles in an attempt to intimidate voters in the first free presidential election ever held in a Chinese state, Kissinger was in China where he met with Rong Yiren, Jiang Zemin, and Li Peng.[20] Shortly before that, on March 31, Kissinger published a syndicated article in which he briefly mentioned "China's militaristic conduct in the Taiwan Strait," but then spent paragaraphs justifying it. The Beijing leaders, he wrote, had to "draw a line" given their discontent over the fact that Taiwan's president Lee Teng-hui had been allowed to travel to the United States; and he warned that China would "fight at any cost" if it felt its sovereignty was at stake.[21]

Kissinger's strategic thinking on China was summed up in an earlier article published in the Washington *Post* in July 1995. Where once China served American interests as a counterbalance to the Soviet Union, he argued, it has become important to the United States in its own right, holding as it does the key to stability in Asia. China is surrounded by countries whose strength is growing and who are not necessarily friendly to it, including Japan, India, and Russia, and it needs the United States to help it prevent any country from achieving hegemony in Asia. Indeed, Kissinger wrote, "Both America and China have their own reasons for opposing the domination of Asia by a single hegemonic power." Therefore, "China wants the United States to help balance its relationship with powerful neighbors . . . at least until it is strong enough to do so on its own."[22]

In our view, Kissinger is conveniently ignoring numerous elements in China's behavior, including the extent of its military buildup, which is aimed, it is true, at preventing domination of Asia by a single power, unless that power is China. Kissinger allows that human rights "must always constitute a central American concern," but that comment, in the absence of any specific recommendations about making that concern central, smacks of lip service. In any event, Kissinger has no reply to those, like us, who show evidence proving that the human rights picture worsened when the United States took the trade pressure off. Kissinger's view of China is, by the way, almost identical to the view put forward in public statements by China's leaders themselves. We think that they are lying and that he is wrong.

What Kissinger does not say as he expresses his views on American China policy is just how much he stands to profit himself by the very policies he urges the government to adopt. Kissinger's company, Kissinger Associates, represents many American corporations seeking to do business in China, and who pay Kissinger large sums of money at least in part because of his unparalleled access to China's most powerful figures. Kissinger always speaks in the language of the American national interest, and he no doubt believes what he says. In 1988, for example, he called for an easing of American technology transfers to China, characterizing China as a friendly, nonaligned country, a view that was quickly echoed by Rong Yiren.[23] But Kissinger is a major paid consultant to companies that might want to sell technology to China. While wearing his geo-strategist's hat, he might believe that technology transfers are justified in order to build a strategic alliance with China, but he is a potential beneficiary of those transfers when he wears his business consultant's hat. Certainly, for Kissinger in 1989 to have stressed shock and revulsion at the murders of students on Tiananmen Square rather than the historic greatness of Deng Xiaoping would have risked his special relationship with China's top leaders, and it can safely be assumed that that special relationship is a key to the China portion of the consulting business of Kissinger Associates.

At the time of his 1989 statements, Kissinger had just formed a limited partnership called China Ventures to carry out joint ventures with the China International Trust and Investment

Corporation, headed by his frequent host in Beijing Rong Yiren. In 1988, he formed the China-America Society with several former American presidents on its board. The society hosts banquets for Chinese leaders visiting the United States and sends delegations to China. Among his corporate clients who do business in China are the Chase Manhattan Bank, Coca-Cola, American Express, the American International Group, Continental Grain, H. J. Heinz, Atlantic Richfield, Midland Bank, and S. G. Warburg.[24] According to Scott Thompson of the National Democratic Policy Committee, at least six of these firms "had billions of dollars of investment at risk in the P.R.C., investments which were likely to be jeopardized if President Bush had implemented the sanctions against the Communist Chinese regime that have been proposed by the U.S. Congress."[25]

When John J. Fialka of *The Wall Street Journal* reported on these business interests, he gave Kissinger a chance to respond to the allegations of conflict of interest. It was "outrageous," he quoted Kissinger as saying, that "I would take a public position to curry favor with the Chinese government for clients."[26] A few months later, complaining about criticism of his China dealings, Kissinger called any linking of his views on China with his business interests a form of "McCarthyism."[27] Again, we do not question Kissinger's sincerity. China's approach is not to force people to express opinions that they disbelieve but to give privileged access to those who speak or write favorably about China while keeping any negative views they have to themselves. Still, to label as "McCarthyism" allegations of conflict of interest when such a conflict so clearly exists is excessive. As Scott Thompson put it before the Senate Foreign Relations Committee, "The fact is that [Kissinger] does receive substantial remuneration from corporations with major investments in China, which stood to benefit from adoption of his positions."[28] The fact is also that the special way that China does business, and the willingness of former senior American officials to help it do business, has resulted in a kind of new and powerful China lobby that, perhaps only by coincidence, has declined to criticize Beijing's human rights record, has warned against "confronting" China or imposing sanctions, and has made substantial profits along the way.

KISSINGER, OF COURSE, is a unique figure, one who might have special treatment in China almost no matter what his public positions were, short of a sustained barrage of anti-Communist condemnation. The Chinese correctly credit Kissinger and President Richard Nixon with the breakthrough that enabled a twenty-year freeze in Sino-American relations to melt and official contacts to begin. But Kissinger is only the best known and most prestigious of a group of former senior officials who have been cultivated by China, who profit from a special relationship with China's leaders, and who have consistently advocated the avoidance of conflict, of sanctions, of harming America's "strategic interests," whatever those might be. It is remarkable the extent to which these individuals, highly respected for their views of the American interest, have come to dominate the discourse on China.

In the wake of the Tiananmen massacre, Kissinger did make one small protest. He postponed a trip to China that had been scheduled for October 1989 and thus was not there to give a keynote speech at a party for the celebration of CITIC's tenth anniversary. Al Haig, a member of Kissinger's America-China Society, went instead. Indeed, it is worth remarking on the extent to which associates or former associates of Kissinger have used the revolving door to do business in China, to conduct American foreign policy, and to speak out on television and in op-ed articles in major newspapers. Not long after the Tiananmen crackdown, President Bush sent his national security adviser, Brent Scowcroft, and his deputy secretary of state, Laurence Eagleburger, on a secret fence-mending trip to Beijing. Scowcroft had been deputy director of Kissinger Associates before going into the Bush administration. Eagleburger was its president before becoming Bush's deputy secretary of state. *The New York Times* reported that in 1988, Eagleburger made

$674,000 from Kissinger Associates; Scowcroft earned $293,000 as a consultant to the group.[29] As early as 1991, only two years after the Tiananmen massacre, Eagleburger was cautioning trade sanctions. "We firmly believe," he wrote in the Washington *Post*, "that renewing China's MFN waiver—without conditions—provides our best interest for promoting positive change and U.S. interests in China." A full "engagement" with China, he argued, is the best way to get the country back "on the path to freedom."[30]

Among the members of the board of Kissinger's America-China Society are Cyrus Vance, Haig, former secretary of state William Rogers, Robert McFarlane, and Zbigniew Brzezinski. Haig is perhaps the figure who, after Kissinger, has most clearly mixed public positions of the sort that Beijing likes with business dealings in China on behalf of corporate clients. As secretary of state, Haig was the key Reagan administration official responsible for the 1982 Chinese-American Joint Communiqué that is one of the three key statements guiding relations between the two countries.* In it, the United States agreed never to pursue a Two Chinas or a One China–One Taiwan policy, to keep arms sales to Taiwan not to exceed, "either in qualitative or in quantitative terms, the level of those supplied in recent years since the establishment of diplomatic relations between the United States and China," and "to reduce gradually its sales of arms to Taiwan, leading over a period of time to a final resolution." Haig left the administration shortly before that agreement was signed. Beijing was grateful for his role in undermining Taiwan. Haig was soon cashing in on that gratitude.

For example, in the mid-1980s, as reported in *The Wall Street Journal*, Haig was paid $600,000 in fees and retainers by the International Signal & Control Group PLC, in part for help in selling weapons fuses to China.[31] He has been for many years a

---

*The others are the Shanghai Communiqué of 1972 and the Joint Communiqué on the Establishment of Diplomatic Relations of 1978.

senior consultant to United Technologies of Hartford, Connecticut, a manufacturer of jet engines and elevators, the world's sixteenth-largest industrial company, America's tenth-largest exporter, and a company that had seventeen joint ventures in China as of 1996. Haig frequently accompanies senior executives of the company to Beijing for meetings. In 1996, for example, he and United Technologies president George David met with Li Peng, during which Haig, not at that time an official of the United States government, reiterated "the U.S. commitment to its 'one-China' policy."[32]

Since 1981, there have been only four years during which Haig did not make at least one trip to China, and on most of those trips he was received by China's top leaders, Li Peng and Jiang Zemin, as well as by CITIC chairman Rong Yiren. Haig was the only American who attended China's 1989 National Day celebrations commemorating the founding of the People's Republic, held only four months after the Tiananmen massacre.[33] Haig appeared on the rostrum beside the top Chinese leaders and a couple of days later was received by Premier Li Peng, who gushed: "The Chinese people will never forget the contributions made by Nixon, Kissinger, Haig and other old friends to the growth of Sino-U.S. relations."[34]

Meanwhile, Haig has written op-ed pieces and made statements in which he has opposed attempts to confront China because of its human rights record and urged the United States to find ever greater means of cooperation. In the spring of 1996, one of the congressmen trying to attach conditions to the renewal of MFN for China was Christopher Cox, a fast-rising California Republican. Earlier that year, Cox played a key role in shepherding a resolution through the House declaring that the United States was obliged to come to Taiwan's aid if China took military action against it. The introduction of the resolution on March 7, with eighty Democratic and Republican cosponsors, was instrumental in President Clinton's decision to send a second aircraft carrier task force to the Taiwan area. The day before the MFN vote, Haig called Cox and berated him, accusing him of trying to destroy U.S.–China relations. "Cox was irate," says his aide, Mark P. Legon. "It was an absolutely unsolicited and inappropriate phone call. We wondered who he's paid by, but we couldn't find out."

The comparison in this regard between Kissinger, Haig, and others like Eagleburger and Scowcroft on the one side and James Lilley, the American ambassador who did not attend that 1989 National Day rite, on the other is instructive. Lilley, a former senior official at the Central Intelligence Agency, has been a critic of China, a believer in the thesis that China's interests clash with those of the United States and that America does have an obligation to protect Taiwan from a forcible takeover by Beijing. Needless to say, it is figures like Haig who are able to gain lucrative access to Li Peng, Jiang Zemin, and Rong Yiren. Does anybody think that, if Lilley decided to go into the consulting business, he would have much success trying to do the same thing?

The argument here is not that Haig's help to United Technologies is wrong, or that there is anything dubious about the company's business in China. United Technologies, it can be assumed, helps the American economy because of that business, and, like other companies, it should use whatever competitive edge it has to make its way in the China market. What is dubious is the double role played by figures like Kissinger and Haig, who use their prestige and influence both publicly and privately to advance policies from which they profit mightily. Most important, perhaps, the New China Lobby fosters a vision of China as an essentially benign, peaceable, and defensive country whose long-term interests and those of the United States are one and the same. "We cannot have a meaningful debate about China policy because almost the entire establishment has, in the final analysis, an interest in the continuation of the status quo," one Senate aide told us.

THE WORDS "CHINA LOBBY," to those with a memory of recent history, recall the likes of Henry Luce and Senator William

Knowland, whose purpose was to advance the cause of the Kuomintang on Taiwan as the legitimate government of all of China. The China lobby today advances the cause of Beijing, and since its victory in the MFN debate of 1994, it has become ever more active. It consists of several loosely connected parts, all of them encouraged through the granting of connections, access, or profit to China. The success of the China lobby in delinking human rights with MFN marked a sea change in American China policy. Ever since, the influence of the business community, especially over China policy, has been enormous—certainly greater than its influence over any other aspect of American foreign policy.

Sometimes it's all in the family. Senator J. Bennett Johnston, the Louisiana Democrat who was chairman of the Senate Energy Committee, took his two sons with him on a trade mission to China paid in part by state and federal funds. Both sons were involved in promoting business deals with China. Johnston then wrote a "dear colleague" letter to members of the Senate Foreign Relations Committee asking them to muffle their support for Chinese-occupied Tibet and offering to arrange meetings with China's ambassador to the United States, Li Daoyu.[35] Some congressional staffers refer to Senator Johnston as the "appointments secretary" for the Chinese ambassador, one congressional insider told us.

A secretive and high-level group, headed by Jiang Zemin himself, is the Central Leading Working Group on the United States Congress. Formed late in 1995 to enhance China's influence in American politics, the Working Group answers only to the seven-member Politburo Standing Committee, and it reflects China's larger awareness of the importance of lobbying directly with members of the legislative branch.[36] China, once utterly ignorant of the American political process and therefore inept in its efforts to influence it, has recently made greater and more skillful efforts in this area. In April 1996 alone, Jiang met three separate congressional delegations led by United States senators.

The Chinese Embassy increased its number of congressional liaison officers from two to five at the beginning of 1995. And the Chinese Academy of Social Sciences was ordered to study the policy-making process to help Chinese leaders better understand how to influence both the executive and legislative branches.[37]

The Chinese initiative can sometimes be humorously unsuccessful. In January 1996, Liu Huaqiu, a deputy foreign minister and reportedly now China's senior official handling relations with the United States, suggested to American senators visiting Beijing that Congress not bring up anything negative about the relationship during the election year. Senator John Glenn of Ohio replied that Liu evidently did not understand how the American government worked, otherwise he would know that no one can order individual congressmen not to bring up something about China.[38] But on other occasions, the China lobby has achieved remarkable and wisely acknowledged power. In 1994, after Secretary of State Warren Christopher's unsuccessful trip to Beijing, during which his demands for human rights concessions from the Chinese were rebuffed, Senator Ernest Hollings told him at a Senate hearing: "Before you even landed [in Beijing], the K-Street crowd down here of lawyers, consultants and special reps told the Chinese: 'Don't worry about him.'"[39]

Other Chinese initiatives are part of the country's long-term effort to influence public opinion. China puts money into several Chinese-language newspapers published in the United States and into Chinese-language cable-television stations, and these media organizations are run almost in the same way as their counterparts inside China itself. (Taiwan also controls its media organizations, but while they take a pro-Taiwan stance, they reflect in style and content the greater democratic freedoms of Taiwan itself.) China has also heard proposals from international public relations companies that have promised to find ways of improving the Chinese image in the United States. "Concurrent with efforts to secure extension of MFN—without conditions— should be activities designed to improve China's overall image in the United States as a valued trading partner with whom we share many common interests" was the way one such proposal, by Hill and Knowlton Public Affairs Worldwide, read.[40]

Most important, however, is the "K-Street crowd," referring to the Washington street where many lobbyists have their offices, led and financed by corporations with the greatest economic stake in China. Among the most prominent (though not the most powerful) organizations involved in lobbying for China are the United States–China Business Council (US–CBC), the Emergency Committee for American Trade, the United States Chamber of Commerce, the National Association of Retailers, and the National Association of Manufacturers. But the most powerful voices on China policy are the chief executive officers of individual companies. "These guys can just pick up the phone and make things happen," one person with close connections to the pro-China organizations told us. A group of these CEOs formed yet another pro-China group early in 1996. It is the China Normalization Initiative and has quickly become the vanguard of the pro-China lobby. It is an ad hoc coalition whose leading members include Boeing, Motorola, Allied Signal, Caterpillar, and American International Group. The China Normalization Initiative operates out of Boeing's lobbying office in Washington, D.C. It appears to have a great deal of money. Among its activities was the distribution of an information packet to educational organizations and to individual teachers around the country. The slick, two-inch-thick package has, for example, reams of data about Pennsylvania's and New Jersey's exports to China, something the written portions of the packet said meant the creation of jobs. It did not mention jobs possibly lost because of imports, however, or the export of American manufacturing operations abroad.

The China Normalization Initiative is one of many signs of increasingly intense lobbying efforts by business. In Chicago in September 1996, for example, a group of corporations including Motorola, United Airlines, Arthur Anderson, Caterpillar, Deere and Company, and others (all with headquarters in the Chicago area) announced the Illinois Coalition to Support U.S.–China Commercial Relations. Motorola's top executive for Asia, Rick Younts, said: "Illinois jobs depend on trade, and trade with China is at the top of the list of future growth opportunities for a wide variety of industries."[41] And in a press release, the group announced that its goal is "to encourage public policy at the federal, state and local level, which supports the normalization of trade relations between the U.S. and China."

What does "normalization of trade relations" mean? First, according to the Illinois group's statement, it is the "permanent extension of China's Most Favored Nation status." Second, it means "China's accession to the World Trade Organization on terms that are commercially acceptable." On this second subject, the group did not specify acceptable to whom, but the reason for Washington's resistance to Beijing's admission to the WTO has been China's trade and tariff policies, which are themselves in part responsible for the $33.8 billion deficit the United States now has with China. Still, the Illinois group did not exactly hide its sympathies. Its creation came with an announcement that its activities would be kicked off by a reception for China's vice premier and foreign minister Qian Qichen, held on September 20 at the Ritz-Carlton Hotel in Chicago. Qian spoke to the group on that day, and remarkably enough his views corresponded exactly with those of the businessmen. He called for MFN to be "renewed indefinitely." He also added an implicit threat, one that was first raised a few years ago by Deng Xiaoping. He effectively warned that the United States will suffer the consequences if it doesn't grant China better trading terms so that the Chinese economy can continue improving. "A China with a stagnant economy, an impoverished population and even social turmoil that produces massive exodus of refugees will indeed be a threat to world peace and stability," he said.[42]

Not coincidentally, the same argument was being made in Washington by businessmen and members of the National Association of Manufacturers who testified at a House committee hearing held the same week as the Chicago reception. Lawrence

Clarkson, senior vice president of Boeing, told the committee that the repeated debate over MFN had created "a lack of predictability" in American China policy that was hurting business: "Europe extends MFN or standard tariff treatment to China, just as it does to the majority of its trading partners on a permanent basis. This contrast in policy has not gone unnoticed in Beijing. And clearly contributed to China's decision to purchase one and a half billion dollars in Airbus aircraft last April." A representative of the National Association of Manufacturers spoke against "demanding immediate social and political change for the privilege of trading with the United States."[43]

The lesson here is that China's efforts to impose its international political agenda on foreign companies doing business in China has shaken up American businessmen. But it hasn't shaken them into leaving China. It has shaken them into doing China's bidding more eagerly than ever.

There is no more dramatic example of this than Boeing, which was selling one of every ten of its planes to Chinese airlines in the 1993–95 period, accounting for about 70 percent of the entire Chinese market. Boeing seems willing to do almost anything for the Chinese government to hold on to that share. In a series of articles in the Seattle *Times* in 1996, Stanley Holmes portrayed Boeing executives frequently reminding Chinese leaders of the political and economic favors they're performing for China and Chinese leaders constantly demanding more.

Holmes reports that the quid pro quo between Boeing and China is crass and clear: "Boeing is not only lobbying to extend MFN for China this year, but also working with other corporate giants to secure 'permanent MFN' status for China. If the aircraft giant doesn't deliver for China, Boeing's chief international strategist, Lawrence Clarkson, conceded, 'we're toast.'"[44] One Senate staff member, speaking of Boeing's lobbyists, put it this way: "When it comes to China . . . they're everywhere and they're smart. They do it through front organizations, they publish studies on exports, they know where their suppliers are and they put pressure on them."[45]

Speaking about the K Street crowd, one senior senatorial staff member told us that those in the policy-making establishment striving to attach some importance to human rights in China tend to be steamrolled by the increasingly powerful business lobby that fights for China on Capitol Hill. "As more and more businesses have invested in China, we have lost more and more people," the staffer told us. "The business community is spending tens of millions of dollars against us every year."

CHAPTER 5

DEFICITS, TECHNOLOGY, AND PLA, INC.

You CAN FIND Spunky the dog and Princess the cat in many American toy stores. They are cute and cuddly. They are also manufactured and imported into the United States by a branch of the Chinese People's Liberation Army—or, to be precise, by a subsidiary of Norinco, the Chinese ordnance company that supplies the PLA with most of its weapons. Norinco now has an estimated ten subsidiary companies spread around the United States.

Many Americans will be surprised to learn that the Chinese military-industrial complex, with the People's Liberation Army at its center, has incorporated many companies in the United States to sell products and obtain technology. Researchers at the AFL-CIO have identified ten of what they call PLA-sponsored business groups in the United States, each of which typically has several subsidiary companies. A lot of these companies move things around: they are freight forwarders and distributors and import-export concerns bringing in a variety of products, from frozen fish and spices to firearms and overhauled engines. Two of the many companies owned by China's armed forces got unwanted publicity in 1996 when the FBI uncovered a San Francisco smuggling ring that had attempted illegally to bring two thousand AK-47 automatic assault rifles into the United States. Two PLA-linked firms—one of them was Norinco; the other a company called Poly Technologies, which is run by the PLA's General Staff Department—were involved in the smuggling. The companies are not only linked to the PLA and China's top political leadership, but they also number among their directors the children or in-laws of senior Chinese leaders.

The army engages in toy and frozen-fish exports to the United States to earn the foreign exchange that it needs for its military modernization program. And exporting to the United States has, since the late 1980s, become China's surest way of earning foreign exchange. Indeed, in August 1996, the United States Commerce Department announced a kind of milestone in Sino-American relations. In June 1996, the American trade deficit with China, growing rapidly for the previous few years, for the first time exceeded its trade deficit with Japan. (China's surplus for that month was $3.3 billion; Japan's was $3.2 billion.)[1] But the gap for August was bigger by far—a $4.7 billion deficit with China, almost $1 billion more than with Japan.[2] These figures, suggesting that the total 1996 American trade deficit with China would probably exceed $40 billion, indicated that the American operations of PLA, Inc., were only one aspect of the Sino-American trade relationship, the fastest growing in the world. Given the problems that the trade imbalance with allied Japan has caused all these years, the gap in the American trade with non-allied China is a portent of serious problems on the horizon.

For many years, China was a stagnant giant, a backwater, less of an economic competitor than far-smaller places like Taiwan or South Korea. That began to change in 1979 when Deng Xiaoping's economic reforms pushed the country forward, creating along the way numerous opportunities for American companies, which began to do real business with China for the first time in several decades. But those trade figures for June 1996 revealed something troubling about the particular mode of foreign trade that China has followed. After so many years of going its own way, China has adopted a consciously mercantilist economic strategy, a strategy that stresses exports, technology transfers, the importation of capital, and high barriers to international competition. The ominous thing about the trade figures is that they showed China following in the footsteps of Japan, which had pioneered the strategy of "guided capitalism" and built up a damaging trade deficit with the United States in the process. And China is ten times the size of Japan.

FOR AMERICANS, the trade surplus with Japan is an old story, one that was told and retold for three decades until, finally in the mid-1990s, the Japanese trade deficit began slowly to shrink. In the case of China, by contrast, the United States seems to have been struck almost overnight. Until the mid-1980s, trade between the United States and China was roughly in balance. In 1988, for example, nine years into the economic takeoff engineered by Deng Xiaoping, China accumulated a surplus of $3.5 billion for the year, a small element in the total American global trade. Seven years later, in 1995, China's trade surplus with the United States had increased nearly tenfold, to roughly $33.8 billion. In that same period, American imports from China had gone up to $45.5 billion; exports were $11.7 billion. That is an extremely lopsided ratio, with China exporting four times as much to the United States as it imported. The ratio has prevailed since 1990; it was holding steady as of mid-1996, the last time that Commerce Department statistics for two-way trade were available. During its entire postwar history of trade competition, by contrast, Japan never came close to putting the United States in such a disadvantaged position. In the first half of 1996, Japan's "export advantage ratio" was 1.6:1. Its exports to the United States were $56.7 billion; its imports $34.5 billion.

Some American experts argue that the situation regarding China is less alarming than these figures indicate. One argument is based on what is called the Hong Kong variable. A great deal of the rise in the China deficit, the argument goes, came when Hong Kong entrepreneurs moved their manufacturing plants into China to take advantage of low wage rates. That meant that a large portion of the swelling deficit was really just an already-existing Hong Kong trade moving into China. And indeed, if you look at American trade data for both China and Hong Kong in the late 1980s and the very early 1990s, you see Hong Kong's trade surplus with the United States fall just as China's trade surplus rises. But the same statistical tables show that this one-time phenomenon had run its course by 1991. After that, Hong Kong–controlled factories continued increasing their production because they had access to a virtually limitless supply of cheap land and labor. The rise in the China trade deficit has not for at least five years been offset by a reduction in the Hong Kong deficit.

Since the mid-1990s, pro-China business lobbying organizations, in particular the United States–China Business Council, have made a different argument minimizing the gravity of the U.S.–China trade imbalance. According to this argument, the Commerce Department's figures for the China trade deficit are overblown because they fail to factor in the role of Hong Kong as a stopover or entrepôt for both exports from China to the United States and exports from the United States to China. Contends a US–CBC paper: "These large statistical errors, by both countries, are due to the ever-expanding role of Hong Kong as entrepôt in the China trade."[3] In fact, this other Hong Kong variable does not alter the picture very much. If Hong Kong is included in the China trade figures, the overall amounts do not change substantially. In 1995, for example, the American surplus with Hong Kong was $3.9 billion (imports, $10.3 billion; exports, $14.2 billion). That would reduce the trade deficit with China by about 10 percent.

A more cogent, but still-flawed, argument often used to discount the importance of the China trade surplus centers on China's virtually infinite supply of cheap labor. Here the idea is that, as time goes by, labor costs will become more expensive (they always do) and that this Chinese advantage will diminish.

Certainly it is true that China does currently enjoy a huge comparative advantage in producing labor-intensive goods for the United States. And indeed those items show up near the top of every list of Chinese exports to the United States—in particular, garments, toys, and footwear. As believers in free trade and the concept of comparative advantage, we aren't moved by those who decry how these goods are "flooding" into America. In fact, we think this "flood" has on balance been a boon to most budget-straitened American families. Indeed, the impact of Chinese-made garments, toys, and footwear on industries manufacturing these products in the United States is hard to gauge. Many American companies are still making profits after having shifted their own production and sourcing to China. That means that a substantial number of low-paid American workers have lost their jobs in these industries. In its much proclaimed series of articles, "America: Who Stole the Dream?" for example, the Philadelphia *Inquirer* contended that in the decade from 1986 to 1996, imports from China had cost the United States 680,000 jobs. "Cancel all their wages, more than $11 billion a year, and taxes paid on that income. Forever," the newspaper said.[4]

But this is economic nonsense. The *Inquirer's* assertion depends on the assumption that none of the people who lost their jobs in garments, toys, or footwear got other jobs someplace else, when, of course, the vast majority of them did exactly that. The new jobs, like the old ones, are low paying, but not lower paying than before. Moreover, the workers who now have jobs in a fast-food restaurant instead of on a garment-factory assembly line are financially slightly better off, like most Americans, because of the lower prices they pay for inexpensive Chinese-made imports.

In any event, as we will see below, the portion of the trade deficit made up by labor-intensive export industries has been steadily going down since the 1980s, while the proportion of the deficit due to high-tech value-added industries has been steadily rising. Increasingly, the deficit is not primarily a function of low Chinese wages. It is a function of a Chinese strategy to target certain industries and to undersell American competition via a system of subsidies and high tariffs. And that is why the deficit is harmful to the American economy and likely to become an area of ever greater conflict in bilateral relations in the future.

A final means of casting the China trade deficit with the United States into a benign light goes something like this: China is a poor and rapidly growing economy, a country whose rates of growth will inevitably slow down in the years ahead. Meanwhile, given its stage of development, it is natural and to be expected that a temporarily high trade deficit will exist between China and its largest trading partner, the United States.

But this too is wrong. Textbook economic theory has it that when an economy is developing rapidly, as China's currently is, it needs large amounts of capital. It usually acquires this capital from foreign investors, that capital qualifying as an import and thus adding to the developing country's deficit. When Asian economies such as those of Japan, Taiwan, and South Korea began to take off, they initially attracted very little foreign capital. Even later, they generated most of the investment capital they needed by exporting cheap, labor-intensive products to their ally, the United States, thereby accumulating large trade surpluses that could be used for new investment.

But China is different. It is the recipient of enormous amounts of investment capital not only from the West but even more so from Greater China—Hong Kong, Taiwan, and the overseas Chinese communities of Southeast Asia. Historically, countries in this situation run large trade deficits. But China has been getting American investment capital and reaping windfall trade surpluses at the same time. As a result, China is one of the leading foreign-exchange-reserve countries in the world—a bizarre situation for a poor and developing country. In fact, China's foreign-exchange reserves reached $91 billion in July 1996, which put it roughly on a par with the two other highest exchange-reserve countries, Taiwan and Japan.[5] Unless current trends reverse themselves, China's reserves will soon surpass Taiwan's and Japan's. And Hong Kong's reserves are estimated at $60 billion.[6]

These foreign exchange-reserve figures represent explosive growth. As of the end of 1993, China's foreign-exchange reserves were $21.2 billion,[7] already a respectable figure. In the following thirty months, they increased by almost $70 billion. During that same period, the total American trade deficit with China was $83 billion.

How has China accomplished this unprecedented economic feat? The primary explanation is that it uses the methods pioneered by Japan, including state subsidies of export industries, a concentration on technology transfer in its dealings with foreign companies, the erection of a labyrinth of nontariff barriers, a currency kept at an artificially low exchange rate, and an industrial policy that targets specific industries and uses unfair trade practices to give those industries a competitive advantage. The American press has picked up on only a small part of the overall Chinese strategy, namely the battle over China's pirating of compact discs, movies, and computer software programs—an issue at least temporarily resolved in 1996 after threats of American sanctions. In fact, the conflict with China over the trade deficit is far more complex than can be represented by any single issue. The larger question is the model of "state capitalism" that China has chosen, which produces a multitude of ways to tilt the contest in its favor.

WITH DENG XIAOPING leading the way, China shucked off Maoist economics in 1979, and the Chinese economy began to take off almost overnight. Deng privatized farming, and rural productivity soared. China's welcome to Hong Kong factories moving across the border into neighboring Guangdong Province also propelled economic growth. Yet with all their fondness for Five-Year Plans and central control of the economy, China's leaders in those early years did not have much in the way of a realistic blueprint for sustaining economic growth.

This changed in the late 1980s when China began consciously to model itself on the other East Asian countries that had used export earnings to foster high-tech industries and achieve re-markably high levels of economic growth. One of the first people to spot this borrowing process was Chalmers Johnson, president of the Japan Policy Research Institute in California, who noted in particular the ways in which China was specifically following the Japanese model of aggressive guided capitalism.[8]

China began with a crude and partial form of export-driven growth. Using a policy of mostly indirect state subsidies and other types of favored treatment for local industries, China achieved a huge and rapid increase in exports. In 1989, exports accounted for 12 percent of China's gross domestic product. Five years later, exports represented 23 percent of GDP.[9] In this same period China began running overall trade surpluses, lapsing back into deficit only once, and by a small amount.[10] It was also during these few years that China's trade surplus with the United States increased tenfold.

Not much noted by the press or the public is an annual report by the Office of the United States Trade Representative (USTR) that has tracked and documented the subsidies and other devices that the Chinese authorities have used to increase exports artificially. The latest of these reports puts the matter diplomatically: "The Chinese Government claims that direct financial subsidies for all exports . . . ended as of January 1, 1991. Nevertheless, Beijing still uses a mixture of subsidies to promote exports."[11] Subsidies cover a range of what the economists call inputs—export-oriented factories are allowed to buy energy and raw materials at below-market prices; they are exempted from paying legally mandated employee benefits like pension plan contributions; and they are given preferential bank loans, which in China may mean not only low interest but also no requirement to repay at all.[12]

Most export subsidies in China are difficult to trace because they are not the product of some central national administration, but are locally arranged and granted. One report, for example, highlighted the very capable manager of a ceramics factory in the Chinese city of Zhengzhou, in Henan Province.

After the state-sector factory effectively went bankrupt, this manager "organized a new production line of holiday plateware, decorated with Christmas trees and holly boughs, to help fill the $10 racks in American shopping malls."[13] Despite its large number of exported plates, the factory continued to lose money. The municipal government, however, concerned about the cost of supporting 1,700 newly unemployed workers, made up the loss, the subsidy being a lot less than the unemployment benefits it would have had to pay if the factory had closed. This is far from an isolated example. There are millions of township and village enterprises (TVEs) in rural China that feed into the export economy and that often depend on various subsidies from local authorities.

No matter at what level they are applied, all of China's export subsidies distort trade relations with China's largest customer, the United States. But even as it subsidizes certain industries, including some that operate at a loss, China is becoming increasingly sophisticated in focusing its subsidies on higher-value-added exports, which are then priced artificially low in the American market, unfairly undercutting what would otherwise have been competitive American-made products. This is one of the more direct ways in which China has learned from earlier Japanese industrial strategy. The method has produced a rapid shift in the nature of Chinese exports, away from low-wage, labor-intensive activities and toward more high-tech, value-added ones. And so, popular perception to the contrary, the share of the American trade deficit with China represented by cheap products made by cheap labor has been declining steadily since 1990.

This surprising fact emerges from our analysis of American trade data over the past several years. We looked at the top-twenty imports from China year to year from 1990 to the first half of 1996. We divided these imports into labor-intensive products, like garments and toys, on the one side and, on the other, products involving increases in value because of technology—telecommunications equipment, electrical machinery, and computers.*

The trend shown in the resulting figures is strong and unambiguous. In 1990, labor-intensive goods accounted for 79 percent of our top-twenty imports from China; value-added items accounted for 12 percent. By the first half of 1996, the picture had changed dramatically. The proportion of labor-intensive imports had dropped by one-third, to 56 percent. And the value-added imports had more than doubled, to 29 percent. These trends have been constant since the 1980s and, if anything, are now accelerating.

Chinese officials are secretive when it comes to their means of subsidizing value-added exports, but now and then they inadvertently disclose some information about their methods. Zhang Ji is the deputy director of the State Mechanical and Electrical Products Import and Export Office. Boasting in late 1995 that China's exports of electrical and machinery goods were running 60 percent ahead of the previous year, he said an important part of the explanation was that a special government bank had given preferential bank loans to the industry.[14] In other words, the industry benefits from a financial subsidy.

As Chalmers Johnson noted, these methods crudely mirror the decades-old Japanese strategy of targeting certain promising industries for growth and then enveloping them with subsidies and protection. While not drawing that parallel, the 1996 USTR report made the similarity with Japanese methods clear:

> China's growing focus on certain "pillar industries"—including machinery, electronics, and autos, among others—is becoming increasingly evident in the composition of China's trade. China's exports for 1995 . . . shifted away

---

*We excluded 9 to 15 percent of the twenty export items—the exact amount varied by year—that did not fit into either category.

from traditional labor-intensive products as exports of electrical and machinery products exceeded textiles for the first
time. Imports of manufactured goods grew sluggishly for
1995, while imports of primary products . . . soared.

One technique Japan and some other East Asian countries
employed—despite the view of most economists that it's usually
ineffective—was import substitution. Here governments rig the
market so that a product being imported in large amounts is produced domestically, even if the cost is greater. In a 1992 agreement with the United States, China declared it had eliminated
all such schemes.[15] But in 1994 it announced an automotive industrial policy that had clear-cut import-substitution requirements. Foreign automobile companies operating in China were
forced to use domestic components, regardless of price or quality. This directly hurt American auto parts manufacturers, as
Mark Anderson, director of the AFL-CIO task force on trade,
explained: "Just before China's auto policy went into effect we
had a surplus of $521 million in our bilateral auto trade. Last year
we ran a deficit of $454 million with them. That's a $1 billion re-
versal in the trade balance in just two years."[16]

China is also a master at much-cruder forms of protectionism
aimed at blocking imports or making those imports much more
expensive. In its April 1996 report, the USTR, which termed
China "highly protectionist," cataloged a bewildering array of
devices that China employs to block imports from the United
States and other foreign countries. "Prohibitively high tariffs" av-
eraging 35 percent and ranging up to 150 percent are only part of
the Chinese wall. There are also import licenses, import quotas,
import restrictions, and standards and certification requirements.[17]

In some instances, Chinese trade bureaucrats have removed
barriers on imports with great public fanfare while simultane-
ously but quietly installing new barriers against the same imports. For instance, the Chinese put their publicity machine into
high gear in November 1995 for an announcement by President
Jiang Zemin himself that tariffs on four thousand categories of

products would be cut by at least 30 percent. But many new non-tariff barriers were then erected before the cuts went into effect in early 1996. Even when such barriers weren't erected, foreign businessmen experienced in trading with China were unimpressed. They reminded journalists that the Chinese government still grants the right to import only to designated firms, most of them state monopolies that ultimately do what the Government tells them to do.[18] In the fall of 1996, after China promised to crack down on the illegal production of copyrighted products, thereby averting threatened American sanctions, Charlene Barshefsky, the U.S. trade representative, continued to stress the underlying problem of unfair Chinese trade practices. "China must stop erecting new trade barriers to replace those previously removed," she said during hearings in Congress in September.[19] Similarly, the USTR report continued to complain of "multiple, overlapping non-tariff barriers that restrict imports."

For example, Guangdong Province arbitrarily announced in June 1996 that it was limiting foreign imports into the province of everything from cars to "various household appliances."[20] Even more recently, Beijing announced it was granting import licensing powers over different types of imports to national, provincial, and local authorities.[21] The authorities being granted this power have their own vested interest in limiting free competition from abroad, because the ministry or other government agency that oversees the manufacture of a product is the same ministry or agency that stands to lose from free and unrestricted competition from abroad.[22]

CHINA'S OVERALL economic strategy is not aimed merely at a kind of mercantilist accumulation of foreign exchange via trade practices weighted in China's favor. It is also aimed at enhancing the acquisition of the most advanced Western technology, including "dual use" technology that can be used for both civilian and military purposes. One way China does this is by requiring foreign companies to manufacture in China some of the components that go into the products sold there. To continue doing business in China, the American company is required not only to transfer advanced manufacturing technology to China but also to train a Chinese workforce, thereby protecting profits in the short term but helping to produce an eventual competitor at the same time. The name normally given to this is "offsetting"—transferring a portion of production work to a foreign country in order to secure sales there. Many countries, including Japan, have done this for years. But China is quickly becoming a master at squeezing the maximum benefit out of offsets.

One in-depth report on China's assiduous pursuit of offsets focused on the creation of a factory in Shanghai by the McDonnell Douglas Corporation, the manufacturer of passenger jets as well as of such mainstays of the American air force as the F-15 fighter plane. In the early 1980s, eager for a share of the China passenger-plane business, McDonnell Douglas went into a cooperative venture with China's state-owned Shanghai Aviation Industrial Corporation.[23] China assured the company a major share of the sales of narrow-body aircraft. In exchange, McDonnell Douglas agreed to have Chinese workers assemble the planes from kits at the Shanghai factory. The arrangement, as *The Wall Street Journal* put it in an investigation of McDonnell Douglas's strenuous efforts to make money in China, involved "one of the largest technology transfers in history." The company, the newspaper said, "provided enough technical data to fill a library." Moreover, the McDonnell Douglas venture became a model for China's deals with other high-tech companies. "No multinational, be it AT&T Corp. or General Motors Corp., can expect an entry pass without divulging technology early and often," the *Journal* reported.[24]

Unlike McDonnell Douglas, the Boeing Corporation has not assembled entire airplanes inside China. Still, as the Seattle *Times* said in 1996: "Boeing quietly accelerated its production in China recently to counter several setbacks and protect its dominant share of the Chinese aircraft market."[25] At Xian Aircraft, Chinese workers have already been producing tail sections for

Boeing 737s being flown by Southwest Airlines and Scandinavian Airlines System, among others. Both McDonnell Douglas and Boeing have come under scrutiny in Congress for giving China technology that has potent military uses. Representative Christopher H. Smith (a New Jersey Republican) worries that Boeing's extensive technology transfer to China not only jeopardizes American jobs but also is giving China the wherewithal to boost its military capacity. "This technology transfer is a very dangerous thing," he has said.[26]

Another example is Motorola, which has a huge and growing business in China, largely manufacturing and selling cellular phones and pagers and related technology. Recently the Chinese have been pressuring not only Motorola to transfer some of its best technology to China but also independent U.S. companies that have supplier relationships with Motorola and would have much preferred to have continued supplying Motorola from the United States. As an American businessman close to one of Motorola's supplier companies told us, the Chinese have issued the company an ultimatum requiring that it begin production in China, using its best technology, or China will look for other suppliers. The businessman cited one company that agonized over the trade-off—keeping their Motorola-related China business but losing some of their best proprietary technology— before taking the plunge into China.

In fact, "technology transfer" is a term that covers a wide variety of activities. Some transfers are open, legal, and on balance good for the American economy. For example, Chinese companies sometimes buy, dismantle, and ship to China obsolete American steel mills and pulp mills that are no longer cost-effective and are often heavy polluters. At the other extreme are activities that are against American law. Most technology transfers to China fall in the gray area between those two poles. "In many cases," *Business Week* said, "companies are testing the limits of U.S. . . . policies."[27]

"They're getting much better at technology transfer," a specialist who monitors both legal and illegal Chinese activities in

this area told us. "Ten years ago, they weren't capable even of asking the right questions. They have more knowledge because they
have more contacts, particularly because they have such a large
number of exchange students in the United States. And they
have more money now; in the United States, money talks." According to another specialist in the American government, some
fifteen Chinese provinces have independently established companies to spot technology that they can get as cheaply as possible. The provincial companies are focused mainly on technology
that will help accelerate their economic growth. But national
companies are more concerned with high tech that has military
as well as advanced civilian use.

A considerable portion of Chinese efforts in this country to
transfer high technology back home are unambiguously illegal.
Recently the Central Intelligence Agency named China as one of
the three top countries "extensively engaged in economic espionage."[28] More explicit and damning were the conclusions
reached by the American Society for Industrial Security, International. In its March 1996 report, *Trends in Intellectual Property
Loss*, it named China as the most likely thief of "sensitive economic information."[29]

THE OPERATIONS of PLA, Inc., in the United States signal the
final way that China shapes its economic relationship with the
United States, both to obtain technology and to earn foreign exchange. In fact, the armed forces are not the only Chinese institution that controls an American branch operation. It is not
certain, in fact, exactly how many Chinese-owned companies
have been established in the United States, but it's generally
agreed they already number in the thousands. *Business Week* estimates that one hundred Chinese-owned companies "have employed sophisticated maneuvers to acquire listed companies in
North America, gaining backdoor access to financial markets."[30]
Buying an already-operating American company is another
method used by Chinese state-run enterprises either to increase

their revenues or to engineer technology transfers. *The Wall Street Journal* has detailed concerted efforts by the American branch of China's aviation trading arm, China National Aero-Technology Import & Export Corporation, or Catic, to acquire highly advanced American machine-tool companies capable of sculpting metal for jet aircraft and missiles.[31]

Another example concerns Southwest Products Company, which makes specialized bearings for all the major aircraft manufacturers in the United States. Its bearings are not only part of civilian airliners but also NASA's space shuttle and the Defense Department's C-17 military transport. Southwest was purchased by Sunbase Asia, Inc., a NASDAQ-listed company controlled by a Chinese–Hong Kong group that has direct, cross-ownership links with a bearing company in Harbin, in China's northeast. Sunbase executives make no secret of the fact that the intention is to transfer technology from California to the Harbin bearing company,[32] an operation that would be perfectly legal under American law.

Still, it appears that the PLA operates most extensively in the United States for both technology and profit. A study carried out by the AFL-CIO, largely by examining shipping records of companies with direct export rights, found: "Not only are the larger Departments and Military Regions involved in trade, but the PLA Navy, Air Force, the 2nd Artillery, all of the military districts [there are twenty-eight of them], and many of the Group Armies [there are twenty-four] also manage their own import/export entities."[33] The largest PLA company appears to be an entity owned by the General Logistics Department. It is called the Xinxing Corporation, which acts as export agent for goods produced by its own plants in China, and also as an import agent for other military-run enterprises. The value of its trade was just under $16 million in 1994. Norinco has several American subsidiaries—Beta Chemical, Beta Toys, Larin, Forte Lighting, and others—that distribute its products throughout the United States. The overall profits of Norinco in 1994 were approximately $31 million. Jeffrey Fielder, an official of the AFL-

CIO, put the situation succinctly to the Senate Foreign Relations Committee in June 1996: "I don't think any member of the House or Senate would say we should support Most Favored Nation status for the PLA. . . . Allowing Chinese military companies to do business in the U.S. . . . is tantamount to subsidizing the modernization of the Chinese military."

SEVERAL CONCLUSIONS can be drawn from these various Chinese efforts. One is that it would be a mistake to think of China as China wishes to be thought of, as a struggling Third World economy whose only difference from other Third World economies is that it is many times larger. It is true, of course, that China was until very recently a poverty-stricken country whose pockets of technological and economic excellence were limited to a very few areas. It was a country able to produce an atomic bomb, but one of whose most important export items was hog bristles. It is also true that there remain vast Chinese areas where the way of life pursued by tens of millions of inhabitants is not all that different from the way of life of centuries past.

China, as the Harvard historian John K. Fairbank used to point out, is divided into three parts: there is the vast interior China of time immemorial; there is bureaucratic China, the country of an enormous, highly educated government administration; and there is the commercial China of the country's east coast, the former treaty-port cities, the China of risk-taking entrepreneurs, universities, scientists and technicians, bankers, industrialists, and global traders. Added to that now is a fourth China, a China of a kind of military-industrial complex that overlays the three other Chinas. Its goal is to aggrandize the nation, to make it wealthy and powerful, to see it achieve its historic mission of renewed grandeur. It is this fourth China especially that distinguishes the country today from any other developing country in the world.

Remarkable things are happening in China. Only twenty years ago, when foreign visitors crossed over into China from

Hong Kong, which was the country's major point of entry, the trip took place in several stages. There was a train from Kowloon to a town called Lowu on the Hong Kong–China border. Passengers disembarked at Lowu and walked across the railroad bridge into China itself at a spot called Shenzhen, a district of agricultural communes. The sounds of chickens in nearby coops could be heard from the sheds where men in baggy uniforms checked the visitors' passports and entry visas.

Now Shenzhen, which was declared a special economic zone in the early 1980s, is a sprawling city of high-rise office and hotel towers, traffic jams, and industrial pollution. Billions of dollars in investments from Hong Kong have flowed into the city. There are shopping centers, expensive restaurants, and nightclubs and karaoke bars; there are prostitutes, drug dealers, antique smugglers. There are stretches of industrial buildings and factories on the banks of the Pearl River, reaching near the ancient city of Guangzhou, formerly called Canton by foreigners, where the British defeated the Chinese in the Opium War and set up the first extraterritorial settlements.

That kind of transformation, which is duplicated all the way up the Chinese coast, in cities like Xiamen (formerly known to foreigners as Amoy), Shanghai, Tianjin, Dalian, and many others, is indeed impressive and exciting. It is one of the remarkable developments in the world in the last years of the twentieth century. The lives of millions of people are vastly better materially than before. And China's growth promises new prospects of trade and exchange for the United States and many other countries. It is possible, indeed, over the long run, especially if China's nationalistic zealousness is abated and the country eventually becomes more democratic, that many of the areas of friction and conflict between the United States and China will diminish. In the meantime, however, as we have already said, it is equally possible that China will harness its economic strength to its strategic goals of domination in Asia, the goals that could put it on a collision course with the United States.

Even if that does not happen, China's rapid economic expansion is a worry as well as an opportunity. China's population is, after all, ten times that of Japan, and the American relationship with Japan has been fraught with conflict and tension at many times in the past forty years. At the very least, the same will be true of the American economic relationship with China over the next forty years. But, unlike Japan, China poses a strategic and a military challenge as well. And there is one important territory that China still wants and that the United States may one day be called upon to defend. We turn to that next.

CHAPTER 6

FLASHPOINT: TAIWAN

The whole relationship between China and the United States is based on an untruth, but it is an untruth that China is prepared to go to war to defend.
—FORMER AMERICAN DIPLOMAT

TAIWAN IS A PLACE that Americans ought to like, a place that has moved steadily over the years from right-wing dictatorship to fully functioning democracy. That does not mean that it is a liberal model. Taiwanese politics are an Asian version of machine politics, reminiscent of the old Tammany Hall, as local opposition figures and other critics (none of them, in contrast to their Mainland counterparts, in prison) never tire of pointing out. But Taiwan is a lively place, with art galleries and theaters, night clubs and publishing houses, chic fashion boutiques and talk-radio programs, traffic jams, and fitness clubs. It has no grinding poverty, almost no violent crime, quite a lot of pollution, a rich artistic and bohemian subculture, a sophisticated, entrepreneurial, well-traveled population—all of it accompanied by a precarious, ambiguous, permanently unsettled international position that is probably unique in world history. That is where the lie comes in, the lie that China is prepared to go to war to defend.

It was forged in a late-night meeting in Shanghai near the end of Richard Nixon's breakthrough trip to China in February 1972.

On one side of the table was then–national security adviser Henry Kissinger, on the other Chinese foreign minister Qiao Guanhua, while President Nixon and Premier Zhou Enlai, who had just toasted each other at a state banquet, waited in nearby state guest houses. Kissinger and Qiao were facing the most delicate and difficult obstacle still standing in the way of the historic rapprochement between China and the United States: Taiwan and its then nearly 20 million people. Their solution was a masterpiece of diplomatic obfuscation that enabled the young relationship to prosper but that threatens to lose its value as time goes on.

From the formal Chinese point of view, Taiwan was a renegade province and therefore a domestic matter for China, in more or less the same way that a dispute between the federal government and the state of California would be for the United States. But in the negotiations that had begun in the spring of 1971 and that led to Nixon's visit to China, China was clearly ready to make major concessions on its formal position toward Taiwan. For twenty-three years, the United States not only had formal diplomatic relations with the "renegade province" but was also committed by a mutual security treaty of 1954 to come to its defense in case of a Chinese attack. Nixon, concerned about criticism from conservatives back home, was not ready to abrogate that treaty.* So finding some formula by which the two countries could agree to disagree on Taiwan was essential, and that is what produced Kissinger's and Qiao's brilliant and necessary untruth. The two of them hammered out a paragraph for the Shanghai Communiqué, setting out the grounds for renewed American ties with China that contained these critical sentences:

---

*The treaty was only abrogated in 1979 when the Carter administration established formal diplomatic relations with Beijing, recognizing the Mainland government as the sole government of all of China and dropping all official ties to Taiwan. Ever since, the United States has maintained a "liaison office" on Taiwan staffed by diplomats temporarily "retired" from the foreign service.

The United States acknowledges that all Chinese on either side of the Taiwan Strait maintain there is but one China and that Taiwan is a part of China. The United States Government does not challenge that position. It reaffirms its interest in a peaceful settlement of the Taiwan question by the Chinese themselves.

"The Taiwan paragraph of the communiqué," Kissinger later wrote, "put the Taiwan issue in abeyance, with each side maintaining its basic principles."[1] In his memoirs Kissinger reports that Secretary of State William Rogers objected to the Taiwan sentences on the grounds that they were an inaccurate description of the objective world. Not all Chinese on both sides of the Taiwan Strait believe that Taiwan is a part of China, Rogers maintained. But Kissinger waved aside those objections as petty and obstructionist and caused by Rogers's pique at being excluded from the negotiations. Some last-minute cosmetic changes were made to the text, but the Taiwan sentences remained unchanged.

Still, Rogers was right as a matter of description, though perhaps wrong to insist on being right just at that moment in history. It was true then as it is now that a substantial number of the Chinese living on the Taiwan side of the strait did not and do not subscribe to the concept embodied in the communiqué. And that is the problem that continues to face China, Taiwan, and the United States. Increasingly, as time has gone by, the people of Taiwan—there are now 21 million of them—have exercised a kind of de facto sovereignty. Taiwan's democratically elected president Lee Teng-hui, an economist educated in Japan and the United States, has said that "the people of Taiwan are sovereign." And so, the United States is committed in theory to the untruth that all of the people involved in this unique historical situation see themselves as belonging to the same country, even as it is in practice committed to preserving the real truth, which is that they do not.

· · ·

THE CONVENTIONAL PREDICTION about the outcome of
Chinese-American-Taiwanese diplomatic jockeying has long
been this: As long as China's claim of sovereignty over Taiwan is
not flouted by any moves on Taiwan toward de jure independence, Beijing will remain content with the status quo. Beijing,
in other words, is playing a game of face, allowing Taiwan to
maintain a separate system and a separate administration as long
as it does not do so in a fashion to humiliate Beijing. An adjunct
to this theory is that over time the contacts between the two entities will foster economic and political convergence, so that at
some time in the future a formal confederation, some sort of unification, will take place. The two countries have already developed an extensive relationship that has given both of them a
stake in being patient and moderate, this reasoning goes. One-
third of the long-distance calls made on Taiwan are to the Mainland. Wealthy Taiwanese businessmen have invested an estimated
$30 billion there; indeed, China is the single most important
area of economic growth for Taiwan, which has the technology
and the capital to mesh with China's land and labor.

Perhaps most important, the passage of time has dulled the
hostility that the two sides once felt for each other. One senses
uncertainty and distrust but no hatred between the people of
Taiwan and the Mainland, who, after all, speak the same national language and share most elements of a common culture.
In addition, virtually all experts agree that any effort by China to
take Taiwan by force, especially by an all-out invasion, would be
costly to China in several ways, not the least of them military,
since Taiwan's armed forces are well prepared to combat an invasion. But aside from that, the damage that China would sustain
to its economy and to its relations with other countries is so great
that recourse to a military invasion will remain a remote and unlikely possibility for the decade to come.

But peace and the national interest are secured not by as-
sumptions of cordial and reasonable behavior on the part of others but by a clearheaded attempt to perceive where matters may
go wrong and where interests may diverge. And it is abundantly

clear that as Taiwanese democracy has flowered and the island has moved to assert an independent image, China has not always behaved cordially or reasonably. This at any rate is one of the lessons to be drawn from the incidents of March 1996.

The public aspects of what we will call the Taiwan Strait Crisis are well known, beginning with China's unhappiness over several well-publicized incidents. One of them was the $6 billion sale of F-16 fighter planes to Taiwan by the United States, a sale approved by the Bush administration and that was itself a response to China's acquisition of SU-27s from Russia. China also condemned a campaign begun by Taiwan's president Lee to get Taiwan readmitted to the United Nations. (It was replaced there by Beijing in 1971.) Then submitting to intense pressure from Congress, the Clinton administration withdrew an earlier ban and allowed Lee to come to the United States to make a speech at his alma mater, Cornell University—an event that Lee used to burnish Taiwan's independent image. This in particular provoked howls of protest from China.

In the early weeks of 1996, American and Taiwanese intelligence agencies watched the PLA mobilize its forces opposite Taiwan. But China waited until March 5 before officially revealing its plans for missile tests and live-fire air and naval exercises in the Taiwan Strait area starting just three days later. The timing was aimed at disrupting the first fully free and democratic election of a president in Taiwan's history, scheduled for March 23. On March 8, just fifteen days before the election, China fired three mobile-launched M-11 intermediate-range missiles at target zones close enough to Taiwan's two largest ports, Keelung in the north and Kaohsiung in the south, to disrupt shipping.

Tensions were made even higher than they might otherwise have been when Chinese officials reiterated their refusal to renounce the use of force to settle the Taiwan question. The Clinton administration revealed the same day that the missile tests began that the aircraft carrier *Independence* and its battle group were only 200 miles east of Taiwan. When the Chinese exercises expanded, the Clinton administration on March 11 ordered a second aircraft carrier, the *Nimitz*, along with its battle group, to the Taiwan region. The dispatch of the two battle groups marked one of the firmest and most adroit shows of force abroad by the United States in many years.

While China complained bitterly that the American action amounted to interference in its internal affairs, it could only conclude that, for the most part, its threats had been neutralized and its bluffs had been called. Early on in the crisis, a Chinese official told a visiting former American State Department official, Chas W. Freeman, that China was prepared to use nuclear missiles targeted on the American West Coast if the United States intervened militarily on Taiwan. Prime Minister Li Peng warned the United States to keep its ships out of the Taiwan Strait. A Beijing-controlled Hong Kong newspaper proclaimed: "With a concentrated fire of guided missiles and artillery, the People's Liberation Army can bury an enemy intruder in a sea of fire."[2] But China in essence lost the confrontation when Lee won the election on Taiwan by a greater margin than expected. China's military exercises stopped, and the United States withdrew its ships.

All of that was reported in the newspapers at the time, giving the impression that the crisis had come and gone rather quickly and would leave no lasting effect. A few elements in the picture did not receive much public notice, however, and they help to explain not only what the effects of the March incident might be but why the Chinese undertook the adventure in the first place. The general impression was that China made a grotesque miscalculation, alienating the people on Taiwan and driving Japan and the United States (as we will see shortly) closer together. China did suffer those losses, and they were considerable. And yet from China's point of view, the exercise may have been worthwhile nonetheless.

Starting late in 1995, American and Taiwan intelligence picked up signals that China was planning more than just a live-fire exercise. Whether the information was false and deliberately planted by China, or whether it was true, is not certain. But the plans called for China to occupy a small island in the Taiwan

Strait near either Quemoy or Matsu—the larger islands off Fujian Province that are controlled by Taiwan. The information was that China's forces would hold the island for a day or two, broadcast their success in seizing it, and then withdraw. The idea would have been to show the inability of Taiwan to resist such an incursion, and the simultaneous inability of the United States to come to Taiwan's aid.

"The Chinese Communists made military preparations to attack our frontline islands to intimidate our presidential elections" was the way the director of Taiwan's National Security Bureau explained this to a local newspaper.[3] The attack, in any case, did not occur. But American intelligence tended to see the information that such a plan was at least being considered as part of an attempt to create an atmosphere of uncertainty and ambiguity around Chinese intentions. In December, for example, the Chinese told Chas W. Freeman that the People's Liberation Army had prepared plans for a missile attack against Taiwan consisting of one strike a day for thirty days—another threat that never materialized.[4] "There were several Chinese actions that were first-time things, and they puzzled us," one American intelligence official told us. "We couldn't be sure what the Chinese were going to do, and they knew that."

The purpose of this atmosphere of uncertainty suggests the underlying purpose of the entire panoply of Chinese actions: it was not just to intimidate the voters of Taiwan but also to test the United States, to see what Washington's response would be. When Clinton sent the *Nimitz* and the *Independence* aircraft carriers to the western Pacific, the American response was the correct one, a clear demonstration that the United States would not stand by idly as China used military force against Taiwan. Indeed, the show of force may have committed the United States more than Clinton intended. The dispatch of the aircraft carriers established a precedent—namely, that there will be American intervention if China attacks Taiwan in the future.

In other ways, however, the American response left room for the Chinese to maneuver. One little-noted aspect of the military exercises was that they constituted a partial blockade of Taiwan by the Mainland—imposed by Chinese warnings to ships of other nations to stay out of the exclusion zone created for the occasion. The fact that the missile targets were near Taiwan's two major ports is further evidence that China was testing the effectiveness of a blockade, and a blockade, a kind of economic strangulation of Taiwan, is the option that many experts find most likely for Beijing to use to force Taiwan toward reunification. China could mount a series of blockades, each one longer and more geographically extensive than the last one.

Such a strategy would make it far more difficult for the United States to know when to intervene than would an outright, frontal assault by China on Taiwan. And indeed, the Clinton administration failed to give a clear answer in response to the blockade of March 1996, even after the arrival of the aircraft carriers. Then, too, when Li Peng warned the United States to stay out of the Taiwan Strait, the Americans did not respond, neither by formally protesting the warning nor, in what would have been a more resolute act, immediately sailing one of the aircraft carriers through the strait to show that they would not permit China to set the rules in this or any future crisis. The previous December, the Clinton administration had appeared to be showing some backbone toward China by sending the aircraft carrier *Enterprise* through the Taiwan Strait. But it transformed that small achievement into a demonstration of vacillation and weakness when it later declared that the *Enterprise* had used the strait only to avoid bad weather—suggesting that it would otherwise be inappropriate for the U.S. Navy to send its vessels through this particular international waterway.

So the results of the Taiwan Strait Crisis were ambiguous. China lost ground diplomatically. But it did convey the message that it would respond if Taiwan made moves that displeased it. China also left open the possibility that there will be further tests of wills with the United States in the western Pacific, especially as China's navy becomes a bigger and more credible force. The parameters of the next confrontation over Taiwan may already have been set.

MANY TAIWANESE CLAIM their island has both the historical and the legal right to be independent. But so far, no large or powerful country in the world has been willing to support that claim. And yet it would also be virtually illogical if the people of Taiwan did not see themselves as ambiguously a part of China and not a part of China at the same time. Except for the civil war years between 1945 and 1949, Taiwan has not been under the control of any government on Mainland China since 1895. During the last fifty years, moreover, while Taiwan was theoretically a part of China, it has largely taken an independent course, becoming a regional economic powerhouse with European-style standards of living and the highest degree of democratic freedom ever achieved by a large Chinese entity. Even the countries that acknowledge Beijing's position on Taiwan maintain a certain ambiguity in their policy. They do not antagonize China by following a Two Chinas policy, but at the same time most of the major countries of the world maintain semi-official trade offices on Taiwan, grant visas to Taiwan citizens, and do not allow Beijing to represent Taiwan's interests in any matter—whether textile export quotas or even, though this is more difficult, arms sales. So, in actual fact, while the world treads a delicate line between reality and the untruth of the Shanghai Communiqué, the world has also by and large treated Taiwan as the special case that it is, not really a part of China, but not actually independent either, a place that is somehow different.

The difference moreover has been part of Taiwan's history all along. While the other Chinese provinces, including disputed regions traditionally controlled by China, have been within the Chinese realm for thousands of years, Taiwan did not become a part of the national territory until the seventeenth century. Until then the island had been considered a wild place of impenetrable mountains and a malarial coastline inhabited by unfriendly aborigines with whom the Chinese had little or no contact. Indeed, the first outsiders to settle in Taiwan were not Mainland Chinese but Portuguese, Spanish, and Dutch traders and explorers who first established forts there in the 1620s, the entire island becoming a Dutch possession around the middle of the century. The Dutch maintained a brisk trade between Taiwan and the islands of the Dutch East Indies (present-day Indonesia). The first Chinese to come to Taiwan were from Fujian Province just across the strait. They brought with them the Fujianese dialect that is still preferred in their private life by millions of Taiwanese and settled in or near the European enclaves.

This was at the beginning of the end of a dynastic cycle, the ruling Ming desperately fighting Manchu invaders from the north, hanging on to portions of coastal China, especially Fujian. As the Ming gave way to the new dynasty founded by the Manchu, however, a remarkable Ming loyalist known to history as Koxinga (the Westernization of a name in the Fujianese dialect) took refuge on Taiwan, rather like the Kuomintang did after losing the Chinese civil war to the Communists in 1949. Like the Kuomintang leaders, Koxinga used Taiwan as a base of operations for an attempt to retake control of the Mainland (in his case to restore the Ming Dynasty), the difference being that Koxinga actually did mount military expeditions to China before being defeated in an assault on Nanjing in 1659. Forced to pull back, Koxinga attacked the Dutch garrison on Taiwan and took control of the island. His presence there, and the threat posed to the new dynasty by his pretender state, was intolerable to the Manchu, as Lee's government is now to the Communists. The new dynasty, which was given the name Qing, sent several expeditions to take Taiwan by force—not as a matter of recapturing Chinese territory, since Taiwan had never been Chinese territory, but to eradicate the Ming loyalists. Eventually, a vast naval force was assembled in Fujian consisting of more than three hundred war vessels under the leadership of a Qing commander named Shi Long, a former Ming loyalist whose father, brother, and son were all murdered by Koxinga when Shi declared allegiance to the Qing. Shi led a successful invasion of Taiwan, whose garrison surrendered in 1683, and the island was absorbed by the great Qing Dynasty emperor Kang Xi.[5]

Taiwan was Chinese territory for the next two hundred years, until, following the dynastic cycle, the Qing too declined, beset from outside by European and Japanese imperialists, from inside by rebellion, mismanagement, and poverty. In 1895, China fought and lost a brief naval war with Japan; as a result of which Taiwan was ceded to the Japanese permanently. In 1943 at the Cairo conference, where Nationalist leader Chiang Kai-shek met with Roosevelt and Churchill, it was decided to give Taiwan back to China after the Japanese were defeated. The Nationalist government took over the island in 1945, governing it in a corrupt and high-handed way—in the same way, in other words, that had led to the Nationalists' lack of support on the Mainland and would lead to their defeat by the Communists. In 1947, Chiang's governor on Taiwan, a former warlord named Chen Yi, brutally crushed a Taiwanese uprising, arresting and executing thousands of Taiwanese intellectuals. With the island secure, Chiang fled there in 1949, ahead of the victorious Communist armies, bringing with him a million Nationalist troops and a large part of the former Kuomintang bureaucracy, its members dreaming of the day when they would retake power in the rest of China.

Chiang was an often mean-spirited dictator who ruled at the head of a martial law regime that imprisoned dissidents, especially those, mostly of Taiwanese descent, who favored independence for the island. Despite that, American support became firm and unambiguous after the Korean War erupted in 1950, the United States and Taiwan signing the mutual defense pact of 1955 that remained in effect until seven years after Nixon's historic trip to China. Taiwan, as the recognized government of all of China, retained a permanent seat on the United Nations Security Council until the UN membership replaced it with Beijing in 1971. For twenty years, the slogan "Recover the Mainland" was plastered on billboards and banners all across

Taiwan, whose government portrayed it as "Free China," the democratic alternative to the rest of China, which, in the Taiwanese view, suffered under Communist enslavement. The propaganda did not reflect the reality of Kuomintang rule, which remained repressive until Chiang's death in 1975, though it was true even at the worst of times that the people of Taiwan enjoyed much more freedom and prosperity than their compatriots living under the Communists. Under Chiang, Taiwan allowed almost complete economic freedom, and the island quickly achieved near-European standards of living.

Under Chiang's son, President Chiang Ching-kuo, martial law was gradually eased, even though dozens of pro-independence dissidents were jailed after kangaroo court procedures. Still, over the course of the 1980s, Taiwan moved toward democracy with substantial press freedoms and the legalization of opposition political parties, including a strong, largely Taiwanese pro-independence party. By the mid 1980s, there were no political prisoners on Taiwan. Indeed, a group of former political detainees formed the largest pro-independence party, the Democratic Progressive Party, whose president in 1995, an ex–political prisoner named Shi Ming-teh, failed by only one vote to be elected president of the National Assembly. Lee Teng-hui, when he was elected president in 1996, ran on a platform whose main unwritten plank involved the continued ability of Taiwan to control its own fate and not be forced into reunification by the Mainland. While Lee is formally opposed to independence for Taiwan, the semiotics of his administration are more subtle and complex than that simple declaration would make it appear.

Lee is a native Taiwanese, and in that sense a representative of the tremendous rise of the Taiwanese to positions of influence and power, largely at the expense of the Mainlanders, who used to run the show. Thanks to China's own blatant attempt to influence the outcome, Lee came to embody a kind of anti-Mainland defiance, the person to whom the population rallied in the face of direct provocation by Beijing. Moreover, Lee ended up with 54 percent of the popular vote, a higher figure than the polls indicated he would get before the Chinese intimidation. It is true, as the Beijing propaganda apparatus claimed after the vote, that the pro-independence Democratic Progressive Party got only 21 percent of the vote in the presidential election, which was down from the 41 percent it had gotten in local elections four years earlier. But that is still a pretty strong indication of substantial antireunification sentiment on Taiwan. Moreover, the combined vote for Lee and for the pro-independence party came to 75 percent of the total, which was widely and correctly interpreted as a stunning rebuke to Beijing. "This was a plebiscite without the label of plebiscite, and I hope that China got the message," one pro-independence legislator, Parris H. Chang, said the day the votes were counted. "And the message is that Taiwan does not want to reunify with the Mainland."[6]

BEIJING PROBABLY did get the message, though it very likely interpreted it differently than Chang. From Beijing's perspective, the humiliating events of 1996 were most logically seen as the culminating failure of the moderate, peaceful approach it had taken toward Taiwan for the past quarter of a century. Rather than luring Taiwan into reunification via economic contacts and exchanges and propaganda barrages about the "Taiwan compatriots" returning to the "embrace of the motherland," China had driven Taiwan ever further into a pro-independence drift. The paradox is that as long as the Communists' mortal enemy, the Kuomintang, held dictatorial power and insisted that it was the legitimate government of all of China, there was no open challenge to the One China principle. But with democracy now installed on Taiwan, the popular will was expressing itself, and while the Taiwanese did not want to provoke Beijing by supporting outright independence, they showed no sign that they wanted to move toward reunification either. And that situation puts Beijing in an awkward position.

"We cannot think of an independent Shanghai or Fujian, so how can we think of an independent Taiwan?" said a senior Chinese foreign-affairs specialist whom we interviewed in Beijing a few months after the elections on Taiwan. "And yet we know that those who are in favor of independence on Taiwan are close to Lee Teng-hui." The analyst continued: "I am worried, because it could become a political issue inside China. If Taiwan veers further in the current direction, there might be a very serious debate as to whether we will have to resort to force, with one side in the debate saying that the only solution is a military solution, because time is not in our favor." In addition, he said, "In history, Chinese leaders have believed in force. Force worked in Tiananmen. It intimidated the intellectuals, and that paved the way for economic growth and political stability. It is realpolitik. And in the Chinese value system, sovereignty, national unification, and preserving the regime have always been higher than peace."

The greatest danger in this sense stems from the evolution of Taiwan itself. At the time that China embarked on its March 1996 exercise in intimidation, a few pundits identified the real issue as not so much Taiwanese independence but Taiwanese democracy. Genuine popular sovereignty on Taiwan threatened to undermine the authority of the dictatorship in Beijing. That would explain one of the reasons why the Mainland government has never raised the possibility of a plebiscite on Taiwan as part of a solution to the problem or, indeed, ever made any suggestion that the desire of the Taiwanese people be taken into account. Merely to talk about the desires of the people on Taiwan would give some support to the revolutionary idea that the people in China should have the same right to choose their leadership as the people on Taiwan—and proclaiming that idea inside China is likely to earn you a few years in prison.

So the dilemma that China faces over Taiwan might actually get worse as time goes by, and therefore the pressures to retake the island by force could grow as well, before the island goes farther down its separate path or before its growing democracy gives people in China the wrong idea. The simple solution, of course, would be for China to follow the political path of Taiwan, becoming not just more prosperous but more democratic as well, leading to an amalgamation of the two societies that would be acceptable to the people of both. But as we have pointed out, China is showing no sign of that at present. This may change in the future, but if it does not, the newly democratic government and people of Taiwan are unlikely to accept reunification on any terms acceptable to Beijing. And with the peaceful solution failing to produce results, Beijing will be faced with two very unattractive alternatives: allowing Taiwan to continue as an independent entity indefinitely or beginning to apply forceful measures, ranging from economic blockade to small-scale military attacks, used mainly as a means of exerting political pressure, to a full-scale military assault.

Even on Taiwan, that last possibility is seen as unlikely. A majority of the analysts on Taiwan that we spoke with shared the general optimism. China, they felt, could not take Taiwan by force without destroying the prize—as well as wrecking its relations with the rest of the world. Some observers were of a different opinion, however. They noticed, for example, that at various times in 1995 and 1996, Chinese television had broadcast ostensible news programs showing off China's developing military hardware. The programs have footage of the deployment of M-9 and M-11 missiles, the mainstays of Chinese medium-range force and the type of missile that was aimed near Taiwan during the military exercises of 1996. The programs showed supersonic aircraft firing air-to-surface missiles and dropping bombs, heavy artillery assaults, and ferocious naval bombardments. There was even some footage of nuclear bomb tests, and there was commentary about what the Chinese call "new and high-tech warfare," involving precision bombing, electronic countermeasures, and mobile missile launchers. The broadcasts always show Chinese soldiers shouting slogans in unison about opposing "splittism" and advancing the cause of national reunification.

China's leaders moreover have indicated a kind of informal timetable for Taiwan, a step-by-step plan for reunification, the accomplishment of which is at the top of China's national agenda. In 1999, China will take control of the Portuguese

colony of Macau. Premier Li Peng has publicly said that after
Macau, it will be Taiwan's turn. By the early years of the next
century, China's economic and military power will have grown,
and its desire to see all of China's historic territory under a single
national roof will be stronger as well. That would be an enormous change, one with huge implications for the United States.
For twenty-five years, it is true, China has been following Mao's
dictum that there was no urgency on Taiwan, that only the larger
strategic issues were important. But there are no larger strategic
issues now. China intends to be a great global power. And great
global powers are not usually patient and accommodating when
it comes to the question of control and sovereignty over what
they deem to be their national territory. The Chinese belief in
the cycles of history cannot be ignored here either. China is on
the rebound, resuming its preeminent place among nations, a
place that it lost because of one of its recurrent periods of decline. The enclaves taken by the imperialists were the first to be
restored to Chinese sovereignty. Taiwan in this view of matters
must be included in the great task of national revival.

The problem for the United States here could be an immense
one. The argument could certainly be made that the Taiwan question truly does not concern Americans, that it is a leftover matter
for China to decide however it sees fit. Why, in any case, should
American soldiers be put at risk for the sake of Taiwan, whose separate status is nothing more than the residue of an unfinished civil
war in China, a purely domestic concern, as Beijing so forcefully
argues? Moreover, what would be so terrible for Taiwan if it were
reabsorbed by the Mainland? This would no longer be a question
of consigning an entire population to the horrors of an orthodox
Stalinist system. China is growing more prosperous and more
capitalist by the day. Reunification might even be a blessing for
Taiwan, which has talent and capital to use in China's economic
growth. Moreover, once Taiwan has been reabsorbed into the
Mainland, the major cause of Sino-American friction will have
been removed. The solution of China's Taiwan problem in this
sense would be the solution of America's China problem.

But if China were to embark on a military offensive against Taiwan, the United States would have little choice except to intervene and to put American forces at risk. Like it or not, Americans are already engaged in the battle, committed to a peaceful solution—that is, a solution agreed to by the people of Taiwan. When the United States sent its two aircraft carriers to the western Pacific during China's intimidate-Taiwan campaign in 1996, the move was endorsed by both Democrats and Republicans.

Despite Beijing's fury, the United States has continued to supply Taiwan with hundreds of millions of dollars' worth of advanced military equipment, most notably the 150 F-16 fighter planes sold to Taiwan to enhance the island's air defenses. The United States must continue to do that for the simple reason that the weaker Taiwan is, the more likely is a Chinese invasion, and an unopposed Chinese invasion would profoundly unsettle the entire balance of power in Asia, a balance of power that has in the past quarter century seen both peaceful conditions and unprecedented prosperity.

Moreover, without an American commitment to intervene in a Taiwan-China conflict, there would be very little standing in the way of Chinese domination of all of East Asia, and this fact is well understood from Australia to Tokyo. The form of an American intervention could vary depending on Taiwan's specific need and the ferocity of China's assault. But whatever form the American involvement took, any war on the Taiwan Strait would be the beginning of a new stage of conflict between China and the United States, a move from strategic posturing across the Pacific to a war that will profit absolutely nobody.

CHAPTER 7

CHINA'S PLAN
FOR JAPAN

On February 23, 1996, Japanese prime minister Ryutaro Hashimoto flew from Tokyo to Los Angeles for a meeting with Bill Clinton that lasted a mere sixty minutes, sandwiched between the American president's golf game at Los Angeles's Hillcrest Country Club and his dinner at movie and record producer David Geffen's Beverly Hills estate. The official explanation, a bit too readily accepted by journalists from both countries, was that the meeting, held at the oceanfront Sheraton Miramar Hotel in Santa Monica, was just a get-acquainted session, a quick *tour d'horizon* of the various bilateral issues that would come up when Clinton went for a scheduled meeting in Tokyo in April.

In other words, the spokesmen for the two leaders wanted their respective publics to believe that the prime minister of Japan would fly all day and well into the night (by his biological clock) for a one-hour chat over routine matters with a president he would see on his home turf two months later anyway. Japanese prime ministers do not usually go to such inconvenient lengths for get-acquainted sessions, even with American presidents. What were the real reasons for Hashimoto's hasty trip?

The timing provides one clue. By February 23, Hashimoto faced the danger of being pulled apart by contradictory forces. One was the China threat. Hashimoto, like many in Japan's political elite, believed that Japan's greatest strategic threat came from an ever more assertive China. By the time plans for the snap summit in Santa Monica were finalized, Japan's intelligence saw a possible full-scale military crisis coming out of the China-Taiwan confrontation. That would have been only the latest Chinese action to worry Japan. The year before, in November 1995, Hashimoto's predecessor as prime minister, socialist Tomiichi Murayama, had approved changes in Japan's National Defense Program Outline (NDPO) that gave the United States–Japan security alliance greater importance than it had even at the height of the Cold War.

The contradictory force was domestic and political. By late 1995, the Japanese public was more discontented than ever before over the alliance with the United States. Indeed, policy makers in Tokyo had long been constrained by the quasi-pacifism and antimilitarism that still dominate opinion among the Japanese people, who, if anything, have generally been far more nervous about the continued American military presence on Japanese soil than about the rapid growth of Chinese power in East Asia. In the fall of 1994, as the crisis of North Korea's nuclear bomb program reached a climax, Tokyo rejected a United States request that Japan deploy minesweepers to support American naval forces in the Yellow Sea. The next year, three American servicemen stationed in Japan raped an Okinawan schoolgirl, spurring a torrent of demands from the Japanese public for a big cutback in the American presence. Seventy-seven percent of Japanese polled in November 1995 said they favored a "major reduction" in American forces.[1] To many at that time, the alliance seemed to be slowly but inexorably unraveling. Speaking of the prevailing mood in that fall of 1995, the United States ambassador to Tokyo, Walter F. Mondale, later said, "The whole security relationship was in question."[2]

When Hashimoto met with Clinton in February, however, Tokyo had decided to move against the trend of public opinion by making its military ties to the United States stronger and publicly declaring their importance. But to make the deed politically acceptable, Hashimoto needed something from Clinton. That is what brought him to Santa Monica. Hashimoto asked for and got from Clinton a commitment to reduce the size of the American military presence in Okinawa, the site of the rape and the home of most American forces. The United States accepted in principle to return one-fifth of the land taken up in Okinawa by American bases. Clinton agreed, as a first step, gradually to close Futenma Air Station, an American base situated in the middle of the city of Ginowan.[3] The Santa Monica quid pro quo was of historic importance.[4] Hashimoto knew that making Japanese-American ties stronger would antagonize Beijing. Nonetheless, for the first time in recent history, Japan acted on the assumption that China was a danger to Asian peace and stability. A few days after returning to Tokyo, Hashimoto declared that Beijing "might be heading in the wrong direction in Asia"[5]—a blunt statement by the diplomatic standards of Japan. In short, Japan was beginning to choose sides in a rivalry that it would have preferred to ignore but could no longer. This is not to say that the future course of Japanese policy regarding China and the United States is fixed forever. Japanese ambivalence, its wish to play both sides, the interests that it perceives in a special relationship with China, the anti-American drift of public opinion, and, perhaps most important, China's growing power all could still operate on Japanese policy makers in the future and lead them away again from a firmer security tie with the United States. But as of the end of 1996, Japan had decided that China's threatening posture required that it move in the direction of the United States.

After Santa Monica, Hashimoto approved of Clinton's decision in the Taiwan Strait Crisis to send first one and then two aircraft carrier task forces to waters near Taiwan, signaling the American determination to block any Chinese attack on Taiwan or even to pose any threat to other countries' shipping lanes. While Japan's desire for a clear-cut demonstration of American resolve in the Taiwan crisis was by no means the sole factor in Clinton's forceful gesture, it played a part. Then at the full-fledged and formal two-day summit in mid-April, the bitter trade disputes that normally dominated the discussion at American-Japanese summit meetings hardly came up. Instead, the centerpiece of Clinton's visit was the formal announcement of a Japan–U.S. Joint Declaration on the Security Alliance for the 21st Century. In it, Japan affirmed that the American military presence in Asia was "essential for preserving peace and stability."[6]

Japan agreed that American military forces could operate from Japan in the event of future crises on the Korean Peninsula and Taiwan, and it promised to keep the number of American troops at roughly the same level as before. Even while some people were still holding demonstrations and branding the United States an "illegal occupant" of Japan, the two sides agreed to review the terms of 1978 guidelines on military cooperation. This was a coded way of saying that Japan would consider revising its interpretation of its Constitution, which prohibits any Japanese military action outside of Japan's territory.

The declaration, hardly noticed in the United States, was immediately seen by China for what it was, a change in Japan's position, aimed at countering China's growing power. China even tried to block, or at least weaken, the Japanese-American security agreement, dispatching its foreign minister, Qian Qichen, to Tokyo two weeks before Clinton's scheduled arrival there in April 1996. Qian publicly worried about the security treaty that was about to be signed, which was a diplomatic way of attempting to dissuade the Japanese from going ahead with it.[7] He failed in this, however. It was one of the costs to Beijing of its aggressive actions in the Taiwan Strait a few weeks before and in Japan's sea-lane, the South China Sea, where China had seized Mischief Reef from the Philippines in 1995.

Once the Japanese-American declaration was announced, China wasted no time in attacking it. The very next day, the Chinese Foreign Ministry spokesman was saying: "Any attempt to have a security arrangement going beyond its bilateral character would certainly be cause for vigilance and concern by other Asian nations."[8] Lu Zhongwei, vice president of the China Institute of Contemporary International Relations, a think tank connected with China's Ministry of State Security, declared: "This accord is a result of a strategic rearrangement of the U.S. policy toward Asia and the Pacific region. The accord is not defensive but offensive."[9] For the several months that followed, anti-Japanese expressions reached the proportions of a campaign in China. When we visited the country in August 1996, scholars and analysts at virtually every policy research institution spoke against the Japanese-American agreement of four months earlier. "The U.S.–Japan alliance was wholly defensive until 1996" was one comment we heard at the Institute of Asia-Pacific Studies in Shanghai. A senior figure at the China Center for Strategic Studies in Beijing said, "We don't care about the American defense of Japan, but we do care about the expansion of the treaty to cover the entire Asia-Pacific region, and about encouraging Japan to play a military role. That is very negative." Months later, Beijing was still denouncing the United States and Japan for transforming their alliance into an "offensive" pact aimed at China.

This reaction also represented a change. In his memoirs, Henry Kissinger talks about how avidly China's leaders in the 1970s urged their American counterparts to maintain a close security relationship with Japan. "On one occasion Mao went so far as to advise me to make sure that when I visited Asia I spend as much time in Tokyo as in Peking; Japan's pride should be respected," Kissinger wrote in 1979. "The Chinese, indeed, came to stress that U.S.–Japanese relations were more important than U.S.–Chinese relations."[10] That was a time when China knew, despite its claims to the contrary, that it was actually very weak, and its global diplomacy was aimed at building a worldwide anti-Soviet bloc.

After the end of the Cold War, China generally became harder on Japan, intensifying its demand that Japan recognize its guilt in World War II more strongly than it ever had before. China's leadership, as we have said, has stirred up nationalist feeling against outside powers, and the bitter words directed against Japan after the collapse of the Soviet Union can be seen as part of that tactic. But the propaganda took a sharp, hostile turn after the announcement of the Japanese-American security agreement, which China correctly saw as something new in Asia, an unwelcome response by other Pacific powers to the growth of China's ambitions.

SINCE CHINA'S GOAL is to become the paramount power in Asia, a concomitant goal must be to keep Japan in a state of what one scholar has called "permanent strategic subordination." China of course does not use so undiplomatic an expression as that, yet it makes no secret of the fact that it wishes Japan to remain demilitarized forever and therefore unable to counter China's own plans for an expansion of its military capability. Put another way, China's strategic goal is to prevent Japan from ever being a "normal" nation, such as the United States or China itself, a nation that has the sovereign right to determine its security needs and to build the armed forces required to meet those needs.

It is an audacious notion to keep a nation of 120 million people, with the world's second-most-powerful economy, in a state of permanent dependence on other countries for its basic security. But no country, not even Japan, has directly and openly disavowed that notion. For fifty years, ever since the end of World War II, Japan's repudiation of offensive military force—which means being an economic powerhouse but a military and diplomatic midget—has become an accepted fact of international relations. And it has been a consistent element of Chinese foreign policy to keep matters that way. In international forums and in its controlled media, China emphasizes the notion that Asia can never trust Japan not to go to war again, that Japan is the real threat to peace.

The stress in the propaganda machinery and in the statements of Beijing's leaders about Japan's wartime atrocities is a major part of China's effort. Japan's atrocities, which include, most notoriously, the "rape of Nanking" in 1937 and innumerable other acts of savagery, were real, and it would be understandable if China wanted to keep the memory of them alive as a matter of moral duty to the victims and historical understanding. But in fact, while many Chinese are sincere in their anger at Japan, there is little doubt that the leadership manipulates the war guilt concept as part of a strategy to keep Japan in a weak and subordinate international position. China's leaders for one thing have been suspiciously vague about which Japanese gestures of remorse or apology would satisfy them. In 1978, the Peace and Friendship Treaty that marked the formal ending of Sino-Japanese hostilities made no reference to war guilt or to any unfinished business of World War II. Since the treaty was signed, however, China has intermittently made demands for formal apologies. This has led several Japanese prime ministers, including two of the most recent, Hosokawa and Murayama, to make official apologies for Japan's past activities. But China has persisted in hammering home the war guilt theme, publishing numerous but sometimes fuzzy and unsubstantiated charges: for example, that Japanese forces waged chemical and biological warfare against Chinese civilians during the war or that they induced cholera outbreaks in occupied villages. Visitors from Japan are pressured by their Chinese hosts to walk through "atrocity" museums with displays said to document Japanese war crimes.

In late 1996, the official control and manipulation of anti-Japanese sentiment became obvious when the government suddenly banned demonstrations planned in several Chinese cities to commemorate the anniversary of Japan's invasion of Manchuria in 1931. Thousands of police were mobilized in this effort; people who organized demonstrations were dispatched to out-of-town guest houses, and others were put under effective house arrest; universities were told to prevent their students from "harming stability." The speculation in China was that the government was worried not that the demonstrations were anti-Japanese, which they were, but that they could turn against the government, as they did at Tiananmen.[11] Whatever the reason, the incident made clear that the Beijing authorities view anti-Japanese sentiment as something to orchestrate primarily for its own international purposes—to strengthen war guilt among Japanese and opposition to Japanese rearmament among the nations of the world. Meanwhile, China's Communist Party shows no concern with any moral accounting for the atrocities that it perpetrated against its own people during the long years of mass imprisonment, labor camps, the politically induced famine of the early 1960s, or, for that matter, the massacre of pro-democracy protesters at Tiananmen.

To make amends for those atrocities—the estimates are that as many as 30 million people died as a result of Communist misrule from 1949 to 1972—would undermine the authority of China's rulers. But to apply a high moral standard to the Japanese bolsters it, and it is consistent with China's strategic interests. "A powerful Japan is not acceptable because China suffered so much in the Japanese invasion," said Xie Xide, a member of the Chinese People's Political Consultative Conference, a kind of advisory body, at Fudan University in Shanghai. "If there's a country that would want to dominate Asia in the future, it would be Japan," a scholar from one of Beijing's semi-official foreign-policy research organizations told us. "In the Asia-Pacific region, the major threat to security comes from the militarization of Japan."

China's ongoing campaign to keep Japan weak includes diplomatic efforts elsewhere in Asia to foster a kind of anti-Japanese front. Diplomats in Thailand and Singapore told us in 1995 and 1996 that Chinese envoys have long put "the Japan threat" at the top of their agenda in closed-door, bilateral discussions. The central message from Beijing's diplomats is that China and the nations of Southeast Asia have a common interest in preventing Japan from acting assertively in Asia and, in particular, from ever becoming a military power in the region. Striking this theme just days after the Japanese-American security declaration, a Foreign Ministry spokesman said: "If Japan's Self-Defense Forces further build up armaments, it is bound to cause concern and vigilance among other Asian nations."[12] And in a commentary on the disputed Senkaku Islands (claimed by China, Taiwan, and Japan), the *People's Daily* commented: "We see some people in Japan have inflated heads, and have lost their minds. The people of all Asian nations must come up with a method to cool off these brains and not allow them to do anything stupid. . . . A high level of vigilance should be given to the actions of Japan."[13]

The Chinese we interviewed in 1996 made clear to us that China's long-range goal is to urge other countries, including the United States, to join in a formal treaty that would ostensibly be aimed at ensuring Japanese security in perpetuity, but would actually build a permanent barrier to its ever returning to the fold of "normal" nations. The signatories would be China, Russia, the United States, and Japan itself, the first three as guarantors of Japan's security, while Japan would commit itself forever to a pacifist-neutralist foreign policy and agree to confine itself to a small defensive force.

FROM THE CHINESE perspective, there was good reason for alarm. The move by Japan to a closer relationship with the United States was exactly what China wanted to avoid—and illustrates the foolishness of its saber rattling in the Taiwan Strait, a policy that helped to bring it about. China knows that on a one-on-one basis—if it was only China versus Japan in any strategic or military confrontation—China would eventually prevail. Its sheer size—measured in area, population, economy, and armed forces—would allow it to dominate Japan, which has one-tenth China's population and the small, untested Self-Defense Force. Likewise, the United States by itself lacks the resources to serve as a permanent counterweight to China's growing power. America must have Japan as its partner—providing land for military bases, wealth to help pay for a credible American military presence in Asia, and eventually manpower in the form of a strengthened military.

Why should the strengthening of the U.S.–Japan relationship in 1996 have come as such a nasty jolt to Chinese strategists? It is true that until at least the mid-1980s, China saw, correctly, that the core of the original U.S.–Japan agreement was a unilateral American commitment to defend Japan against external attack. That commitment was the natural outgrowth of the "Peace Constitution" that the United States imposed on Japan after defeating it in World War II, by which Japan renounced war and restricted itself to the modest Self-Defense Force that, despite its name, is too small to defend Japan against an invasion by any major military power, let alone a nuclear attack. Nor is the SDF capable of defending the sea-lanes that are vital to Japan's survival as a trading nation. Instead, the understanding was, and is, that the United States would fulfill that need, in part by maintaining military bases in Japan, from Okinawa in the south to Hokkaido in the north.

At the height of the Cold War, when China and Japan both felt threatened by the Soviet Union, China was pleased that Japan was firmly allied to the anti-Soviet forces led by the United States. After the Soviet threat ebbed and the Cold War ended, China concluded at first that the American military presence could still serve China's interests, at least temporarily. As long as the United States defended Japan, China seemed confident that Japan would never seek to build a military force sufficient to defend itself and its sea-lanes. From China's viewpoint, the United States was helping keep Japan down.

What China did not expect was that the U.S.–Japan defense arrangement would start shifting in the direction of a real alliance, largely to counter China's growing strength. Beijing hoped that the status quo would continue as long as possible, but it also expected that the arrangement would slowly unravel of its own accord. Anti-American sentiment in Japan would play a role in this. China also believed that Americans would grow tired of defending Japan free of charge while Japan racked up huge trade surpluses at American expense. Clear-eyed Chinese strategic thinkers understood that American lawmakers or the American public would eventually balk at such a one-sided arrangement.

With the weakening of Japanese-American ties, China's strategists believed, would come other important developments, most important the eventual collapse of North Korea and the re-unification of the Korean Peninsula. It is awkward for the Chinese to acknowledge this publicly given their long relationship to the ultraorthodox Communist regime in North Korea, but Beijing has to realize that that regime, which has literally bank-rupted the country it rules, is doomed and that reunification under South Korea is likely in the next decade or two. Foreign-affairs experts in China told us that they doubted American troops would remain in Korea long after reunification began, a prediction that seems realistic, since the reason for the troops, the North Korean threat, would have disappeared. One Chinese we interviewed pointed out that this would bring the entire issue of the American military presence in Asia into acutely sharp focus. The United States would then have permanent bases in only one country, Japan. He suggested that that would place both the United States and Japan in uncomfortable positions and force an international debate on the issues of the American military role in Asia and on Japan's international status. That would be the time for China to press for a final resolution of the Japan question, very likely via the multilateral treaty already being discussed in Chinese research institutes.

Such a treaty would strongly favor the Chinese domination of Asia. American troops in Japan would be there only to prevent Japanese rearmament, not to use Japan as a base of offensive op-erations. Russia would still be too weak militarily to challenge China's domination. Even many Japanese would be seduced by the Chinese scheme, since it would hold out the promise of a low-cost national defense. There would be substantial American sentiment favoring it as well, especially if the United States, hav-ing lost its bases in the Philippines, were to depart from Korea as well. It would appear to Americans a way of reducing military expenditures, of ending the American role as the world's policeman, a role that leaves many Americans uncomfortable anyway. Very likely there would be Chinese "peace offensives" rather like the Soviet "peace movement" of the 1970s and 1980s. But the truth is that if Beijing one day broaches such an arrangement with Washington, it will in effect be asking the United States to acquiesce in China's domination of Asia and in presenting Japan with Chinese hegemony as a fait accompli.

WHILE CHINA has long identified Japan as a strategic foe, Japan was until recently relatively relaxed about China. As late as 1993, a major book on Japanese security issues hardly mentioned China.[14] For several years before that, the usually pessimistic Japanese had started believing their own press notices about Japan as No. 1 (the title of a book by an American scholar that became a best-seller in Japan). There was a rise in the belief that the United States was of diminishing importance to Japan, which should devote itself to being the leader of Asia.

At the beginning of the 1990s, despite such warning signals as the crash of Japan's real estate and stock markets, Japanese power did seem to loom over Asia. A Yen Bloc, an economic association under firm Japanese economic leadership, was supposedly imminent. The metaphor heard in Tokyo for the economies of Asia was "a flock of geese." While the Asian countries were at different stages of economic and technical development, all were flying forward following Japan's lead and flight plan. Japan was at the head of the "V." Just behind it were Taiwan, South Korea, and Singapore, whose factories were producing products that Japan had made only a decade earlier. Then came Malaysia and Indonesia, with countries like Burma and Vietnam at the rear.

At first, the Japanese viewed China as a very big but slow goose. To their credit, however, Japanese political and business leaders recognized in the period following the Tiananmen crisis that China was emerging as an economic and military power to be reckoned with. At that time the Japanese were almost alone; China hands in the United States and elsewhere in the West were speculating about the downfall of the regime. But Japan began a major effort at the start of the 1990s to improve relations with China. While the Japanese private sector continued to move slowly on the trade and investment front, the Japanese government stepped up its foreign aid and economic assistance program for China. By the mid-1990s, Japan's aid package for China totaled almost $5.5 billion a year in grants and soft loans. Japan's government dispatched its emperor and empress to China for a royal visit, a powerful symbol of Japanese respect. Tokyo also emerged as a voice in international forums for taking a conciliatory approach to Beijing in an effort to integrate China more with the world community. Finally, Japanese leaders issued those apologies to China and other nations for Japanese actions in World War II.

As we've seen, Japan's efforts at rapprochement with China have not succeeded. China accepted Japanese aid and investment but encouraged anti-Japanese sentiment among its own people and abroad. Meanwhile, the Japanese government's manipulation of market forces and its overregulation of the domestic market had saddled Japan with an economy that had severe and fundamental structural problems. By 1996, a majority of economists both Japanese and foreign agreed that Japan's economic problems were chronic and long-term. By world standards, Japan will remain healthy and prosperous, but the growth rates that propelled Japan's miraculous leap from a rubble economy in 1945 to a contender for the world's number one economy are history. Indeed, it is a certainty that in the next several years, China will overtake Japan in the total size of its economic output, pushing Japan into third place in the world.

An apt reflection of the mood of uncertainty that gripped Japan by the mid-1990s was the result of a poll conducted by the newspaper *Asahi Shimbun* in August 1994. Asked what nation would have the greatest influence on Asia in the twenty-first century, 54 percent of the Japanese respondents said China, 30 percent said the United States, and only 16 percent said Japan.[15]

This mood of pessimism and anxiety no doubt contributed to the decision to seek closer strategic ties with the United States. Another factor was China's continuing barrage of anti-Japanese propaganda. But what finally persuaded Japan of the need for a tilt toward the United States was a series of aggressive political and military moves by China that took place over a period of little more than one year and threatened Japan's fundamental security interests.

Japan was particularly alarmed by China's aggressive moves in the East and South China Seas, which threatened Japan's economic lifelines. Most of Japan's energy and raw materials pass through the South China Sea, where China had begun in the 1970s to seize islands belonging to a much weaker Vietnam. China's increasingly assertive claims of sovereignty over the entire South China Sea also alarmed the Southeast Asian states such as the Philippines and Malaysia, which had long claimed or occupied several islets. Other countries, Indonesia and Singapore in particular, had no public disputes with China over the South China Sea but had a vital interest in preventing conflict.

In November 1994, Jiang Zemin visited several countries in Southeast Asia to proclaim China's peaceful intentions. Referring to the Spratly Islands, which are a good deal closer to Vietnam, Malaysia, and the Philippines than they are to China, he told a press conference in Singapore: "China's position has been consistent and clear-cut. We advocate the settlement of relevant disputes through bilateral negotiations. All sorts of statements stemming from the proposition that 'China will pose a threat' are groundless."[16]

As it happened, however, almost as Jiang was declaring China's commitment to the peaceful settlement of disputes over reefs and islets in the sea, the Chinese navy was preparing to seize one of them. The Philippines had long been considered the "owner" of Mischief Reef, about 135 miles or so west of the

Philippine island of Palawan, but its small and poorly equipped armed forces had never succeeded in adequately patrolling Philippine territory (the United States gave up the job when its military bases in the Philippines were shut down). The Chinese had already built a structure on Mischief Reef when a Philippine fisherman by chance discovered that the Chinese were there in January 1995. The Chinese government claimed that the occupiers were fishermen, but nobody believed it. What Beijing called "simple fishermen's structures" included bunkers, satellite dishes, and radar equipment. It was clear to everyone that China's occupation of Mischief Reef was a navy operation.

What alarmed Japan, as well as the Southeast Asians, was China's duplicity (Jiang's announcements having been only the latest and most authoritative assurances of peaceful intent) and China's seeming determination to take control of the South China Sea no matter what regional opinion might hold. Although Chinese ambitions are focused on the islets and reefs, they have also claimed the right—which they say, for now, that they will not exercise—to "regulate" navigation through those waters. For Japan, of course, China's exercise of that "right" would involve regulation of its most important trade routes. But the prospect of the South China Sea's being turned into a Chinese lake had serious implications for Japanese investment as well. A huge amount of Japanese wealth is invested in the Southeast Asian nations that border on a waterway that might soon be controlled by the Chinese navy. Japan, by contrast, doesn't even have the constitutional right to send a warship to the South China Sea to protect those investments. Instead, it must depend on the willingness of the United States to send American forces to die for Sony and NEC. Never before, as one observer noted, has an important and powerful country allowed large amounts of its wealth to flow overseas without being able to protect it.

Also in 1995, Chinese leaders stepped up their maneuvering in Korea, where they took an explicitly anti-Japanese stance. While anti-Japanese sentiment is evaporating in Southeast Asia, it is still ferocious among Koreans, whose feelings about Japan's long and brutal occupation of their country, which lasted from 1895 to 1945, are intense, even among people born well after World War II. In a historical state visit to South Korea in November 1995, Jiang Zemin appealed to Koreans' animus toward Japan at every opportunity. Evoking memories of Japan's colonial rule of Korea, Jiang joined with Korean president Kim Young-sam in condemning Japan's history of "aggression," with Jiang suggesting further that Japan's "militarists" were still a threat to both Chinese and Korean well-being.[17]

To the West, Jiang's initiative in Korea seemed a healthy sign of China's willingness to extend the sphere of its good relations. Actually, however, China's initiative in Korea, based on the assumption that the Pyongyang regime will eventually crumble, encourages the Japanese nightmare: a reunified, nuclear-armed Korea that tilts toward China and against Japan. "Japanese geopolitics have not changed over the centuries," Hisahiko Okazaki, a Japanese strategic analyst, has said. "The strategic importance of the Korean Peninsula remains as it always has been."[18] If China wielded decisive influence in a nuclear-armed and unified Korea, it would have enormous leverage on Japan by in effect forcing Japan to seek China's protection against Korea.

The American alternative to this is to propose four-power talks with the two Koreas as well as the United States and China. So far this proposal has gone nowhere. In the meantime, there are persistent reports that China is secretly facilitating contacts between the North and South, advancing its agenda of being the decisive outside player on the peninsula. Despite American military assets on the peninsula itself, the United States seems to have no policy, and this alarms Japan all the more.

At the same time, China's growing entente with Russia, while not explicitly aimed at Japan, is, by any strategist's definition, contrary to Japan's interests. It further tilts the balance of power in Northeast Asia in China's favor and against the interests of Japan and the United States. Even though it is in part coincidental and not causal, the Sino-Russian entente seems to be running closely parallel to the Japanese-American entente. Indeed, in 1996, Russian president Boris Yeltsin and Jiang Zemin declared a Sino-Russian strategic accord the same month, April, that Clinton and Hashimoto issued their joint declaration in Tokyo.

For Japan, the Taiwan Strait Crisis has to be seen against this background. Taiwan is crucially important to Japanese security. It in effect helps guard Japan's southern flank. Since the Korean War, its close ties with the United States and its pro-Western, pro-trade policies have made Taiwan a comforting presence. What is nearly always completely overlooked is that Taiwan also guards the eastern entrances to the South China Sea—the Taiwan Strait, which Taiwan shares with China, and the Bashi Channel in the Luzon Strait, which it shares with the Philippines. Little attention has been paid to this important strategic fact because Taiwan's commitment to trade and to freedom of navigation is such a given that the prospect of Taiwan's bottling up those waterways has never arisen. But the prospect of eventual Chinese control of Taiwan, a prospect certainly brought to mind by the confrontation on the Taiwan Strait in 1996, forces Japanese strategists to appreciate anew the immense strategic importance of Taiwan to Japan.

In any case, these various incidents and statements, all of them taking place in the post–Cold War world, have led to several Japanese-American undertakings. Taken together, they represent a remarkable increase in military cooperation between the two countries:

- In February 1996 the United States and Japan signed a memorandum of understanding regarding the sharing of detailed information about missile defense. In April 1995, the Japan Defense Agency had set up the Ballistic Missile Defense Research Office, whose mission is to decide whether to deploy the THAAD (theater high-altitude area defense) antimissile system.
- In April 1996 there was the joint security declaration.
- In May 1996 the Japanese government was reported to be looking into setting up new guidelines for Japan "to act in con-

cert with Washington in tackling all emergencies . . . that occur in the surrounding region." This was an outgrowth of the April declaration. One newspaper reported that Japan was looking for the right language to rationalize Japan's taking a more active military role on the side of the United States in the event of war.[19]

- In June 1996 the Pentagon agreed to supply the Japan Defense Agency with early-warning data from spy satellites, that is, early warning of a missile attack.

- In July 1996 Japan's annual defense white paper was issued with assessments of strategic threats to Japan. Although it sounded diplomatic to outsiders, its references to China were the sternest yet: "[China's] continuous promotion of modernizing nuclear, naval and air forces; its expansion of . . . naval activities; and tensions caused by its military exercises around Taiwan all suggest the need for us to pay close attention . . . to Beijing's behavior."[20]

- In August 1996 defense industry associations in Japan and the United States agreed to set up a coordinating body to foster joint development of high-tech military equipment.[21]

The most significant trend to emerge from these events was the increasing momentum in favor of a missile defense system for Japan. THAAD would constitute an antiballistic missile shield around Japan and South Korea to be erected by 2005. It is still in development in the United States, and major questions about what share of the development costs would be footed by Japan are still far from resolution. However, if THAAD is adopted, it would be a further major step toward a closer U.S.–Japan strategic alliance aimed primarily at China. Beijing once again recognizes a challenge when it sees one, and its media have been strongly attacking both the United States and Japan for even considering a missile defense system. "The Chinese are concerned because THAAD would negate the modernization of its own missiles and nuclear weapons systems," David Lampton, president of the National Committee for U.S.–China Relations, said.[22]

China, unhappy about this trend to say the least, can be expected to step up its pressure on Japan. For example, a Chinese official announced in June 1996 that political considerations will affect the final selection of contractors for China's huge Three Gorges Project, a series of dams and hydroelectric stations it intends to build on the Yangtze River. Qin Zhongyi, vice president of the China Yangtze Three Gorges Development Corporation, was quoted in Beijing's *China Daily* saying that the chances for a Japanese consortium (Mitsubishi Heavy Industries, Mitsubishi Electric, Toshiba, Hitachi) to win its bids for $4 billion in contracts "look doubtful, since Japan's close association with objectionable American policies is not easily forgotten." Qin, who is in charge of all international bidding for the project, said a German-Canadian consortium is the front-runner because of "the conducive relations between their home countries and China."[21]

IT WOULD BE DIFFICULT to exaggerate the extent to which the future balance of power in Asia depends on Japanese-American cooperation. As one Japanese commentator put it to Thomas L. Friedman of *The New York Times*, "Japan alone cannot handle China, Japan alone cannot handle a unified Korea, and Japan alone cannot protect its own sea lanes—so for all these reasons we need the U.S. alliance."[23] That, however, does not mean that Japan will firmly ally itself to the United States. Many elements of Japan's dominant bureaucratic and corporate interests will probably resist a revived alliance explicitly aimed at balancing China because it will threaten the profits Japan can make in China. There is also resistance from the general public, which has a collective dread of the disasters that unbridled militarism once brought to Japan. After half a century of pacifism, the Japanese self-perception may simply not permit the country to accept a genuine great-power role, even in its own backyard. As Friedman put it, the problem is that "the Japanese government does not want to talk about the C-word or the K-word."[24]

For much of this century, it was China's weakness and Japan's strength that destroyed any possibility of a stable Asian balance of power. As a result, since World War II it has become axiomatic that a rearmed Japan would threaten peace and stability in Asia. But if that was once true, it no longer is. In the post–Cold War world it is Japan's weakness that threatens peace and stability by creating a power vacuum that the United States cannot fill, but that China can. A strong Japan in genuine partnership with the United States is vital to a new balance of power in Asia. A weak Japan benefits only China, which, the evidence indicates, aims not at a new balance of power but at Chinese hegemony, under which Japan, if it yields to that fate, would serve as China's richest and most useful tributary state.

CHAPTER 8

CHINA VERSUS AMERICA: A WAR GAME

WE DO NOT THINK that a war between China and the United States is likely. But there could be conflict in the South China Sea if Chinese moves there threaten the sea-lanes, and the United States, asked by the Philippines or (ironically) Vietnam, feels it has to intervene. But the most likely occasion for the unlikely war between China and America would come over Taiwan. Say it is the year 2004. Hong Kong and Macau are safely in the embrace of the Chinese motherland. A crisis develops even as certain conditions exist that push China toward an armed attempt to force Taiwan into the Chinese fold.

China itself is in some domestic turmoil. The economy has slowed down; there is labor unrest; masses of the unemployed have become vagabonds drifting here and there through the provinces looking for work. Students and intellectuals are tired of the regime of Jiang Zemin, which is still as intolerant of criticism and dissent as ever. The system's endemic corruption has reached astonishing levels, with the friends and relatives of senior officials enjoying glittering lives of conspicuous wealth as the heads of the various enterprises associated with the government. Formerly Communist China has become a country of controlled capitalism, and the most controlling capitalists are the relatives of the former Communists. Public cynicism has grown strong, in other words, and the party leaders understand that a national emergency centering around an issue sacred to patriotic feeling, an issue that requires unity, self-sacrifice, an end to private grumbling, and devotion to the Great Cause, would quell that cynicism.

Moreover, figures like Jiang and his premier want to secure their places in history. Do they want to be remembered as the butchers of Beijing, or as the revolutionaries who presided over the McDonaldization of China, especially when Taiwan gives them an opportunity to complete the reunification of the motherland?

To be sure, that goal has occasioned intense debate inside the Politburo. Moderates in the leadership warn that a war over Taiwan will cost China dearly in terms of international public opinion and in relations with Japan and Southeast Asia. Some countries might even use China's absorption by a war in the Taiwan Strait to try to take back the islands in the South China Sea that China seized in 2001 in a coordinated amphibious assault, with air cover provided by the new fleet of Russian SU-27 fighter-bombers. But while those risks are clear, the pro-war, unification-at-any-cost party also knows that once hostilities have broken out, anybody who criticizes the leadership will be buried under an avalanche of manipulated patriotic sentiment.

Then there is the factor of military readiness, proved to some extent by the success of the South China Sea operation of a year and a half before. For years, everybody has known that a frontal assault on Taiwan would be extremely risky and costly to both sides. Indeed, it would risk leaving Taiwan in such a state of devastation that any success in retaking it would ring hollow and create a generation's worth of renewed animosity between Taiwanese and Mainlanders. Nonetheless, China, acting on its threat to resolve the Taiwan issue militarily, has been secretly building three times as many submarines, landing craft, and warships as the world believes, giving it the arsenal necessary for an operation aimed at taking the island in three days—before the international community, and especially the Americans, have time to react.

Several military advances have made the task of conquering Taiwan, impossible to carry out as recently as 1999, feasible in 2004, the country's army leaders are saying. China now possesses a fleet of Tomahawk-class cruise missiles. Another major development is its purchase from the Russians of a full regiment— twenty-four planes—of supersonic TU-22 long-range backfire bombers, to go with its fleet of two hundred SU-27 fighter planes and the IL-76 transport planes that now are fitted out as AWACS. Four new Luhu- and eight Luda-class destroyers have come into service, based at China's new modern naval base on Stonecutters Island in the Hong Kong Special Administrative Region. The Luhu destroyer in particular is a formidable ship, powered by General Electric LM2500 gas-turbine engines and equipped with solid-fueled surface-to-surface missile launchers, a French-made Crotale surface-to-air missile air defense system, and 324-millimeter Whitehead torpedo launchers, coupled with improved radar, fire-control systems, variable-depth sonar equipment, and two Harbin Z9A helicopters.[1]

In the years since the military modernization gained real momentum, China has gotten ten Kilo-class submarines to go with its existing and improved fleet of nuclear-powered Han-, Ming-, and Romeo-class vessels, the new arrivals in China's fleet far quieter than the previous generation and difficult to detect even by American antisubmarine warfare technology. The Kilo-class ships in particular are equipped with Soviet-built 533-millimeter passive wake-homing torpedoes with effective ranges up to 26 kilometers.[2] The expanded submarine force could be used to seed minefields in Taiwan's sea-lanes, and more generally to encircle Taiwan either to enforce a commercial blockade or to prevent efforts to bring in military supplies by ship. China has bought or built one thousand T-72 tanks, the most fearsome of the battle tanks of the former Soviet Union, along with several dozen large high-speed air-cushion boats, each capable of carrying five hundred fully equipped infantry troops and ten tanks for an amphibious landing. China has developed its radar-jamming equipment, its command and control operations, its electronic countermeasure equipment, to the point where military planners are confident that they can seriously disrupt communications between enemy troops in the field and Taiwan's major command center in Taipei. China's satellite reconaissance is world-class and can keep the country almost immediately informed of Taiwan's military moves. China has several dozen DF-15 and DF-11 missiles (otherwise known as M-9 and M-11), the same kind that were fired in the famous, long-ago military exercises of 1996, whose mobile launchers can be put into place, fired, and dismantled in less than thirty minutes, and they can be counted on to land within 20 meters of their targets when fired at a distance of 300 kilometers.

As China's military force has reached world-class levels, its efforts at peaceful reunification have been frustrated by the continued trend on Taiwan toward independence. One reason for this is the by-now well-known heavy-handedness of China's takeover of Hong Kong a few years before, when members of the main pro-democracy party there were jailed, and, following that, newspapers that supported them closed down and demonstrations in support of them suppressed by the Public Security Bureau. That made a bad impression on Taiwan, which has gotten used to a free and unrestricted political life.

China then embarked on military exercises that equally backfired on the regime in Beijing. Following a variation of the script it first tried in 1996, China mounted a blockade of Taiwan without calling it that—since international law defines a blockade per se as an act of war. Instead Beijing announced a series of submarine warfare exercises and warned merchant ships away from the island. As several shipping lines suspended service to Taiwan, the stock market went into a brief but steep downward spiral. But the United States, with enthusiastic support from Congress and the Pentagon, turned the tables on China. Taking advantage of the opportunity presented by China's submarine warfare exercises, the American navy promptly started its largest-ever exercise in antisubmarine warfare. For three weeks, American submarines and ASW aircraft, displaying their formidable advantage in technology, constantly bathed every Chinese submarine in a cloak of electronic detection signals. The American message to China: If this was real war, we'd sink every single sub you have. The Americans were pleased with themselves, overly pleased as it would turn out. They declared that this marked the effective end of any Chinese hope that escalating de facto blockades would break Taiwan's will.

Later, to save face, Chinese leaders floated rumors that they would fire missiles into remote mountain sites on Taiwan. If this was also meant to intimidate the Taiwanese, the move failed. Instead, it provoked defiant, pro-independence demonstrations in front of Taipei's presidential palace.

The year after that, again in the guise of military exercises, China flew a squadron of fifty MIG-21 fighters along the northern edge of Taiwan, just outside the country's area of air sovereignty. In response, Taiwan scrambled two squadrons of F-16s and Mirage 2000s, which it acquired from the United States and France a few years before. Within twelve minutes or so, while the Taiwan planes were still in the air, China dispatched a second batch of fifty planes off the island's southern coast. When another squadron of Taiwanese planes were in the air, yet a third group of fifty planes was sent aloft by China, this one flashing south to north parallel to the island's western coast. Eventually, as wave after wave of Chinese planes were put into the air, Taiwan had no more aircraft to scramble. Yet the Chinese continued to fly by, almost daring the Taiwanese to provoke an incident by using one of their surface-to-air batteries to shoot a plane down.

In all, nearly eight hundred Chinese planes took part in the "exercise," which was actually a dramatic lesson to Taiwan in the numerical, though not technical, superiority of China's air force. China has roughly five thousand planes, ranging from Qian-5 ground-attack planes, with advanced French-made range-finder avionics, to Chao-7 fighters, modeled on the old Soviet MIG-29 standby, to the SU-27 supersonic fighter-bombers. Taiwan has roughly one-tenth the number of planes as China.

Still, even that demonstration of China's airpower failed to push stubborn Taipei toward negotiations, as tens of thousands of Taiwanese again demonstrated in favor of independence. China's actions, so far from persuading Taiwan that it needs to face the inevitability of Beijing's control of the island, seemed instead to provoke a lively movement stressing the separate Taiwanese culture and history. Several pro-independence newspapers and radio stations are flourishing on Taiwan. Then in March 2004 came a new presidential election, in which the pro-unification party's candidate was likely, if the polls were accurate, to get less than 18 percent of the popular vote. The Kuomintang incumbent, who had become in everything but name the pro-independence candidate, appeared ready to sweep to a landslide victory. During his last term, he had actually succeeded in getting some additional small countries to extend full diplomatic ties to what was still called the Republic of China on Taiwan, a move that especially infuriated Beijing. Meanwhile, the Americans were still willing to sell Taiwan the high-tech military equipment it needs to deter a Chinese attack.

Beijing, in other words, feels that time is running out. The election will consolidate the pro-independence forces in the presidential palace for another four years. It is time to do something, something that might risk an American intervention, which China wants to avoid, but something that will be effective in forcing Taiwan back to the motherland's embrace.

First came the causus belli. During an election campaign demonstration in front of the presidential palace in Taipei, a group carrying pro-independence placards provoked a melee. It never became clear whether the incident was a spontaneous one or whether it had been engineered from Beijing, which, as everyone knew, had spent years putting "sleepers" into place on the island, agents who remain quiet for years before undertaking any action.

In any case, the confrontation in front of the palace got worse. Suddenly there were squadrons of demonstrators bearing pro-Beijing and pro-reunification banners running in small groups through the crowd. A group of them broke through the gates of the Ministry of National Defense, across the square from the palace, and when the antiriot police were called out to quell the disturbance, several of the pro-Beijing demonstrators were injured. Then just as the disturbance seemed to be quieting down, there was a burst of fire from an automatic weapon. Three of the pro-Beijing demonstrators were killed, several others injured.

Within minutes, Jiang Zemin, China's party chairman (he got that title, Mao's old one, in 1999), was meeting inside Beijing's heavily guarded Zhongnanhai complex with the chiefs of staff, the commander of the Nanjing military region, along with the members of the Politburo Standing Committee. Jiang solemnly announced the historic duty of China to restore order on Taiwan and to satisfy the deep and abiding longing of Chinese people on both sides of the strait to live under the same roof. Clenching his fist, Jiang declared that China could no longer tolerate the sabotage and subversion of splittists and others who would never give up their efforts to implement a One China–One Taiwan policy. The blame lay with the chief splittist, the president himself, who had made no secret of his plans to create an independent Taiwan. "We will never allow China to be divided," the normally soft-spoken Jiang declared, his voice filling up the meeting room, his teeth clenched, his face red. "One billion Chinese would never forgive us."

THE FIRST BLOCKADE came just two weeks later in the guise of renewed military exercises in the Taiwan Strait. This time China warned all shipping not only to stay out of the strait itself but to keep more than one hundred nautical miles from both the northern and southern coasts of Taiwan, where Chinese submarines and surface ships would be engaged in maneuvers. The American ambassador was called into the Foreign Ministry and told that the exercises would last about a week. He was asked for patience and understanding and to convey to his government assurances that China had no aggressive intent.

The exercises made front-page headlines all over the world. They were denounced by Taiwan. The Americans sent the *Nimitz* and a flotilla of support vessels, two destroyers, four cruisers, a torpedo boat, and several submarines, to the western Pacific about 150 nautical miles east of Taiwan. The United States protested to Beijing about the closure of international waterways, as did the Japanese, the Americans warning that China would pay the consequences if any American ships were hit or damaged as a result of the "exercises."

China deployed its Han- and Kilo-class submarines around Taiwan and conducted almost hourly surveillance flights up to three hundred miles offshore. It also deployed several dozen fast patrol boats near Keelung and Kaohsiung Harbors. Two of its Luhu destroyers and support vessels stood ready, one outside Hong Kong, the other offshore Xiamen, the main port on the coast of Fujian, directly opposite Taiwan. When the week ended, China announced the successful completion of its exercises and pulled its forces back into port.

And then, a month later, having had only the mildest protest so far from the United States, China announced a similar exercise, this one of indefinite duration. In Taipei and in Washington, it was by now obvious that the Chinese action represented a disguised blockade of Taiwan's ports, which are, needless to say, a major part of the island's economic lifeline. Beijing sent several battalions of rapid deployment forces to Fujian in a state of full battle readiness. As the crisis built, Beijing made a diplomatic overture. It invited the Taiwan president to open talks leading to the eventual reunification of the motherland and let it be known through several informal channels that the "military exercises" would continue until Taiwan came to the table. Taiwan's response, as expected, was an angry refusal to be forced into negotiations at gunpoint, a refusal portrayed in the Chinese press as the triumph of a "splittist war party" on Taiwan, which wants a showdown with China.

Meanwhile, as ships began accumulating in the waters outside of the exclusion zone, the Americans moved a second carrier task force south of Taiwan so that it was stationed roughly between Kaohsiung and Hong Kong in the northern part of the South China Sea. Then it sent surveillance planes and submarines to keep track of China's vessels. In all, the United States had sixteen warships in the area, with 120 F-14s on the carriers, as well as cruise missiles and S-3A/B antisubmarine warfare aircraft. The Chinese newspapers published articles about how the Americans would be "pulverized" by China's airpower, missiles, and sea-borne artillery if it tried to interfere in China's internal affairs, meaning the blockade of Taiwan.

TAIWAN STRUCK BACK on the ninth day in a coordinated attack aimed at ending the blockade. Its shore batteries fired on four Chinese patrol boats in the strait, and a Mirage 2000 fighter-bomber, escorted by F-16s, knocked out a Luda-class destroyer in a direct hit by an Exocet missile. In a brief aerial dogfight, two Chinese MIG-21s were downed, and Taiwan lost an F-16, apparently to missile fire from a ship. There were banner headlines the world over as the first armed clash in more than half a century took place in China's still unended civil war.

The Chinese retaliation was swift and devastating. At 5 a.m. the day after the Taiwanese retaliation, DF-15 and DF-11 missiles were fired from mobile launch sites in Fujian and Guangdong Provinces at targets on Taiwan itself. Then at first light, several waves of Chinese planes hit additional targets on Taiwan in an effort to cripple the island's main defense installations. The bomber attack provoked fierce resistance from Taiwan, which sent aloft its F-16s and Mirage 2000s and its first batteries of surface-to-air missiles, knocking out seventeen of the attacking planes, but which had kept its best planes in reserve and sent up a squadron of backfire bombers in a second-wave attack that proved to be devastating.

Struck in the coordinated assault were Taiwan's eight military airports, its five naval harbors, its five radar centers, and two signal intelligence centers located in the mountains that form the island's north-south spine. An hour after these first attacks, there was a third bombing wave from China, aimed at secondary targets: the Chongshan Science and Technology Institute in Taoyuan, where Taiwan develops its missiles and electronic weapons; the San Hsia Missile Production Center outside of Taipei; the Aircraft Production Center in Taichung; and the several Military Combined Logistical Services in Taipei, Tainan, and Kaohsiung.

Suddenly it was full-scale war, but a war involving psychological pressure and matériel destruction, rather than an attempt to occupy territory. China still held back its Fist units on Fujian, knowing that their mere presence would unsettle Taiwan's rulers, who would not know if an invasion was actually going to take place or not. If China did send troops, Taiwan's objective would not be to defeat them. In the long run it couldn't do that. The objective would be to last long enough for international pressure to build up against China and for American help to arrive. The idea would be to exact as high a price as possible from China while buying time. That is why when the first missile and air strikes came, Taiwan took no retaliatory action. Its advanced planes, kept in hardened underground bunkers, had not been damaged. Its warships, in anticipation of the attack, had left their ports and steamed to the eastern side of the island for protection. Taiwan would continue to attack the naval blockade force, but it would keep its main forces in reserve in case China tried a land invasion.

Meanwhile, Taiwan sent an urgent appeal to the United States. It needed F-16s to improve its air defenses. It needed more submarines and ASW ships and aircraft to fight the blockade. It needed Patriot missiles to defend against further missile attacks. It asked for satellite intelligence help in locating Chinese forces. And, if possible, it wanted the United States to use its ships to break the blockade. In Taipei they knew what they had known all through the years: in the face of a determined military action by China, only an active American intervention in the war could preserve Taiwan's freedom from Mainland control.

THE PRESIDENT of the United States, meeting in the White House Situation Room with his chiefs of staff, his national security adviser, the director of Central Intelligence, and his secretary of defense, wanted to know what the American options were.

"If we wanted to break the blockade and guard against an invasion, what could we do?" was his first question.

Answer: The Seventh Fleet, which is only a day's sail away, could overwhelm China's blockade force, though there would probably be some American losses. We have the capability, using cruise and Exocet missiles and the standard arsenal of antisubmarine weapons, to destroy enough of the ships and submarines of the Chinese navy to break the blockade. Once the fleet was in place, we could quickly establish air control over the Taiwan Strait, which would enable Taiwan's own defenses to repel any invasion from the sea. And if we have control of the air, the Chinese would be unable to bring troops or equipment into their foothold at the airport, and the Taiwanese forces would thus presumably be able to deal with them as well.

"Are we still far enough ahead of the Chinese to do that without taking any major losses ourselves?"

The Chinese have advanced surface-to-air missiles and very good MIG-29s and SU-27s, which might mean a loss of some American planes. China might try an airborne attack on some parts of our fleet, and while we believe it would be repelled, there is always the danger of losing a ship either to submarine-launched missiles or to torpedoes fired from the air. We cannot count on a Gulf War situation, where the enemy would have almost no capacity to hit our forces at all.

"What other risks do we face?"

At the worst, they could use nuclear weapons against us. It's not that well known, but China has been the world's third-biggest nuclear power since the late 1970s, in terms of the total number of delivery vehicles. They have actually been able to hit us since at least the early 1980s, with what they call their Long March 2 rocket, sometimes called the Dongfeng, or DF-5. It has a range of about nine thousand miles, so it could definitely hit targets on the West Coast. China has been able to put as many as three independently targeted warheads on each rocket since about 1988.

China also has some nuclear submarines—they are called Xia-class submarines—armed with nuclear-tipped SLBMs, submarine-launched ballistic missiles. We have detected one of these submarines as close as several hundred miles off the California coast. We're not sure how many of them they have, but we think it's about twelve now. The missiles are accurate to within a mile. So China definitely has a survivable nuclear deterrent. The question is, would they use it?

"What can we do in the way of a more limited involvement?"

The best approach might be a gradually scaled escalation. We take out one ship, say a cruiser or a destroyer, and warn Beijing that if the attacks and the blockade continue, we are ready to take out the rest of their navy one ship at a time. Or we could patrol an air corridor over the Taiwan Strait and only shoot at them if they cross the line that we establish—in other words a no-fly zone like the one we used to have in Iraq.

"What can we do to help Taiwan without getting into a shooting war with China ourselves?"

We can help them out quite a bit with intelligence information. We have satellite reconnaissance that can give them a clear idea of the exact nature of the Chinese deployment. We can supply an AWACS plane, to give them airborne control and command. For some time now they have needed a couple more Knox-class frigates, some S-70C ASW helicopters, acoustic processors to help them detect subs, and advanced air-search radars, but we haven't sold them the stuff because we were afraid of stimulating a new arms race in Asia, but Taiwan needs all of that to use against the blockading force. We could reinforce their air force by sending in more F-16s and delivering them right away from our own stocks. We could bring in some Patriot missile batteries to improve their air defense.

"Would it make a difference?"

The key right now is for Taiwan to be able to break the blockade, and if we send them subs and ASW aircraft and technology, they'll make China pay a heavy price. But China could always use any Taiwan counterattack as a pretext for launching an invasion. And if China is determined to win this war and they are willing to take heavy casualties—and they have traditionally been willing to take heavy casualties—then over the long run they are going to win, unless we get directly involved ourselves.

"What is the cost to us if Taiwan loses?"

Well, all the other countries near China, from Japan to Indonesia and even Australia, will feel that the United States has failed to keep the peace in Asia. Japan especially could well see its alliance with us as a liability, one that makes the Chinese angry and doesn't give the Japanese any credible security guarantee in exchange. American prestige will drop precipitously elsewhere in Asia where countries, whether or not they actually come right out and say so, are afraid of China and want our protection. In other words, if we can't stop China from taking over Taiwan, China will immediately become the Asian superpower, and nobody in the region, whether it's Japan or Korea or the Philippines or Vietnam, will be in a position to maintain a foreign policy that doesn't take account of China's preferences first.

"Speaking of Japan, Prime Minister Murakami called me a couple of hours ago. He gave us an unconditional go-ahead to use our air and naval bases in Okinawa for military operations in the Taiwan theater. But his voice was trembling as he told me this. It's obvious he's hoping and praying we won't have to take him up on his offer. What else on Japan?"

The military alert announced by Tokyo a week ago is now in full effect. Japan's Self-Defense Force is about as close to a war footing as it'll ever be. Almost every warship it has is now on the high seas south of the home islands. And its air force is flying as many patrols as it's capable of. But we know the Japanese won't get directly involved in any hostilities unless they're attacked. And if that happens, we don't know if their forces will stand and fight.

Anyway, Murakami's already out on a limb. A hundred thousand people marched in Tokyo today—demanding that Japan preserve its "pacifist purity," whatever that is. It's the middle of the night there now, but about three thousand protesters are staging a sit-down in front of the Imperial Palace pleading with the emperor to intervene. Yoko Ono just flew in—she's leading them in choruses of "Give Peace a Chance." They're singing in Japanese, but whenever CNN and FOX go live, they switch to English.

If we hold firm, and win this one, these people are going to evaporate.

"And if we don't?"

For starters, Murakami would be finished politically. Second, if we let Taiwan go down the tubes, our alliance with Japan is finished. The doves in the Foreign Ministry will be on the next plane to Beijing with a promise that Japan will be China's good friend and tributary forever.

"What are the Russians going to do, especially if we intervene?"

The Russians are so dependent now on China's buying half their weapons production that whatever they say is going to be pro-Beijing. But in case you're worried about them sending their Pacific fleet toward Taiwan, the question is, what Pacific fleet? Russian weapons in China's hands are kept a lot better than the Russians keep them themselves. Our satellites are watching that so-called fleet trying to get out of Vladivostok. A couple of nuclear-armed submarines have left their berths, but what good are they in a crisis like this? And we've seen four rustbucket warships leave port, but one of them is already dead in the water, and the other three are sailing aimlessly in the Sea of Japan.

"Well, where do we stand with our friends in Southeast Asia, then?"

Well, it's a somewhat-mixed but not very good picture. In Singapore, Lee Kuan Yew, who is very old now but still has influence, called on all parties to end the crisis, but, very pointedly, he mentioned only Beijing by name. But that doesn't help much. The Thais are calling for peace but not saying anything helpful to us or to Taiwan. The new Indonesian leader has been boxed in by ethnic Chinese businessmen who are pleading with him to stay neutral. That could change; our Australian friends are pushing him hard to stand up and be counted. But don't hold your breath. In the Philippines, we're getting very conflicting messages from the new government. Some of our navy people are saying we should just sail into Subic Bay and take over our old base there, and quote some recent Philippine message saying we could do that. But the Filipinos are terrified of China, and they're just not going to take a public and unambiguous stance and stick with it. And, to some extent, we have only ourselves to blame. We weren't there for them back in 1995 on Mischief Reef. We played it ambiguously during the last Taiwan crisis. But if we act decisively and forcefully on Taiwan this time, not only the Filipinos but the Indonesians too will line up with us for decades to come. We'll be finally able to put together that Asia-Pacific Alliance for Peace and Stability that we proposed in the last election campaign. We'll have a balance of power that will last generations.

"But there's China to deal with, a China armed with nuclear weapons. Isn't it normal that it has paramount influence in its own region?"

You could make the argument that the whole Taiwan question is just a detail left over from history, and once China has it, a lot of the problems between the United States and China will disappear. Certainly China will be happy with us if we don't interfere. But there's another way of looking at this. It may be true that Taiwan is not like any other country, but it's an important country. It's a big economy. It's also a democracy, a real democracy. And it has 21 million people who do not want to live under Beijing's control. Taiwan is also an old friend. Can the greatest country in the world really just stand by and do nothing while a friend is conquered by its neighbor?

"Will China threaten the United States even if it does take Taiwan?"

Not directly. China is pretty unlikely to attack Hawaii or Alaska. China has no interest in doing that. But if it gains disproportionate power in Asia, it will limit our ability to protect our interests there—in keeping open the sea-lanes, in participating in free trade and economic development, and in preventing war. So, yes, you could say let China have Taiwan, it's not our problem. But American credibility and the American interest would both be seriously affected if China takes Taiwan by force, and we just stand by and do nothing about it.

"So your unequivocal recommendation is to intervene?"

We have to. The choice is not whether to intervene, but how to intervene. And no matter how we intervene, there's going to be a good chance of some kind of direct shooting war with China. Either they will hit an American merchant ship, and we will have to retaliate, or they will fire a missile at one of our planes, and then we will be involved whether we like it or not.

IT IS UNLIKELY but not unimaginable that such a conversation might take place in the White House before we have gotten very far into the next century. The more China continues to be aggressive and the more America continues to be naïve about China's long-range interests and goals, the more likely it is that such a conversation might someday take place. If it did come to war between China and the United States over the Taiwan Strait, the precise military result, while certainly important, would not be the longest-term consequence. Whatever the result, whether the United States preserved a Taiwan of de facto independence or whether it failed to do so, the cost to both China and the United States would be staggering. China would be set back by years in its economic development plans. Beijing would have destroyed the fragile confidence it has built up around the world in its ultimately peaceful intentions. As for the United States, a long and beneficial era would be at an end, the era of the Pax

Americana in Asia, to be replaced by a new era of open super-power conflict.

The point, of course, is to avoid such a confrontation. The point indeed is to avoid other, less dramatic difficulties in the Sino-American relationship in the future. Striving to do that will be the most important task of American foreign policy for the next decade at least. The cost of failing will be very high. How, then, can we ensure success? What follow are some concrete suggestions for managing the American relationship with China, aimed at isolating the issues where China must be confronted, in the hopes that a firm, consistent, and sensible policy, attached to a clear and unchanging goal of maintaining the balance of power, can avoid any emergency discussion in the White House like the one just imagined.

CONCLUSION: COPING WITH CHINA

When China awakes, it will shake the world.
—NAPOLEON BONAPARTE

CHINA HAS BEEN a great power for most of the last two thousand years, and it is now the largest nation on earth, so it should not be surprising as it undergoes its long-expected awakening that it is destined to become a global power. But as China resumes its historic place among the world's powerful nations, what can be done to encourage that emergence to be beneficial rather than harmful? Put another way, how can the conflict with China be managed?

No matter what happens in China, American policy toward that country should be guided by a clear and firm sense of American national interests. Today, that is not the case. Indeed, largely framed by China's own propaganda machinery and the Clinton administration's confused rhetoric, the discussion assumes that we have only two options: "engagement" versus "containment." The terms are so vague as to be nearly meaningless as prescriptions for policy. At best, "engagement" stands for little more than the process of increasing contacts with China in all fields based on that noble but naïve American idea that better communications automatically lead to better relations. But "engagement" is also coming to suggest something much worse: the idea that making concessions to China and shrinking from imposing sanctions on it no matter how bad its behavior will encourage it to act with greater restraint and responsibility in the international community.

"Containment," on the other hand, prescribes a permanent distrust and hostility modeled on the policy pursued by the West toward the Soviet Union in the late 1940s and 1950s. But China is not the Soviet Union, which was a territorially and ideologically expansionist country with a rigidly controlled economy and a messianic, world-conquering vision of itself. China's situation and its stance toward the rest of the world resemble more the emergent Russia of the nineteenth century than the Soviet Union in the twentieth. China is a backwater superpower, weak and poor on a per capita basis but immense on an absolute scale and therefore able to concentrate its resources and abilities into the forms of strength needed to dominate its region. Moreover, while it does not covet its neighbor's territory—except for the unique case of Taiwan—it is a profoundly dissatisfied power. There is a kind of collective desperation in China to make up for lost time, to use whatever means are necessary, from deceitfulness to bluster, legitimate competition to outright theft, to achieve its goal of renewed greatness.

The goal of the United States is not a weak and poor China; it is a China that is stable and democratic, that does not upset the balance of power in Asia, and that plays within the rules on such matters as trade and arms proliferation. The single most important change, one that would, almost at a stroke, eliminate the sharpest areas of conflict with the United States, would be for China to follow the global trend toward democracy. Insofar as Beijing needs to be responsive to the needs and desires of its own people, and insofar as the policies it pursues are subject to real scrutiny and debate, China would be less threatening to the interests of other countries. We do not mean by this that all antagonism would disappear, but only that democratic countries, even when they are fiercely angry at each other, usually respect their own populations' reluctance to go to war.

All that would be required, for example, to resolve the Taiwan question would be for Beijing to give formal recognition to the democratically expressed preferences of the 21 million people who live on Taiwan. With Taiwan already democratic, a democratic Mainland would lead almost inevitably to reunification, very likely at first in some sort of federal arrangement. The possibility that a frustrated China eager for a nationalistic cause would send troops to conquer Taiwan would be virtually eliminated.

And so, how to deal with China? The standard answer to that question usually puts forward the notion of balance as the first principle. We must achieve a balance of often-inconsistent goals, encouragement of human rights and economic interchange being the most conspicuous. As such, American policy gets pulled from one extreme to the other and appears inconsistent and detached from underlying goals. When China cracks down on human rights, as it did so violently in 1989, the human rights component of American policy moves to the fore, and we forget that the too-ardent pursuit of that policy will sacrifice other interests. A few months later, when we have lost a couple of key contracts to Japanese or European competitors, the economic interest comes to the fore, and human rights is jettisoned as naïvely idealistic.

The basis for any policy is a clear definition of goals and a clear and consistent policy aimed at achieving those goals. There are three goals: one, to ensure peace in Asia by maintaining a stable balance of power there; two, to encourage the largest and potentially most powerful country in the region, namely China, to be a responsible state committed to nonproliferation, the peaceful resolution of disputes, and honest free trade; and three, to induce China to become more democratic and to respect the human rights of its own people, partly on the grounds that democracy and the peaceful resolution of disputes go hand in hand.

· · ·

THE ECONOMIC RELATIONSHIP with China is the area in which the United States can be more effective than it has been in defending its national interests. The conventional American response to unfair trade practices has been to negotiate, then to issue threats of sanctions when the negotiations fail, followed by agreement on specific issues, compliance with which has then to be monitored and is often subject to a renewal of the negotiation-threat-agreement cycle. The best example of that has to do with the widely publicized problem of Chinese piracy of computer software and compact discs. Amid heated negotiations and threats and counterthreats, the United States managed to wrest two agreements from the Chinese to curb such piracy. The Chinese made only a halfhearted attempt to enforce a first agreement on that subject reached in 1995. Circles sympathetic to Beijing said the central government didn't have enough political power to shut down factories owned by the People's Liberation Army or local power holders and producing pirate CDs. Nevertheless, on the apparent verge of a trade war, an agreement was reached between the two sides after Beijing authorities made a public show of pursuing the pirate producers. Even after the second agreement, only a few weeks passed before peddlers of illegal CDs were once again aggressively approaching Western tourists on the streets of Beijing. "It's business as usual," a cheerful peddler of CDs told an American visitor in the summer of 1996, only weeks after the agreement was reached.[1]

At least with international property rights, the problem remains relatively constant even if a solution remains elusive. But other agreements with the Chinese have later proved even more frustrating. We have already cited the United States trade report for 1996, which pointed out how agreements on ending protectionist tariffs made between China and the United States in 1992 were undermined when Chinese authorities introduced new protectionist measures that negated parts of the original understanding. So too did newly introduced nontariff barriers make a mockery of many of the tariff cuts, enacted with such fanfare from the Chinese in early 1996.

That is the pattern. Every time a new trade barrier or market-distorting trick is introduced by the Chinese, the small American trade bureaucracy has to identify and document it, then open negotiations with the Chinese to discuss the issue. China, in short, is using a strategy eerily like the People's War strategy favored by Mao for defending China from foreign military invasion. Let the invader thrust deep into China and then slaughter him with the deadly pinpricks of guerrilla warfare. Today the United States is allowing itself to be pricked into defeat by a similar kind of guerrilla strategy, one in which we fight one battle after another with China, winning each one, but then exhaust our forces and lose the war. We could have a bureaucratic army of ten thousand trade warriors fighting through a Chinese forest of protectionist measures and still not win.

Experts on the American trade war with Japan pointed out long ago that the trade barriers and market-distorting mechanisms that Japan had created weren't aberrations in the Japanese system that we could negotiate away if only we were patient enough. Japanese practice represented the state of development that Japan had reached. That conclusion applies to China as well. The techniques it has adopted, consciously modeled on those of Japan, are parts of a strategy aimed at achieving accelerated economic growth. In the case of Japan, the United States was often willing to pay the price of trade deficits and even to lose entire industries in order to foster both economic development and political stability in Japan during the Cold War. China, however, is unlike Japan. It is several times larger, and it is not a strategic partner in a larger struggle against a more important enemy. There is no strategic or geopolitical prize to win in exchange for letting China cheat economically.

Indeed, look at what China is doing with the huge trade surplus that it has accumulated at American expense:

- It has built what will soon be the world's largest foreign-exchange reserve, a future source of political as well as economic power.

- It is using billions of American dollars to buy state-of-the-art weapons systems from Russia and Western Europe.
- It is subsidizing its own trade deficits with countries that are not as open to Chinese exports as the United States.

To put it simply, our current economic relationship with China is fundamentally against the national interests of the United States. To remedy this, we must start by taking steps that will reduce the trade deficit with China. It is important to note here that it is not necessary to reduce imports from China. Many imports from China, as we stated above, are beneficial to Americans, and they are beneficial to the cause of economic development in China as well. The goal should not be reducing sales of Chinese goods in the United States but increasing American exports to China, something that will happen once China drops its various barriers to imported goods. How?

The United States should allow China to export all it can sell in the United States but on one condition: that the trade-deficit ratio be gradually reduced by an increase in American exports, brought about by the elimination of China's unilateral trade barriers. China's imports from the United States are currently 25 percent of its exports to the United States. Washington should simply declare that next year that figure must increase to 30 percent, then 35 percent the year after, and so on. Only if China falls below those benchmarks would punitive tariffs and other measures against imports from China be imposed automatically—ideally against high-value-added imports like computers and other electronic goods rather than against the labor-intensive products for which China enjoys a genuine competitive advantage.

We should not insist on reducing the trade deficit to zero. When American exports equal 65 percent of China's exports, the United States might not need any longer to insist on a five-percentage-point improvement each year.

The disadvantage of such a scheme is obvious: the very idea of managed, balanced trade seems contrary to the notion of genuinely market-driven trade, which the authors of this book have long favored. But the advantages far outweigh the disadvantages. For one thing such a policy would be consistent with a growing economic relationship with China, rather than force a cutback in that relationship. It would avoid the painstaking and impossible issue-by-issue negotiations that take place today. It would also interfere with China's method of waging economic warfare against the United States by turning to European and Japanese suppliers in order to punish the United States for political offenses. There would, in other words, be an economic cost to China if it buys Airbus Industrie airplanes instead of Boeings as part of a campaign to pressure the United States to drop its concern for Chinese human rights. In addition, the arrangement would implicitly guarantee China that the American market, its best export market by far, will remain wide open to Chinese goods as long as China plays fair. That is a much better way to go about dealing with the trade deficit than a recourse to unilateral protectionism.

Indeed, while our proposal would appear to be a kind of managed trade, it would actually bring about something closer to genuine free trade than the current system allows. Today we have free trade in only one direction: we allow China to export almost anything it wants to the United States. As we have seen, China in turn uses numerous ways to pervert market forces and limit imports of American goods. That, moreover, has kept American exports not just out of balance with imports but low on an absolute scale as well. For the entire calendar year 1995, American exports to China were equivalent to an average five weeks' worth of exports to Canada that same year. They were about the same as just the increase in exports to Canada over the previous year.[2] In fact, trade between the United States and China would probably be roughly in balance, as it was for most of the 1980s, if the trade-distorting measures that China has introduced since the late 1980s were withdrawn.

We can be certain that Chinese officials will protest loudly at any such solution to the trade-deficit problem, but it is also certain that China would have little choice but to comply. The simple fact is that the United States is the only country willing and able to buy such a huge amount of Chinese-produced goods. China wants both to export freely to the United States and to engineer a high trade surplus. If given the choice between the exports and the surplus, China would have to choose the exports.

In short, the United States has a great deal of potential leverage on the trade front if it is willing to use it. But the New China Lobby is pressing Washington not to use it. Its first demand is to make most-favored-nation status for China permanent, rather than to consider its renewal each year. We agree that MFN status should not be withheld for political reasons, but we do not agree that it should be automatically granted no matter what China's trade practices are. The reason is not complicated: once MFN is permanent, it would become almost impossible for the United States to pressure China to abandon its unfair practices via the method that we are proposing.

Indeed, we believe that at the next debate, Congress should suspend China's MFN status, giving the administration full authority to raise tariffs on any Chinese goods whenever aggregate American exports fail to make the required incremental increases. With that power should go the clear directive that the administration must use its newly granted leverage to seek balanced trade with China.

The second demand of the China lobby is for the United States to drop its opposition to Chinese membership in the World Trade Organization, the successor group to the General Agreement on Tariffs and Trade (GATT). China has wanted to be a part of the WTO since it was formed in 1994, but the United States has blocked its admission, demanding that China reduce or eliminate many of the trade-distorting abuses that have been documented in this book. For its part, China is demanding to be admitted to the WTO as a developing country, which would exempt it from many of WTO's requirements for fair and open trade.

Chalmers Johnson has explained the danger of China's being admitted to the WTO as a developing country: "China would not have to open its markets to foreign competitors on an equitable basis, it would be exempt from provisions of the WTO treaty concerning subsidies, investments in China, and intellectual property rights."[3] There were signs at the end of 1996 that American and Chinese officials were close to a compromise on WTO membership, one by which China would gain entry into the organization as part of a package that included Jiang Zemin's visit to Washington and Bill Clinton's to Beijing. But any such deal would give away the store to China without gaining any compensating advantages for the United States. It would give Third World privileges to a Chinese economy that, as we have shown, has developed large, First World enclaves ready to compete head-on, but unfairly, with the United States.

In addition, WTO membership for China would virtually prohibit the United States from taking meaningful action in its trade disputes with China, since China would have the right to insist that any dispute be resolved via the WTO's system of binding arbitration. Like its predecessor, the GATT, the WTO moves cautiously and slowly, rarely assertively or bravely. Disputes will take years to resolve. And even if the United States wins every time, it will be back to the issue-by-issue approach that China can always win by following its People's War strategy.

AMERICAN POLICY on human rights in China is currently inconsistent, even hypocritical. It consists of making a rhetorical fuss about their violation and threatening reprisals but then failing to take meaningful action. The reason for this has to do in part with the ebb and flow of the pressure of public opinion on this question, but the American failure to induce China to change is also a measure of China's growing international strength and influence, one of whose consequences is its ability to ignore demands and threats that come from abroad. In the end, no matter how much of a verbal fuss we might make, the United States has essentially no power to force China, or anybody else, to respect what we regard as inalienable rights. In addition, it makes no sense to impose sanctions on China when sanctions are likely to hurt Americans even while they do little to accomplish the goals they were put in place to accomplish. This was the mistake made by the Clinton administration when it tried to make most-favored-nation status contingent on specific human rights improvements. The toothless moralism of that attempt only led to humiliation when the administration had to back down. Meanwhile, human rights in China did not improve.

There are two essential and contradictory points to be made about human rights. One is that the United States cannot hold its policy toward an emerging military and economic superpower hostage either to imprisoned Chinese dissidents or to the Tibetans. No nation can abandon its material interests, economic or military, in what would be a futile effort to ensure fair treatment of the citizens of other countries. And yet the United States also cannot follow the recommendations of the more slavish of the "engage China" school by abandoning human rights altogether. How can these two mutually contradictory needs be satisfied?

With regard to human rights inside China itself, the United States ought to implement the measures it announced when it delinked trade relations and human rights. It should continue giving strong support to Radio Free Asia, which started operations in the fall of 1996 and whose approach is to deluge China with information and news about China, not as propaganda but in the tradition of objective, professional Western-style journalism. The United States should continue to provide funds to the various Chinese groups living in the West who publicize Chinese human rights violations and who themselves strive to form the nucleus of a democratic movement in China—and it should do this even though these groups have often not been effective. Washington should press vigorously—not, as it does, halfheartedly and ineffectually—for the official scrutiny of Chinese human rights violations in various international forums, especially the United Nations Commission on Human Rights, but also in other organizations such as UNESCO and the International Labor Organization. It should do this even knowing that in many cases the organizations themselves will show no eagerness to air issues that many countries see as purely Western cultural preferences. It should insist on the right of Chinese nongovernmental organizations to make themselves heard in these forums, rather than acquiesce to the Chinese government's often-successful efforts to silence them or to promote their own government-supported nongovernmental organizations as substitutes for them.

The amounts involved in the programs that will require money would be modest, and so, it must be admitted, might be the gains. China has been a dictatorship for many centuries, and it will probably remain one for a while longer. But taking positions on human rights and taking some sensible measures to advance them is America's way of keeping faith with its democratic ideals and its commitment to open societies. If we stand only for our material interests, then we cannot be a very proud superpower.

The issue comes down to a calculatedly correct tone in a necessary relationship with leaders whom President Clinton at one point correctly called "tyrants." This relationship should be cool and correct. American officials should not, in the interests of trumpeting their brilliance in the handling of our foreign affairs, lose sight of the nasty things the Chinese are saying about us, of the ways our values and practices differ, or of our conflicting interests. We would have preferred that the administration not invite China's president Jiang Zemin to the White House for a twenty-one-gun salute. There are other ways of having contacts with Chinese leaders. But when Jiang does come to the United States, the affair should be organized in businesslike fashion and not turned into a festival of friendship. The essential thing is to avoid going from a moralistic extreme to a kind of uncritical gushing. There is no need to be stampeded by Chinese unhappiness with us into celebrating relations with those responsible for the imprisonment, torture, harassment, and, in 1989, the murder of people fighting for democracy. Summit meetings especially should not be occasions for tyrants to bask in glory. They should be occasions for a tough-minded airing of differences and an effort to obtain the adoption of policies that are in the interests, moral as well as material, of the United States.

THERE ARE TWO other places where human rights concerns either do or might bedevil relations between Washington and Beijing. One of them is Hong Kong, where human rights and other issues will arise if China mishandles its takeover. In the few, limited democratic elections preceding the takeover, the people of Hong Kong have registered their deep distrust of the People's Republic, giving a majority, for example, to the pro-democratic party of Hong Kong's leading critic of Beijing, Martin Lee. It would be no surprise if Beijing begins curtailing human rights, arresting dissidents, closing down newspapers, restricting religious observance to what it calls "patriotic churches," interfering with academic freedom at Hong Kong's schools and universities, and, if it does, the United States, whose economic interest in Hong Kong is immense, will face the usual dilemma: wanting to take steps to stop the violations but having little real power to do so.

In Hong Kong, however, China has in principle committed itself to recognizing the former colony's special status and separate way of life. It did so in the treaty it signed with Britain in 1984 that settled the Hong Kong question. The United States, which can legitimately claim the rule of law in Hong Kong to be in its economic interest, should insist that China respect its commitments and protest loudly and vigorously if it doesn't.

On Tibet, the general policy on human rights elsewhere in China should apply. Americans need to recognize that, for better or worse, we have no practical alternative to Chinese sovereignty in Tibet, even if, in an ideal world, Tibet would be an independent country, as it has been at various times in the past. It would be pointless to make independence a goal when there is virtually no chance that such a goal can be realized.

Still, the United States can maintain a respectful relationship with those who represent the aspirations of Tibetans to practice their way of life and to maintain their culture, especially their desire to recognize the Dalai Lama as their spiritual leader. American policy in this regard has been sensible and firm, with senior American officials, including the president in an impromptu and discreet way, meeting with the Dalai Lama when he has been in the United States. The prime ministers of Australia and New Zealand provided a model in this regard when they defied Chinese warnings and held full, formal meetings with the Dalai Lama, making it clear that efforts by China to intimidate other countries into submission on Tibet will not have the desired effect.

Private citizens and organizations as well as parliaments can contribute mightily to the cause of Tibetan freedom by embarrassing China and providing moral support for the Tibetans. In 1996, the German parliament passed a resolution condemning China's human rights record in Tibet. China responded with its usual hyperbolic vitriol, calling the resolution an "open, flagrant violation of international law and a serious case of interference in China's internal affairs."[4] China then canceled a visit to Beijing by Germany's foreign minister Klaus Kinkel. A day or two later, the German chancellor Helmut Kohl, though eager to maintain the China trade, said it was ridiculous to call the resolution either a violation of international law or an interference in China's internal affairs.

China will not easily give up its oppressive and inhumane control of Tibet, and, indeed, that may not even be necessary. Over the long run, as China becomes more democratic itself, conditions in Tibet will improve, until it may be possible for a voluntary confederation between the two entities, if that is what the Tibetan and the Chinese people choose to have. In the meantime, the United States should adopt the same policies on Tibet that it maintains on other human rights issues in China, including the censure of Beijing at international meetings. China responds to criticism of its practices in Tibet with rhetorical excess, but that excess is a measure of China's concern with international public opinion, a concern that could someday produce an easing of its repression of the Tibetan people and culture.

IN THE SUMMER OF 1996, a prestigious commission composed of twenty-four American strategic thinkers and political leaders from both the Republican and Democratic parties issued a report entitled *America's National Interests.* The commission concluded that of the large number of supposed American interests in the world, only five could be deemed vital, that designation given only when commission members responded yes to the following question: "Is the preservation of this interest, value, or condition strictly necessary for the United States to safeguard and enhance the well-being of Americans in a free and secure nation?"

Most supposed "vital interests" did not meet this test, the commission agreed. First among those that did was preventing a devastating nuclear, biological, or chemical weapons attack on the United States. In second place was the need to "prevent the emergence of a hostile hegemon in Europe or Asia."⁵ The commission considered that American vital interest so self-evident that it felt no need to explain its reasoning, but its definition of a vital interest in this sense has always guided American policy in both Europe, where no such hegemonic danger currently exists, and Asia, where one does. Nevertheless, very few Americans could articulate why our vital interests would be at stake if China did succeed in its goal of dominating Asia, especially when, unlike, say, Japan of a half century ago, China has no intention of sending its troops to conquer the territory of other Asian countries.

"It's commonsense geopolitics even though the American people have no appetite for it," says Walter McDougall, the Pulitzer Prize–winning historian and strategic thinker at the University of Pennsylvania, answering that question. A hegemon that can genuinely dominate Europe or Asia would by definition be very big and strong, and it would therefore have no local enemies able to prevent it from projecting its power unopposed throughout its region. In Asia, for example, a China that was free to devote itself not only to development of a blue-water navy but also to long-range airpower—both planes and missiles—would be able to hinder or even block the United States if it felt it necessary to send forces to Asia to protect our interests there. Our trade routes and energy routes in particular would be vulnerable. Fortress America might even have to pay tribute to China in order to trade with the other countries of East Asia.

Without any military assets in East Asia, the United States would lose the ability to fight limited, regional wars similar to the Gulf War for the simple reason that China, if it chose to do so, could prevent other countries from providing necessary territory and cooperation. The United States would have to choose between no war—in other words, acquiescing to China in a confrontation—and world war.

One of China's long-term goals is, as we have seen, to prevent American armed forces from having any permanent bases in Asia from which it could wage offensive warfare in case of an emergency. At the moment, China is too weak to insist on achieving that goal. But we have seen how it is looking ahead to the day when American forces will have no choice but to leave Korea and to keep forces in Japan only for the purpose of preventing Japanese rearmament. China, as we have also seen, successfully has pressured Thailand to reject our innocuous request for storing military equipment aboard freighters in Thai territorial waters. After that, Bangkok unexpectedly turned down a request from Radio Free Asia to use transmitters in Thailand to broadcast programs to China, a decision that China immediately praised.[6]

What would China's reaction be if the United States needed to position actual troops in Thailand in order, say, to intervene in a conflict between China and the Philippines over the exploitation of resources in the South China Sea? China would no doubt pressure the Thais to keep American forces out of Thai territory, and, if China had the hegemonic power it seeks, it would succeed in exerting that pressure. Samuel P. Huntington lists in his book *The Clash of Civilizations* eleven ways in which China's regional hegemony could oblige other countries to submit to Beijing's will: they range from acquiescing to Chinese control of the South China Sea to supporting China in any conflicts that might arise with the West over human rights, weapons proliferation, or economics.

So, the primary American objective in Asia is quite clear: to prevent China from becoming the hostile hegemon that could interfere with the American pursuit of its interests in Asia. The first element in achieving that goal is to maintain the American military presence in Asia and to keep it vastly more powerful and effective than China's military. The United States needs to watch China's own military buildup and to react accordingly. The technological edge enjoyed by the American side is so great that China will probably never catch up, provided the United States does what is necessary to maintain that edge.

Second, it should clearly be an American goal to prevent China from building up its nuclear weapons arsenal. In the worst case, as we have imagined in the preceding chapter, China could use even the vaguest threats of a nuclear attack to preempt decisive American action in a matter that China felt affected its sovereignty or national pride—such as coming to the aid of Taiwan in the event of a Chinese invasion. The worst outcome of Sino-American relations would be the reappearance of a kind of nuclear standoff reminiscent of the Cold War, with each side relying on the doctrine of mutually assured destruction to prevent an attack from the other.

In fact, China has numerous incentives to avoid a nuclear arms race. It would be immensely costly for one, and, perhaps more important from China's point of view, it would encourage other countries, Japan and India especially, to match China's nuclear arsenals with arsenals of their own. The United States should play a quiet but effective role in building up international pressure to persuade China to make its current moratorium on nuclear weapons testing permanent, and it should fight very actively against nuclear proliferation in China and elsewhere. Unlike human rights, any increase in nuclear weapons in Asia does affect the American vital interest, and almost any well-conceived policy, including economic sanctions and diplomatic isolation, is justified to prevent such an increase.

The third element of the balance of power involves Taiwan. The worst result of the mismanagement of the balance of power in Asia would come about if the United States were drawn into a conflict between China and Taiwan. The single most important measure for avoiding that result is to ensure that Taiwan maintains a credible defensive deterrent, so that if reunification comes about, it will be voluntary. Whatever Chinese threats and warnings and protests may come, the United States must continue to provide Taiwan with the weapons that it needs, with air defense and antisubmarine warfare especially important to guard against a possible Chinese blockade.

Beyond that, preserving the balance of power in Asia essentially means one thing: strengthening Japan. The growth of Chinese power has made much of the recent American attitude toward Japan obsolete. We can no longer operate on the assumption that a weak Japan is a good Japan. Japan can be encouraged to reject China's guilt and intimidation campaign, not by repudiating its war guilt (Japan certainly should acknowledge that, not only toward China but toward the United States as well), but by building a credible military force even in the face of it. Japan's war readiness is untested and suspect, one expert warns. Its Self-Defense Force could easily crumble in war despite its expensive hardware. Even the lines of command for a military emergency are uncertain.[7]

For half a century, it has been American strategic doctrine that a rearmed Japan would threaten peace and stability in Asia. If that was once true, it was only true because China was poor and weak. That is no longer the case. Indeed, in the post–Cold War world, it is Japan's weakness that threatens peace and stability by creating a power vacuum that the United States alone can no longer fill. A strong Japan, in genuine partnership with the United States, is vital to a new balance of power in Asia. A weak

Japan benefits only China, which wants not a stabilizing balance of power in Asia but Chinese hegemony, under which Japan would be little more than China's most useful tributary state.

This means that the United States needs to cease viewing Japan as an abnormal nation existing in a state of permanent military weakness and diplomatic pariah-hood. The dilemma here is considerable. The United States cannot block Chinese hegemony in Asia unless Japan is an equal and willing partner in the process. But if the United States pushes Japan, the result could well be an anti-American reaction there. Resolving that dilemma will be the most important single task of American diplomacy in the near future. The United States has to demonstrate that it is a reliable and trustworthy ally, as it did this spring in the waters near Taiwan, while waiting for Japan to come to grips with a security environment that is increasingly threatening to it. China's determination to achieve hegemonic status in Asia will probably serve the American interest in this regard. But there is no doubt that the United States and Japan must realize they need each other.

The United States, its relative power declining, is deluding itself if it thinks it can continue to guarantee peace and order in all of Asia without a more active support role from Japan. The navies of the two countries, for example, should be planning joint training exercises that cover a growing area of the Pacific from Alaska and Siberia to Micronesia and eventually Southeast Asia. That kind of cooperation can anchor a new balance of power in East Asia.

ONE LAST THING must be noted. It is not in the American interest to be an enemy of China. It is not impossible to envisage a cordial relationship with a resurgent, ever more democratic China that values close ties with the United States and is willing to forgo an adventurist foreign and military policy for that purpose. In this sense, the most dangerous period is the one immediately facing us, when China will still be governed by the old generation of Communists whose ideological and cultural formation took place in the years of Maoism and who still remember China's humiliation at the hands of the outside world. A new generation is waiting in the wings to take its place, a more modern generation, schooled in part in American and European universities, a more open-minded and tolerant, less reflexively defensive and chauvinistic, generation, many of whose members sympathized with the Tiananmen uprising.

We do not pretend to know what is in the minds of all young Chinese, and how many of them are susceptible to the chauvinistic, anti-American appeal of the current leadership, how many of them, indeed, may someday take the lead in pressing that appeal. We have noted, as one small sign, that the authors of the vitriolic, anti-American *China Can Say No* are all young intellectuals of the sort that one might hope would part company with their elders. But we have also met many Chinese in their twenties, thirties, and forties for whom antagonistic nationalism has no appeal. Another of the great tasks of American diplomacy will be to remain on good terms with the more cosmopolitan and liberal segments of the vast Chinese nation. The surest way to avert the conflict with China would be for that strain in Chinese life to triumph and to guide China as a whole into the twenty-first century.

NOTES

INTRODUCTION

1 *Megatrends China* (Beijing: Hualing Publishing House, 1996), cited in Bruce Gilley, "Potboiler Nationalism," *Far Eastern Economic Review*, Oct. 3, 1996.
2 Karl W. Eikenberry, *Explaining and Influencing Chinese Arms Transfers* McNair Paper no. 36, (Washington, D.C.: National Defense University, Institute for National Strategic Studies, February 1995), cited in Samuel P. Huntington, *The Clash of Civilizations and the Remaking of World Order* (New York: Simon & Schuster, 1996), pp. 189–90.
3 David E. Sanger, "China's Arms Aides Are Sought by U.S. in Smuggling Plot," *The New York Times*, May 22, 1996.
4 Robert D. Hershey, "China Has Become Chief Contributor to U.S. Trade Gap," *The New York Times*, August 20, 1996.
5 Richard F. Grimmett, "Conventional Arms Transfers to Developing Nations, 1988–1995," *Congressional Research Service Report for Congress*, August 15, 1996, p. 9.
6 Philip Shenon, "Russia Outstrips U.S. As Chief Arms Seller to Developing Nations," *The New York Times*, August 20, 1996.
7 Patrick Tyler, "Rebels' New Cause: A Book for Yankee Bashing," *The New York Times*, September 4, 1996.
8 Jim Mann, "A Confident China No Longer Wants America's Military Muscle in Asia," Los Angeles *Times*, August 7, 1995.

I AMERICA IS THE ENEMY

1 Henry Kissinger, *White House Years* (Boston: Little, Brown & Company, 1979), p. 1091.
2 Lo Bing and Li Tzu-ching, "Military Leaders Pursuing Hard Anti-USA Stance," *Cheng Ming*, May 1, 1994, cited in *BBC Summary of World Broadcasts*, May 13, 1994.
3 Ibid.

4 Ibid.

5 Patrick E. Tyler, "China Holds Christian Visitors 4 Days," *The New York Times,* February 18, 1994.

6 Human Rights in China, *China: Use of Criminal Charges Against Political Dissidents,* October 3, 1994.

7 Patrick E. Tyler, "Abuses of Rights Persist in China Despite U.S. Pleas," *The New York Times,* August 29, 1994.

8 Zhang Li, "Fighting Back on Provocation on the Sino-US Naval Vessel Confrontation in the Huang Hai," *Beijing Qingnian Bao,* Jan. 6, 1995, cited in *BBC Summary of World Broadcasts,* January 15, 1995.

9 Jim Mann and Art Pine, "Faceoff Between U.S. Ship, Chinese Sub Is Revealed," Los Angeles *Times,* December 14, 1994.

10 Wei Wei, "Who Is Threatening World Peace?" *Liberation Army Daily,* July 4, 1996. Text carried by the New China News Agency, same date.

11 Song Yimin, "New Alignment of World Forces," *People's Daily,* April 19, 1996.

12 "Can the Chinese Army Win the Next War?," cited in *FBIS,* May 5, 1994. Originally published in Chinese in June 1993.

13 Bu Wen, "U.S. Should Look Inward Before Launching Human Rights Crusade," *China Daily,* June 6, 1996.

14 Ren Yanshi, "Please See the Situation of American Children," New China News Agency Domestic Service, February 22, 1996, translated in *FBIS,* February 23, 1996.

15 Lu Guoying, "Firmly Resist Infiltration of Colonial Culture," *National Defense Daily,* June 19, 1996, translated in *FBIS,* July 2, 1996.

16 He Fang, "With a Multi-Polar Order Now Evolving, the Superpowers Are Going to Become History," *Liberation Daily,* April 22, 1996, translated in *FBIS,* July 8, 1996.

17 Zhou Hao, "The Core of Politics, Political Direction and Political Stance," *Pursuit of Truth,* no. 3, March 1996. Cited in *FBIS,* July 24, 1996.

18 Lin Bainiao, "CPC Formulates New Policy toward United States," *Cheng Ming,* December 1, 1991, cited in *FBIS,* April 6, 1991.

19 Cheng Te-lin, "Deng Says China Will Neither Seek Hegemony nor Ally Itself with the North," *Ching Pao,* April 5, 1992, cited in *FBIS,* April 6, 1992.

20 Lo Ping and Li Tzu-ching, "One Hundred and Sixteen Generals Write to Deng Xiaoping on Policy toward the United States," *Cheng Ming,* June 1, 1993, cited in *BBC Summary of World Broadcasts,* June 4, 1993.

21 Ibid.

22 Donald Zagoria, *American Foreign Policy* (newsletter), October 1993, cited in Huntington, *Clash of Civilizations,* p. 223.

23 Chang Lan-hai, "National Counterespionage Work Meeting Held in Xingshan," *Cheng Ming,* November 1, 1993, cited in *FBIS,* November 8, 1993.

24 Tsung Lan-hai, "CPC Decides on Its International Archenemy," *Cheng Ming,* January 1, 1994, cited in *FBIS,* January 25, 1994.

25 "Cigarettes Bid Is 'New Opium War,'" Hong Kong *Standard,* July 1, 1996.

26 "China's Taiwan Policy Swayed by Anti-U.S. People, Woolsey Says," Jiji *Press,* March 15, 1996.

27 Orville Schell, "Tell China That America Will Wait for Beijing to Settle Down," *International Herald Tribune,* August 15, 1995.

28 Willy Wo-lap Lam, "Funds Set Aside to Head Off Protests," *South China Morning Post*, February 9, 1996.

2 "WE WILL NEVER SEEK HEGEMONY"

1 Xing Shizhong, "China Threat Theory Can Be Forgotten," *Qiushi* (*Pursuit of Truth*), June 27, 1996.
2 "Says Nation No Threat," New China News Agency, November 14, 1995.
3 Yan Xuetong, "China Security Goals Do Not Pose a Threat to World," *China Daily*, March 4, 1996.
4 Colin S. Gray, "How Geography Still Shapes Security," *Orbis*, Spring 1996.
5 Huntington, *Clash of Civilizations*, pp. 169–71.
6 Estimates of China's per capita income by the World Bank and the Central Intelligence Agency place it between $1,800 and $3,000.
7 Chong-Pin Lin, "Chinese Military Modernization: Perceptions, Progress, and Prospects," paper given at the Fifth Annual American Enterprise Institute Conference on the People's Liberation Army, Staunton Hill, June 17–19, 1994, p. 11.
8 This summary draws on David Shambaugh, "China's Military: Real or Paper Tiger?" *The Washington Quarterly*, Spring 1996.
9 Ibid.
10 "A Major Step for Building Up a Strong Army Through Science and Technology," *Jiefangjun Bao*, Beijing, June 21, 1996, cited in *FBIS*, July 17, 1996.
11 "Lax Security Puts Plans into China's Hands," *Asia Times*, August 16, 1996.
12 Bill Gertz, "Russia, Ukraine Get Stern Missile Warning," Washington *Times*, May 21, 1996.
13 Ibid.
14 "Deputy Foreign Minister Panov Denies Sale of Missile Technology to China," Interfax News Agency, May 22, 1996.
15 "Military Commission Reportedly to Reduce Army by 500,000 Troops," *Ming Pao*, July 1996.
16 Nicholas D. Kristof, "China Raises Military Budget Despite Deficit," *The New York Times*, March 17, 1993.
17 June Teufel Dreyer, "Chinese Strategy in Asia and the World," paper prepared for the First Annual Strategy Forum Conference on China, United States Naval Academy, April 27–28, 1996.
18 Stockholm International Peace Research Institute, *SIPRI Yearbook 1996* (New York: Oxford University Press, 1996), p. 465.
19 Tai Ming Cheung, "Can PLA Inc. Be Tamed?" *Institutional Investor*, July 1996, p. 41.
20 Xinhua News Agency, November 16, 1995.
21 Reported by Agence France Presse, March 5, 1995.
22 "China Announces New War Games," Inter Press Service, Beijing, March 6, 1996.
23 Li Cheng and Lynn White, "The Army in the Succession to Deng Xiaoping," *Asian Survey* 32:8, August 1993.
24 Ibid.
25 *Ming Pao*, Hong Kong, November 9, 1992.

26 *Ming Pao*, Hong Kong, July 17, 1996.

27 These figures are based on Chong-Pin Lin's reading of several Chinese and foreign sources. "The Military Balance in the Taiwan Strait" (unpublished paper).

28 Ibid.

29 Ibid.

30 "New Developments in the Chinese Air Force," *Kuang Chiao Ching*, Hong Kong, Jan. 16, 1996.

31 Bill Gertz, "Chinese Arms Buildup Increases Attack Range," Washington *Times*, March 12, 1996. See also Bruce Blance, "Taiwanese Facilities to Be at Subic Bay, Philippines," *Jane's Intelligence Review*, August 1, 1996.

32 Michael Richardson, "Growing Military Might Worries Southeast Asians," *International Herald Tribune*, April 24, 1995.

33 Gertz, "Chinese Arms Buildup."

34 David B. H. Denoon and Wendy Friedman, "China's Security Strategy: The View from Beijing, ASEAN, and Washington," *Asian Survey*, April 1996. The Washington *Times*, which has reported accurately on the Chinese military ahead of other newspapers, reported in 1994 on a U.S. Senate report revealing Chinese efforts to develop the DF-41, an ICBM with a range of 7,440 miles, which would make it capable of reaching the American West Coast. See Washington *Times*, May 5, 1994. The BBC World Service reported from Beijing on August 1, 1996, that China, with help from Russian scientists, is developing an ICBM with a range of 8,000 miles. See also Shambaugh, "China's Military."

35 Denoon and Friedman, "China's Security Strategy."

36 Shambaugh, "China's Military."

37 Chong-Pin Lin, "Chinese Military Modernization."

38 *Jane's Fighting Ships 1994/1995* (London: Jane's Information Group Limited, 1994).

39 Nayan Chanda, "No-Cash Carrier," *Far Eastern Economic Review*, Oct. 10, 1996; "Britain to Supply China with Advanced Navy Radar," *Financial Times*, August 6, 1996; "China Poised to Seal AWACS Deal with British Firm," *Agence France Presse*, October 8, 1996.

3 SPEAK LOUDLY BUT CARRY A SMALL STICK

1 U.S. Department of State, *China Human Rights Practices*, 1995.

2 Wang Dan, "Give China a Chance," *The New York Times*, September 23, 1993.

3 This account of the crackdown in Tibet in May 1996 draws heavily on Human Rights Watch/Asia, *China: The Cost of Putting Business First*, July 1996, pp. 13–15.

4 Pico Iyer, "China's Buddha Complex," *The New York Times*, December 3, 1995.

5 "China Accuses U.S. on Tibet," *International Herald Tribune*, September 25, 1995.

6 Agence France Presse, "China Warns Tibet 'Terrorists,'" *International Herald Tribune*, June 27, 1996.

7 Reuters News Agency, "Tibet's Goals Target God-King," Washington *Times*, June 17, 1996.

8 "Bush's China Policy: No More Mr. Nice Guy?" Transcript of *American Interest*, broadcast May 4, 1991, Federal News Service, May 3, 1991.

9 Elaine Sciolino, "China Trip Begins on a Frosty Note for Christopher," *The New York Times*, March 12, 1994.

10 Elaine Sciolino, "China Rejects Call from Christopher for Rights Gains," *The New York Times*, March 13, 1994.

11 Elaine Sciolino, "Clinton and China: How Promise Self-Destructed," *The New York Times*, May 29, 1994.

12 Mark Clifford, "Tribute Time," *Far Eastern Economic Review*, March 31, 1994.

4 THE NEW CHINA LOBBY

1 Reuters News Agency, "Strong Demand Expected on China $1 Billion Global Bond," January 30, 1994.

2 Reuters News Service, "Ford Names James Paulsen Head of China Office," February 28, 1994.

3 New China News Agency, March 30, 1995.

4 Jeff Cole, "Boeing Nears Major Order from China," *The Wall Street Journal*, May 26, 1994.

5 Mark O'Neill, "KFC Announces $200 Million Investment in China," Reuters World Service, May 28, 1994.

6 "New York Signs Trade Pact with China Province," United Press International, April 29, 1994.

7 "High Power Trade Delegation Hits DC," *The China Business Review*, 21:3, May 1994, p. 8.

8 Sally D. Goll and Laurence Zuckerman, "Few Companies Are Expected to Follow Levi's Example in Pulling Out of China," *The Asian Wall Street Journal*, May 10, 1993.

9 David E. Sanger, "U.S. Blames Allies for Undercutting Its China Policy," *The New York Times*, June 12, 1996.

10 Ibid.

11 Gary Milhollin and Meg Dennison, "China's Cynical Calculation," *The New York Times*, April 24, 1995.

12 Mark Crudele, "Princeton Prof and Human Rights Critic Unwelcome in China," Associated Press, Beijing, August 14, 1996.

13 Orville Schell, correspondence with the authors.

14 Lilley quoted in Susumu Awanohara, "Asian Lobbies: The K-Street Crowd," *Far Eastern Economic Review*, June 2, 1994.

15 Reported in John J. Fialka, "Mr. Kissinger Has Opinions on China—and Business Ties," *The Wall Street Journal*, September 12, 1989.

16 Henry A. Kissinger, "For China, Economic Reforms Spark Eruptions," Los Angeles *Times*, June 4, 1989.

17 Henry A. Kissinger, "China: Push for Reform, Not Rupture," Los Angeles *Times*, July 30, 1989.

18 "Deng Xiaoping Meets Henry Kissinger," New China News Agency, November 10, 1989.

19 A Chinese spokesman said that Kissinger's talks with Li took place in a

"friendly, light and sincere atmosphere." "Li Peng Meets Kissinger," New China News Agency, September 8, 1990.

20 "Chinese President Meets Dr. Kissinger," New China News Agency, April 19, 1996.

21 The article was summarized in a dispatch from Bonn of the New China News Agency, March 31, 1996.

22 Henry Kissinger, "Heading for a Collision in Asia," Washington *Post,* July 21, 1995.

23 "Kissinger Calls for Ease on Tech Transfer to China," New China News Agency, July 17, 1988.

24 Reported in Fialka, "Mr. Kissinger," and by Scott Thompson in U.S. Senate Foreign Relations Committee, *Hearings on U.S. Policy Toward China,* February 13, 1990.

25 Thompson, *Hearings.*

26 Fialka, "Mr. Kissinger."

27 Walter Pincus, "Kissinger Says He Had No Role in China Mission," Washington *Post,* December 14, 1989.

28 Thompson, *Hearings.*

29 Jeff Gerth with Sarah Bartlett, "Kissinger and Friends and Revolving Doors," *The New York Times,* April 30, 1989.

30 Lawrence S. Eagleburger, "How to Get China to Change," Washington *Post,* June 20, 1991.

31 Edward T. Pound and Andry Pasztor, "American Arms Dealer Was Amazing Success, or So Ferranti Believed," *The Wall Street Journal,* January 23, 1990.

32 Barbara A. Nagy, "UTC Wins Friends with Cultural Philanthropy," Hartford *Courant,* April 5, 1996.

33 Nicholas D. Kristof, "'People's China' Celebrates, but Without the People," *The New York Times,* October 2, 1989.

34 "Li Peng Meets Former U.S. State Secretary Haig," New China News Agency, October 3, 1989.

35 Juliet Eilperin, "Johnston's Letter on China Raises Questions," State News Service, April 22, 1994. See also Joan Lowy, "Senator's Sons Get a Boost in China," Atlanta *Journal and Constitution,* December 31, 1993.

36 Benjamin Kang Lim, "China Forms High-Level Group Eyeing U.S. Congress," Reuters News Agency, Beijing, January 18, 1996.

37 "Beijing Woos US Congressmen to Lessen Taipei's Influence," *Straits Times* (Singapore), April 12, 1996.

38 Sciolino, "Clinton and China."

39 Awanohara, "Asian Lobbies."

40 Hill and Knowlton Public Affairs Worldwide, *Proposal for the People's Republic of China (PRC)* , June 1, 1991, p. 9.

41 Business *Wire* (Schaumburg, Ill.), September 18, 1996.

42 Qian speech was reported by the Voice of America, September 20, 1996, broadcast from Chicago.

43 The account of this meeting comes from a broadcast of the Voice of America, September 20, 1996.

44 Stanley Holmes, "Boeing's Campaign to Protest a Market—Corporations Lobby to Save China Trade," Seattle *Times,* May 27, 1996.

45 Ibid.

5 DEFICITS, TECHNOLOGY, AND PLA, INC.

1 All Sino-American trade data cited in this chapter are drawn from Commerce Department reports.

2 Richard W. Stevenson, "Trade Deficit Narrow, but Just Slightly," *The New York Times,* October 19, 1996.

3 Cited in Los Angeles *Times,* September 23, 1996.

4 "America: Who Stole the Dream?" Philadelphia *Inquirer,* September 17, 1996.

5 Reuters News Agency, Beijing, September 8, 1996.

6 Reuters News Agency, Hong Kong, September 11, 1996.

7 New China News Agency, Beijing, September 4, 1996.

8 Chalmers Johnson, "Nationalism and the Market: China As a Superpower" (unpublished paper), April 1996.

9 Jeffrey Sachs and Wing Thye Woo, "China's Transition Experience Re-examined," *Transition,* The World Bank, March–April 1996.

10 "Keep Knocking, Keep Opening," *The Economist,* May 11, 1996.

11 Office of the U.S. Trade Representative, *1996 National Trade Estimate Report on Foreign Trade Barriers,* April 1996. Hereafter the "USTR report."

12 Ibid.

13 Matt Forney, "Trials by Fire," *Far Eastern Economic Review,* September 12, 1996.

14 "China Bank Privileges Help Increase Exports of Electrical Goods," *The Wall Street Journal,* October 27, 1995.

15 USTR report.

16 House Ways and Means Committee, *Hearings of the Trade Subcommittee,* June 11, 1996.

17 USTR report.

18 These events are described in *International Tax Review,* June 1996; *China Business Review,* May 1996; *The Economist,* May 11, 1996.

19 *Congress Daily,* September 19, 1996.

20 "Protectionist Temptations Tugging at Beijing, *International Herald Tribune,* June 20, 1996.

21 "Commodity Import Licensing Authorities Detailed," *Guoji Shangbao,* June 11, 1996. In FBIS, September 19, 1996.

22 USTR report.

23 This account of McDonnell Douglas's activities in China draws heavily on Joseph Kahn, "McDonnell Douglas's High Hopes for China Never Really Soared," *The Wall Street Journal,* May 22, 1996.

24 Ibid.

25 Stanley Holmes, "How Boeing Woos Beijing," Seattle *Times,* May 26, 1996.

26 Sandra Sugawara, "With Billions at Stake, Boeing Goes to Bat for China," Washington *Post,* July 7, 1996.

27 Bruce Einhorn, "The China Connection," *Business Week,* August 5, 1996.

28 U.S. Senate, *Hearing before the Select Committee on Intelligence,* February 22, 1996.

29 American Society for Industrial Security, International, *Trends in Intellectual Property Loss* (Arlington, Va., 1996).

30 Einhorn, "The China Connection."

31 Kahn, "McDonnell Douglas's High Hopes."

32 Einhorn, "The China Connection."

33 This information drawn from the AFL-CIO study, portions of which were provided to the authors.

6 FLASHPOINT: TAIWAN

1   Our description of the Sino-American late-night negotiations in Shanghai draws substantially on Kissinger's account of this episode in his memoirs, *White House Years.*

2   Seth Faison, "Tension in Taiwan: The Polemics," *The New York Times,* March 22, 1996.

3   "Security Chief Says China Cancelled Attack Plan," Agence France Presse, April 14, 1996, citing Taiwan's *United Evening News,* same day.

4   Patrick E. Tyler, "As China Threatens Taiwan, It Makes Sure U.S. Listens," *The New York Times,* January 23, 1996.

5   Jonathan D. Spence, *The Search for Modern China* (New York: W. W. Norton & Co., 1990), pp. 53–57.

6   Patrick E. Tyler, "Taiwan's Leader Wins Its Election and a Mandate," *The New York Times,* March 24, 1996.

7 CHINA'S PLAN FOR JAPAN

1   Mary Jordan, "Japan Turns Assertive," Washington *Post,* November 15, 1995.

2   Nicholas D. Kristof, "Angry Islanders Dig In for a Battle over Bases," *The New York Times,* May 25, 1996.

3   Nicholas D. Kristof, "Angry Islanders Dig In for Battle over Bases," *The New York Times,* May 25, 1996.

4   Our account of Japan's shifting strategic position draws on Michael J. Green and Benjamin L. Self, "Japan's Changing China Policy: From Commercial Liberalism to Reluctant Realism," *Survival,* Summer 1996.

5   Tokyo *Shimbun,* March 2, 1996.

6   Alison Mitchell, "U.S. Military Role in East Asia Gets Support in Tokyo," *The New York Times,* April 17, 1996.

7   "China Warns over U.S.–Japan Ties," *Financial Times,* April 2, 1996.

8   Reported in Agence France Presse, Beijing, April 18, 1996.

9   "U.S.–Japan Pact Does More Harm Than Good," *China Daily,* May 23, 1996, cited in *FBIS,* May 24, 1996.

10 Kissinger, *White House Years,* p. 1089.

11 Patrick E. Tyler, "Shifting Gears, Beijing Reins in Anti-Japanese Campaign," *The New York Times,* September 19, 1996.

12 Cited in the *International Herald Tribune,* April 19, 1996.

13 *People's Daily*, August 30, 1996.
14 Peter J. Katzenstein and Nobuo Okawara, *Japan's National Security* (Ithaca, N.Y.: Cornell East Asia Series, 1993).
15 Edith Terry, "China Checks Japan's Power in Asia," *Christian Science Monitor*, January 10, 1995.
16 New China News Agency, November 10, 1994.
17 "Jiang Cements Ties with Seoul," *Financial Times*, November 15, 1995.
18 Cited in George Friedman and Meredith LeBard, *The Coming War with Japan* (New York: St. Martin's Press, 1992), p. 266.
19 Kwan Weng Kin, "Japan Wants Joint Role with U.S. to Fight Crises," *Straits Times* (Singapore), May 3, 1996, citing *Asahi Shimbun*, May 2, 1996.
20 Defense Agency Japan, "Defense of Japan: Response to a New Era" (Tokyo: Government of Japan, 1996), translated in *Japan Times*.
21 Armed Forces Newswire Service, August 15, 1996.
22 *Asiaweek*, July 12, 1996.
23 "Political Bias May Influence Award of Three Gorges Job," *Straits Times* (Singapore), June 17, 1996.
24 Thomas L. Friedman, "J-a-p-a-n and C-h-i-n-a," *The New York Times*, February 12, 1996.
25 Ibid.

8 CHINA VERSUS AMERICA: A WAR GAME

1 The authors have drawn on information about China's military modernization and capabilities as described in papers presented at the American Enterprise Institute Conference on the People's Liberation Army, held at Staunton Hill, June 17–19, 1994. These papers include: Paul Godwin and John Caldwell, "PLA Power Projections: Year 2000?" and Chong-Pin Lin, "Chinese Military Modernization."
2 Some of the technical information we cite on China's likely military modernization program comes from Felix K. Chang, "Conventional War across the Taiwan Strait," *Orbis*, Fall 1996, pp. 577–607.

CONCLUSION: COPING WITH CHINA

1 "Bootlegging Is Back in China," *The Journal of Commerce*, August 12, 1996.
2 United States Commerce Department trade data.
3 Johnson, "Nationalism and the Market."
4 Alan Cowell, "Germany's Concerns over Rights in Tibet Clash with Trade Ties to China," *The New York Times*, June 25, 1996.
5 *America's National Interests: A Report from the Commission on America's National Interests* (Cambridge: Center for Science and International Affairs, John F. Kennedy School of Government, Harvard University, July 1996).
6 *Far Eastern Economic Review*, September 12, 1996.
7 This argument made in Andrew K. Hanami, "Japan and the Military Balance of Power in Northeast Asia," *Journal of East Asian Affairs*, 8:1, Winter/Spring 1994.

ACKNOWLEDGMENTS

WE ARE GRATEFUL to the Chinese scholars and analysts who allowed us to visit their organizations in the People's Republic of China and who discussed their views with us.

In Shanghai, we visited the Institute for Peace and Development Studies, the Institute of Asia-Pacific Studies of the Shanghai Academy of Social Sciences, the Center for American Studies at Fudan University, and the Shanghai Institute for International Studies.

In Beijing, we visited the Institute of American Studies of the Chinese Academy of Social Sciences, the China Institute of Contemporary International Relations, the China Center for International Studies, and the China Society for Strategy and Management Research.

We owe a special debt to Al Wilhelm and Karen Sutter of the Atlantic Council in Washington, D.C., for the work they did in helping arrange our visit to Shanghai and Beijing. They did so in the truest spirit of scholarly inquiry and open debate, knowing that the views in this book would probably differ in many ways from their own.

We also express our gratitude to the director and staff of the Government Information Office on Taiwan, where our requests for information were met with prompt and scrupulous attention.

We would like to thank Sharon Fennimore, David K. Kim, Jane Tsou, and Eunice Yang for the contributions they made to this book. Special thanks are due to researcher Nam C. Kim for devoting several months to ferreting out essential information that can be found throughout this volume.

Inevitably, many people who helped us, especially private Chinese citizens in both the United States and China, must remain unnamed, though we are grateful for their help in quietly advancing our understanding of the issues. In Washington, China hands in both Congress and the executive branch provided invaluable insights.

The opinions expressed in this book are exclusively those of the authors and in no way represent the opinions of the Foreign Policy Research Institute or any other institution.

We express also our warmest appreciation to Jonathan Segal of Alfred A. Knopf, and to our agent, Kathy Robbins.

INDEX